YOUNG MAN
IN A HURRY

ALSO BY GAVIN NEWSOM

Citizenville

Young Man in a Hurry

A Memoir of Discovery

GAVIN NEWSOM

PENGUIN PRESS

NEW YORK

2026

PENGUIN PRESS
An imprint of Penguin Random House LLC
1745 Broadway, New York, NY 10019
penguinrandomhouse.com

Designed by Amanda Dewey

LIBRARY OF CONGRESS CATALOGING-IN-PUBLICATION DATA
Names: Newsom, Gavin, 1967– author.
Title: Young man in a hurry : a memoir of discovery / Gavin Newsom.
Description: New York : Penguin Press, 2026. | Includes index. |
Identifiers: LCCN 2024051249 (print) | LCCN 2024051250 (ebook) |
ISBN 9781984881939 (hardcover) | ISBN 9781984881946 (ebook)
Subjects: LCSH: Newsom, Gavin, 1967– | Newsom, Gavin, 1967—Family. |
Newsome family. | Governors—California—Biography. |
Mayors—California—San Francisco—Biography. | California—Politics and
government—1951– | San Francisco (Calif.)—Biography.
Classification: LCC F866.4.N48 A3 2025 (print) |
LCC F866.4.N48 (ebook) | DDC 979.4/054092 [B]—dc23/eng/20250206
LC record available at https://lccn.loc.gov/2024051249
LC ebook record available at https://lccn.loc.gov/2024051250

Printed in the United States of America
1st Printing

The authorized representative in the EU for product safety and compliance is
Penguin Random House Ireland, Morrison Chambers, 32 Nassau Street,
Dublin D02 YH68, Ireland, https://eu-contact.penguin.ie.

To Montana, Hunter, Brooklynn, and Dutch, my four children.

May they carry on the story.

YOUNG MAN
IN A HURRY

Prologue

....

I am sitting in the office of our Mediterranean-style house in a greenbelt of Sacramento, a landscape that still feels foreign to me. All my life, the air I breathed blew in from the Pacific, the smell of sea and redwoods along the San Francisco coast. The bluff we now call home is rare high ground in the great flatland of the Central Valley. Our yard is studded with oaks and overlooks a river, the American, that carries a different scent. This is the river where the story of California—at least the Gold Rush version we like to tell ourselves, the shout of "Eureka! Eureka!"—began.

It is five thirty in the morning in the middle of summer. I am writing this from a time and place when the seasons have already begun to lose their capacity to tell us what time and place it is. Spring used to mean the abundant snowmelt that recharged the rivers that flowed across the California plain. Spring, rivers deceived, now means another year of record drought. Summer as a boy meant traversing the Sierra Nevada with my father, William

Newsom, explorations that always carried added meaning because he left us when I was so young, for reasons that neither he nor my mother ever made clear. In those years when he was most alive, he was determined to pass on to me his veneration of California's rivers and mountains. I now leave his old cabin in Dutch Flat, in the hills of Gold Country, wondering if I might never see it again, for summer has become the season of fire.

My time in office has been altered by twenty-first-century pandemic and climate change, by drought and wildfire and the rise of authoritarian forces whose contempt for democracy is its own flame. As the calamities have piled one on top of the other and challenged the very notion of governance, I cannot help but consider what remnant of state, what remnant of nation, I will pass down to my four young children. In a life where my every movement as father and governor can feel orchestrated, the early morning allows me a sliver of space to call my own, where my mind can wander and find contemplation and reflection, if not a way out of catastrophe.

If I were merely the governor of California, I might let the darkness sink deeper inside me. But I am a husband and father who doesn't want the convulsions of nature and politics to be all that his children remember of this time. And so on this day, the eve of the Fourth of July, my wife, Jen, and I have decided to take the kids on a family excursion, a kayaking trip. Beyond our backyard, on the other side of a sandbar and a park, is the American River. I want to teach them the history its waters carry.

Upstream from our house, in the year 1848, James Marshall, a dream seeker from New Jersey, found himself diverting enough of the river's flow to build a lumber mill for Johann August Sutter. Captain Sutter, as he liked to be called, was a fugitive who had traveled an even greater distance than Marshall to reinvent himself. The captain had erected a fort in present-day Midtown Sacramento and was looking to build the first empire of California. He couldn't very well see his way without lumber. The mill was nearly finished when, on the morning of January 24, 1848, Marshall caught sight of three shiny nuggets in the ditch beside the river. The cry of "Gold!" echoed. Tens of thousands of miners who knew little about mining arrived that first year from every corner of the globe. Madness ensued. As the newcomers rushed the Sierra foothills, running right past Sutter's Fort, the captain could see the spoiling of his dream, if not the ruin that would soon befall him.

Of course, the true invention of California was a story the schoolchildren of my generation were never taught. Certainly not by the nuns at Notre Dame des Victoires, where we wore little sailor outfits and blue socks up to our knees and I got booted out in the third grade for one shortcoming or another. Surely not by my teachers at Neil Cummins K–8 or Redwood High School. The story of California's original sin would have required a more forthright narration: how a century before gold's finding, the decimation of California's Indigenous had commenced. While it played out haphazardly, there was no mistaking the result. California was born in genocide.

I often find myself measuring this history, wondering about the warp speed at which the Gold Rush shot us forward and whether so many of our challenges today are because we've never really rid our spirit of its voracious impulse. I weigh the water we are now mining from hundreds of feet belowground and the oil we keep on fracking. The lessons of the Gold Rush—the mountains it melted, the rivers it fouled—we Californians did not heed. Our collective forgetfulness, the grooved pattern by which we reach too far and grab too much, again and again, is its own force of nature to behold.

At the same time, I marvel at our capacity to invent and reinvent, the grit and ingenuity that run deep in that same spirit and imagine a new way forward that changes not only California's future but also America's future, the world's future. The doomsayers in the East have been predicting the demise of the California Dream for as long as we've been dreaming it. And yet here we are: three iconic cities along the coast; a Central Valley that stands as the most productive farm belt in the world; a smaller valley called Silicon that gives birth to a new age of technology; wine-making in the North, moviemaking in the South, an organic foods movement hatched on counterculture farms and in the mom-and-pop grocery stores of Santa Cruz and Berkeley. Together the regions of California are creating a new Green Economy that lessens our reliance on fossil fuels and offers a prototype that might yet stave off the worst of climate change. The talking heads on cable TV can pore over the numbers of California's in-migration and out-migration all they want, pronounce a mass exodus where none exists, but the fact remains: it is this regenerative California that continues to act as a powerful lure to a new generation of dreamers—all races, all creeds, from all places—not so different from those 49ers.

I learned first from my father, on those summer trips to the upper American River, where water and fish ran wild, that California's open arms must inevitably extend to saints and scoundrels alike. Often they are in search of the same thing: proper dirt on which to stage their next revival, be it a second act or a third act. What they find at continent's edge, in the real and the imagined of the Golden Land, isn't always what they were looking for. As a judge who sat on county and state appellate benches, my father saw his share of these dreamers, at their highest and lowest. I've seen my share of them, too. Whatever frontier legend invigorates them, they come with the same look in their eyes. They needn't be completely true, and they needn't be completely loyal. They tap into our spirit, and hundreds of millions of dollars in subsidies, and sometimes they move on to Texas or Florida. May their landing places greet them with great fanfare, for it is California they take with them.

It was this same fever that brought the Newsoms here from County Cork, Ireland, six generations ago. My great-great-grandfather, the first to land, was a cop who walked a beat in San Francisco. The year of his arrival was never given a specific date. Whenever my father was asked how far back our family traced its San Francisco roots, he would add to the myth. "It seems the policeman didn't come here. He *was* here. As San Francisco appeared, he appeared." Policeman to politician took 150 years, and it is thanks to the American story, the California story, that I now find myself the governor of the most daring, magical, cursed, blessed state in the United States.

Before I took office and moved to this private bluff in a Sacramento burg called Fair Oaks, all my years had been shaped by the city of San Francisco. Growing up, my sister, Hilary, and I stayed with our mother, Tessa, who juggled three jobs to keep a roof over our heads because our father was so inattentive to money. In those first years after their divorce, he fled two hundred miles away to Lake Tahoe and I struggled to find ways to reach him. Out in nature, kayaking down the American, something would open up in him. We'd paddle toward a sandbar and he'd tell me a story or recite a line from Yeats. "That the future years had come, dancing to a frenzied drum, out of the murderous innocence of the sea." We'd find a spot where the river calmed and a large rock stuck its flat head out of the water, and I'd climb atop it and stretch out my long, skinny body to the sun and push off with both legs. No matter that it was summer, the water was ice cold. As I dove beneath and swam, I kept my eyes open, for this was the American and there was no telling what I might find on its sandy bottom. I was looking for an artifact or treasure to add to our story.

While my father's physical presence remained episodic throughout my childhood, he became an intellectual and spiritual force for me when I got older. I only needed to dial his number or sit across the table from him over dinner to benefit from his knowledge and wisdom. In my more solitary moments as governor, it hits me that I have no one I can call on to fill his absence, no one who might listen to my fears and anger and respond with understanding, savvy, and an erudition that brings with it history and philosophy and literature. I struggle at times to make sense of the challenge of governance before me, in part because it is a challenge that has few precedents in history and in part because the means to meet it are not always within my grasp.

Today another unprecedented heat wave sits down on the West Coast. My experts tell me that this wildfire season could outdo last year's, which was the worst in recorded history. Huge chunks of landmass are primed to explode. As many as ten thousand of our giant sequoias, among the oldest living organisms on earth, perished in last year's blazes. The trees, which can grow as tall as three hundred feet and as wide as thirty feet, evolved not only to withstand fire but to thrive as a species because of it.

Their bark is practically fireproof and their cones utilize flame to produce seedlings. But these are not the blazes that have shared three thousand years of history with the oldest of the trees. These conflagrations are born of a different nature—tornadoes of fire, really, that incinerate tree crowns dating back to the Sumerians.

I try not to worry about any of this as we paddle down the American River on the eve of the Fourth of July. As it turned out, only Hunter, our oldest boy, wanted to come along. He and I sit in one kayak, Jen in the other, the water so cold and clear we can see the fish swimming beneath us. I do not have to reach for sentimentality to hear an echo from my own childhood; I just need a memory of the season. The stretch we're kayaking isn't quite the wild American my father and I first rafted and fished more than forty years ago. I am not a replica of my dad, a board member of the Friends of the River who fought to keep another dam from being built on the American, and Hunter isn't a replica of me, though he has the same fascination with the old historic bridges we pass under and the same ache to jump from a rock into the river. About halfway down, he finds his rock, climbs upon it, and leaps in. He is now swimming with the steelhead, shad, stripers, and rainbows. It is summertime.

CHAPTER ONE

""

I t's been three years since my father's death, and his stories, with their perfect beginnings, middles, and ends, come back to me at the oddest times. He was an intellectual who spent almost all his solitary hours reading. He didn't leave Hilary and me much in the way of an estate, but he did pass on his prized collection of novels, short stories, memoirs, tomes of history and poetry. He left us the Russian greats, the English greats, and, most proudly, the Irish greats. My luck, I've never been able to decipher a single classic of literature. Who would have guessed—certainly not my father—that his only son would be dyslexic. One of the struggles in my life is that my brain has trouble processing words on a page. If the text is too crowded, the story too woven, I lose track. My brain does better with nonfiction, but only if the words have room to breathe.

People curious about my lifelong jousting with a neurological disorder naturally wonder how it complicates my job. They might notice that in my speeches and press conferences I sometimes weigh down my sentences with words like *iterative* and *demonstrable* and *contextualize* and *foundational*. When I was in my early twenties, I found a dictionary that was typographically friendly and studied it front to back, as a way to command words that would show my facility with the English language. This was no doubt compensation for my peculiar wiring. Through hard work and persistence, I have overcome a lot of obstacles on the path to becoming a more confident public speaker, but I have yet to find comfort reading a typewritten speech. I can't manage the spatial tracking of looking down and up. It feels like vertigo. Reading from a teleprompter is easier only because the lines appear with plenty of space.

Dyslexia explains my compulsion to master every facet of policy and every number in the state budget and maybe even my fastidious note-taking and recordkeeping. In a banker's box filled with objects from my growing-up years, I can find my report cards from grammar school. "Gavin mixes up his letters," my third-grade teacher wrote. "His Ds are Bs. He can't read the alphabet." I couldn't say *dress*. It came out "bress." I couldn't say *order*. It came out "orer." By the fourth grade, I was taking speech-therapy classes after school. "Gavin can correctly pronounce S sounds in isolation in words but not in conversation. When he speaks, he substitutes TH for S." But year after year, the word *dyslexia* never showed up in my school records. The actual name of the affliction I suffered from remained a mystery to the school and to me.

I got through childhood by compartmentalizing the world. Because I did not have the words, so many of my experiences as a kid never got imprinted as memories. I didn't have the ease with language my sister had. The vividness with which Hilary can summon the past—it's almost as if she is the older sibling.

Storytelling and drinking ran together on the Newsom side of my family. They might as well have been Irish twins the way one prepared the ground for the other, the way one watched out for the other. Storytelling kept drinking from getting sloppy. Liquor transmuted into lore. If the stories were told well and repeated enough times to be firmly planted into the next generation, vice might yet be redeemed, or so believed my great-grandmother, Belinda Newsom, aka Belle, the dowager with snow-white hair whose trips around the rosary beads were all-day affairs.

To tell a good story, you had to live a good life, and to live a good life, you had to engage with worlds different from your own. In San Francisco, a foreign place could be found on the other side of the hill, so that a boy growing up in the Marina District in the late 1970s needed only to venture to North Beach or Chinatown or the Mission or the Fillmore to interact with people whose music, art, dress, food, scene, felt nearly like the occult. If you timed your adventure right and stayed open to its possibility, you might even come home with a story worth passing on. Even the friends you chose from your own station were selected in part because of the eccentricities they brought to the game. Pick them correctly, keep them for life, and they became the subjects of endless stories, too. Of course, no well yielded more storytelling than the family well, and no tale was told with more shine than the one that began with a knotty problem at city hall and ended with a greased palm.

My father's fascination with the theater of politics came to him, like the name *William*, through his father and his father's father. The first William, my great-grandfather, was an associate of A. P. Giannini, founder of the Bank of Italy, who after the great earthquake and fire of 1906, when all the big banks had vanished, set up two planks on the Washington Street wharf to continue serving his customers. This first William Newsom, a man with a good sense of humor and a bad marriage, opened Giannini's branch at Twenty-ninth and Mission and extended his loans to common folk on a handshake. The fact that the Mission District was filled with Irish immigrants who needed a familiar touch made the branch an early model of community banking and my great-grandfather a trusted figure among his tribe. The Bank of Italy, replicating this community model, eventually became the Bank of America. It was said that my great-grandfather turned into a Democrat out of his compassion for the working man. He served as the San Francisco commissioner of public works, a member of the kitchen cabinet of Mayor James Rolph (later Governor Rolph), and then a builder who erected Commerce and Lowell High Schools.

His son William, my grandfather, saw the boom after World War II as his chance to build housing tracts that looked out to the bay. This turned him into the first wealthy member of the Newsom clan, but it didn't turn him into a Republican. He was a kingmaker, and the first king he helped make was Edmund "Pat" Brown. My grandfather, whose nickname was "the Boss," served as manager or treasurer for several of Brown's campaigns, from district attorney to attorney general to the thirty-second governor of California. He was one of the thinkers behind the throne, and the trust between the two men was such that Brown asked the Boss to be godfather to his daughter, Kathleen. And then, as such things happen, the two men had a falling-out over Governor Brown's refusal to appoint my grandfather to a board regulating the banking industry. As the Newsom version goes, this was because Governor Brown knew that my grandfather held views that would have brought the hammer down on bankers abusing the citizenry. The old pals parted ways and never talked again. Whenever Pat Brown needed to compare notes with my grandfather, he did so through my father, the third William, who happily played intermediary, if for no other reason than the material it might furnish for a story.

My father had literary ambitions as he pursued his bachelor's degree in French literature at the University of San Francisco. His dreams of a life of letters were not discouraged. In fact, they were nourished by his father, who once admonished him, "You leave the moneymaking to me and I'll leave the Shakespeare to you." By the mid-1950s, my father had determined that he didn't have the chops to be a writer. Was there a stab at a novel or a book of poems? A manuscript he squirreled away? He never said, and I've never found evidence of such. Clutching his degree in French literature and not sure what to do next with his life, he decided to pursue both law school and a master's degree in English. He attended Berkeley Law, left partway through, graduated from Stanford Law, and then stayed on campus to earn an MA in English, taking classes from Professor Newell Ford, an eminent Shelley scholar.

This is how my father found himself, in the late 1950s, "flat broke and alert to a modest financial opportunity which arose at the Palo Alto Mental Health Facility." In Dad's telling, the clinic was offering two hundred dollars a day for any brave soul willing to submit to experiments that Dr. Russel Lee was conducting with the drug LSD, which was barely known and still quite legal. My father accepted the offer to spend two days under the influence of the psychedelic, during which time he was prompted by the doctors to recite the poems of Gerard Manley Hopkins and other "tactile" verse and to document any relevant insights from the drug on a tape recorder.

It was not long thereafter that my father divined a fork in the road: a career teaching literature to college students or a career practicing the law. Out of no special ardor, he picked the latter. Where to hang his shingle? In pursuit of an answer, he scooped up his T. S. Eliot and William Blake and headed to Lake Tahoe, to the old Squaw Valley ski resort, which had played host to the 1960 Winter Olympics. This was the same resort that his father, thanks to that past friendship with Governor Brown, had been leasing for one dollar a year, a deal that Richard Nixon, running for governor against Brown, tried to turn into a scandal. There, beside the resort's swimming pool sometime in the summer of 1965, William Newsom III made the acquaintance of my mother, Tessa Menzies, a "tall brunette with long legs" and a wicked overhead tennis serve who had only recently graduated from Lowell High School in San Francisco.

Tessa came from a family of brilliant and daring misfits who had carved new paths in botany and medicine and left-wing politics. Her father, Arthur Menzies, who had served in the army during World War II and endured a brutal captivity in a Japanese prisoner of war camp, was an expert in horticulture, especially California wildflowers. Among the family secrets was his decades-long battle with alcoholism and depression. His life of flora, it was said, wasn't enough to blot out the monsters of his wartime confinement. To the horror of my mother and her two sisters, he ended up committing suicide in his bedroom with a .38-caliber bullet to the head. He was fifty-seven years old and left behind no note. There's a four-acre botanical garden full of native plants in Golden Gate Park named after my grandfather

Menzies, whose letters home from the war I keep in a black binder.

My mother's mother, Jean Addis Menzies, was a nurse and an actress who spoke French and Russian and founded an avant-garde theater group in San Francisco. She was said to bear an uncanny resemblance to Katharine Hepburn and went by the odd stage name of Trigger Addis. In the 1930s, when she was barely twenty, her socialist passion took her to Soviet Russia, where she mixed it up with other young American Reds. This was my grandma Jean who understood my childhood struggles with dyslexia like no one else in the family. She was the daughter of Dr. Thomas Addis Jr., a pioneer in kidney-disease research at Stanford University who conceived the so-called Addis count, a method to diagnose kidney function. My great-grandfather worked to devise a special diet for patients suffering from deadly forms of nephritis, especially Bright's disease. Dr. Addis was a tall and lanky Scotsman, which explained the tallness and lankiness of my mother and me, and he was said to be a man of great humility who smoked a pipe as he listened with much care and discernment. When he talked, he spoke in a near whisper. My great-grandfather's antifascist politics, however, were so fierce during the McCarthy era that the FBI suspected him of being a communist and tapped his phones.

I tried now and then to piece together our history, but it remained a narrative shot full of holes. When it came to her past, my mother was almost completely mute. There was no use probing her. She saw no need to revisit or share any part of it. My father, whose highest regard was reserved for literature and history and storytelling, tended to mythologize, if not sanitize, the family history of both sides. I'm not sure he believed that the messy truth of it was relevant or even interesting to me, that it served any purpose, or that I would derive any lessons from it for my own life. California was a grand stage of reinvention, a place where you whitewashed the past and painted afresh, and so it would be with his only son, he must have thought. In his defense, the kid I was gave him plenty of reason to believe that any such transmission of history was fated not to hold. This is not to say that later in my life, when I became a San Francisco supervisor and then the mayor of the city, I did not press him to give me more and he did not regale me with his best stories. And yet, looking back, I have the sense that he used his gift of gab and wit as a shield that would not allow me to peek deeper inside him to understand the ways family history had bent him and thus me.

Our past, it now seems to me, was all too painful for either of my parents to touch. In her deference to silence and secrets, my mother did not possess the language to delve into the complications and tragedies of her parents and grandparents, much less convey the story to me and my sister, Hilary. My mother lived an entire life never making sense of it to herself and believed to the day she died that this was okay. My father was harder to figure. He had the language in all its abundance. And yet the times he decided to share his stories with me, his telling of the past felt like the same performance over and over, a script all too familiar.

And so I am left to guess, among many other details, how all that Menzies and Addis family lore, English and Scottish to boot, got added to the Irish Newsoms. In their hasty courtship, did my mother find a way to reach inside herself and share her family history with my father? Did this then become the glue that bound them? My search for answers sooner or later led me to the transcript of a 2008 interview that historian Martin Meeker conducted with my father for UC Berkeley's Bancroft Library. Among the many colorful stories he passed on to the historian are glimpses into his infatuation with my mother. "I just fell for her," he said. "She was eighteen when we met and going to Chico State. She was nineteen when we married in 1966 and I was thirty-two. Scandalous."

I was born on October 10, 1967, accompanied by the apparently weighty decision to not name me William IV. My father named me Gavin in honor of Gavin Maxwell, who wrote the literary masterpiece *Ring of Bright Water* about his remote house in coastal Scotland, where he raised several wild otters as pets. Hilary was born on December 24, 1968, which made us close to but not quite Irish twins. We lived in an apartment on Octavia Street that bordered the Marina District, with a pet otter named Potter who would fall asleep at the edge of our parents' bed. The animal was so well trained that Dad would play a game of hiding his keys in the couch and Potter would slide over and retrieve them. I was still an infant when Potter developed the habit of nibbling on my toes. Mom apparently laid down an ultimatum. "It's either the otter or us," she informed Dad. He found a wildlife sanctuary for Potter, and we replaced him with bunny rabbits, a guinea pig, and a horse named Tanka that we stabled in the foothills.

My father, a dedicated board member of the Environmental Defense Fund, made it his practice to take on legal cases that were causes. This almost always meant a lot of work rewarded with modest pay. When he later found his way onto the bench, he presided over cases that challenged California institutions such as the Bohemian Grove, the 2,700-acre campground in Sonoma County where some of the world's most powerful men communed among the redwoods. The Grove's management enforced an all-male hiring policy for its workers that my father decided wasn't exempt from the state's fair-employment law. His ruling against the Grove did not sit well with the bigwigs of San Francisco, several of them his good buddies.

As to the question of why our parents divorced after a few years of marriage and Dad moved to Lake Tahoe, two hundred miles away, he had a rather inadequate answer. In a story that lacked his usual flourishes, he told the historian that the blame rested with politics. During the very period in which his children were born, he had made the mistake of running for office not once but twice. This he did at the vehement suggestion of a group of men who were, or would shortly become, the most prominent and powerful politicians in Northern California, including Willie Brown, George Moscone, and Phil and John Burton. Oddly, my father's first campaign, for San Francisco County supervisor, had him running against several candidates, including his brother-in-law, Ron Pelosi, and though Dad won almost fifty-seven thousand votes, a respectable showing, he lost. The second race, for state senator, was against the even more formidable Milton Marks, a Republican who had earned considerable support among Democrats in San Francisco. It wasn't a landslide by any means, but he lost again.

Looking back, my father considered both stabs at elected office to have been fool's errands. In his estimation, he had let his ego get the best of him. The back-to-back campaigns, he explained, left him in such deep financial debt that he could no longer face our mother. He did not mention to the oral historian any need to face his two children, and I am left to conclude that it was his calculation that he could, and would, make it up to me and my sister. "I had, in effect, a kind of breakdown, nervous breakdown," he said. "I was in financial tatters. I'd lost two elections and I thought, *Get me out of here*, or something. We went to marriage counselors for a while. Didn't work. I remember one marriage counselor and every time we would go see him, he would fall asleep. Tessa said to me, 'Bill, let's leave and save the money.' I was in bad shape emotionally, and that is the principal reason I moved to the Lake Tahoe area. I needed a complete change of scenery."

""

D ad wasn't the only Newsom in the room when he sat down to record his oral history. Beside him were his sister, Barbara, and brother, Brennan, the last surviving children of William "the Boss" and Christine Newsom. Their three other siblings had died of cancer at ages far too young. On the transcript pages, the voices of my father, aunt, and uncle are all too alive. Their memories hadn't yet dimmed, and their storytelling skills remained potent, if not at their absolute peak. It didn't hurt that each of them happened to have lived a remarkable life.

Uncle Brennan, as was family tradition, had attended Notre Dame des Victoires and St. Ignatius College Prep before thinking he might become a priest. He spent two years at the Jesuit seminary and then went off to earn his law degree. He was a boxer and a lover of nature, a trial attorney who was a fierce advocate for those without a voice. He possessed a wit that lit up rooms and could expound on a wide range of topics, from Russian military development to the verse of Valéry, without ever sounding like a know-it-all.

Aunt Barbara, whose political acumen came to the aid of Governor Pat Brown more than once, had gone back east for college before marrying a Bay Area boy, Ron Pelosi, Nancy Pelosi's brother-in-law. In 1970, my aunt Barbara and uncle Ron were out to dinner when an electrical fire ignited their home in Presidio Heights, killing their two daughters. My cousin Cynthia, who presided as godmother at my baptism, was only thirteen years old. Her little sister, Caroline, was one. Their Chinese American babysitter, Gwen Yang, who was thirty-five, died in the blaze. My two other Pelosi cousins, Matthew, nine, and Brennan, eleven, somehow survived. This was the great challenge thrust in front of my aunt Barbara during her middle years, and she responded by delving deeper into knowledge, into paleontology and archeology, and into founding an educational retreat for women in Marin County. She and my uncle eventually divorced, and she went back to using her Newsom name. In 1980, President Carter appointed her to represent the United States at the United Nations, and later she directed Georgetown University's Italian studies program outside Florence, Italy.

For the first half hour of the oral history session, my father, Judge Newsom, mostly kept quiet, deferring to his younger brother and sister, which made sense because he wasn't the domineering type and there were two more interview sessions planned with him alone. When he did join in, the three siblings began to aid and abet and sometimes correct each other's recollections. They practically made a sport out of seeing which one of them could furnish the ultimate adornment to the perfect family story.

There's the classic one about their grandmother Anna Brennan, an indefatigable spirit who lived in their home as they were growing up on Jefferson Street in the Marina District. She was an elfin lady whose father had been a horse trainer in a place called Tubbercurry in County Sligo, Ireland. Here in America, her husband, John Brennan, a San Francisco longshoreman by way of County Sligo, too, died in his forties, leaving her to raise their seven children alone. My father recalled that his grandma Anna would awaken at 5:00 a.m. sharp to bake him and his brothers and sisters soda biscuits in the shape of fish. She had an easy sense of humor in spite of the tough life she was called to live, and she liked nothing more than to read the greenish paper on which the *San Francisco Chronicle* printed its sports news, including the pony races at Bay Meadows racetrack. She would dope out the horses at night and decide which ones to wager on the next morning.

One night in her bed she was visited by a vision of Saint Theresa, who was holding up five fingers on one hand and three fingers on the other. This she considered propitious. This she took to mean the fifth horse in the third race. "I'm going to walk up and make a bet with Moon," she told my young father. Moon was her bookie, who operated on the corner of Scott and Chestnut, where he sold four newspapers, the *Call Bulletin*, the *News*, the *Chronicle*, and the *Examiner*, for a nickel each. His work as a newspaper hawker surely didn't explain how Moon was able to tool around town in a brand new 1949 Lincoln Continental. "Dad, I can't quite figure it out," my father, a curious boy, said to his father. "Moon is a paper seller. And he's driving a Lincoln Continental?" His father's reply was close to deadpan. "A substantial inheritance Moon's parents left him. A substantial inheritance."

My great-grandmother Anna grabbed her little maroon coat with a fur collar, her fancy hat with flowers, her round glasses and wood cane, and hightailed it to catch the next bus out to Bay

Meadows. This would not be family legend if the fifth horse in the third race had not placed first and she had not come home the winner of the daily double. She knocked on my father's bedroom door the next morning and asked him, "Want to come get the money? Let's take the F car to Scott and Chestnut." When they arrived at Moon's corner, the bookie looked to be in a panic. "Mrs. Brennan," Moon pleaded, "get lost." Great-grandma Anna was sure that Moon was in a reneging mood. "You owe me twenty-three dollars. I've got the bet right here." Moon looked pained. As it turned out, he wasn't looking to cheat her; he was under surveillance by the cops at that very moment. As they arrested Moon and dragged him away, my great-grandmother began to tear up. It wasn't the money she was crying over. Rather, she was certain it was her stupidity that had gotten Moon busted.

My father's father, Boss Newsom, made a few phone calls to the judge and the district attorney. Moon got off light. If the bookie held anything against my great-grandmother, he didn't hold it for very long. My grandfather treated Moon and his wife to a free vacation at the Newsoms' inn in Sonoma County along the Russian River. My grandfather even dug into his own pocket to cover the winnings Moon owed. The Boss quietly handed the twenty-three dollars to my father and said to give it to my great-grandmother, with a little white lie attached. "Moon sent you this money," my father told her. "He says no hard feelings."

Sixty years later, my father was laughing as he finished telling the story to the oral historian. "That's a true story," he said.

My aunt Barbara nodded. "It's so true," she said.

My father wanted the historian to know that his grandma Anna was the one elder in the family not afraid to display her love. "Nobody ever could get me to eat peas. I would never eat peas. She mashed them in the mashed potatoes, and I ate peas. . . . She was a marvelous person."

She had come from a clan completely sympathetic to the Irish Republican Army and made her loyalties freely known. "'Up the long ladder' . . . she taught me that," Uncle Brennan recalled the old Irish ditty. And then the three siblings began to recite the verse: "Up the long ladder and down the short rope. To hell with King Billy and God bless the Pope."

CHAPTER TWO

....

My father left us in the early 1970s and moved back to the same place where he had plucked my mother off her lifeguard tower: old Squaw Valley. The split in our lives became a geographic one. He opened a small law office near the Truckee River, which flows out of Lake Tahoe. On weekends he'd place a book of poems on the steering wheel of his Volkswagen bug and read aloud as he drove out of the Sierra and across the Central Valley and on to San Francisco to see us. At some point, he wanted to give Hilary and me the choice of spending every third or fourth weekend with him, and Mom was fine with it. They agreed to a midway point for drop-offs and pickups, a legendary road stop along Interstate 80 called the Nut Tree. We couldn't have been more than six and seven, and while I remember almost nothing about those transfers of custody, Hilary remembers a great deal.

During one such exchange, she recalls, Dad had treated us to hamburgers and milkshakes at the Nut Tree's restaurant and was

watching as we rode the carousel and choo-choo train and marveled at the sleek twin-engine airplanes parked one behind the
other in an exhibit of flying machines. We were sucking on treats
from the Nut Tree's candy store and riding these big rocking
horses when Mom, still youthful and starting to date again,
pulled up to take us home. "You were devastated to leave Dad,"
Hilary told me. "You were holding on to him and crying, and you
wouldn't let go. It was just agonizing to watch. I remember feeling crushed for Mom because she had to see that. *That has to hurt
her*, I remember thinking. *Gavin doesn't want to come home.* It hurt
me to see how much pain you were in."

I had buried the experience deep enough inside that it seemed
like it was someone else's life. The little I remember about those
transfers of custody at the Nut Tree I remember with fondness. I
remember my father sitting there with a book in his hand. I remember my mother, years before the ravages of breast cancer,
excited to see us. I do not remember anything even remotely
wrenching. And yet I have no doubt that I threw just such a fit. I
was a difficult kid, and the worst of my acting out came at night,
when it was time for bed. Tired to the core, I could not shut down.
I'd scream and yell to get my mother's attention, and she'd do her
best to ignore me, often with the aid of a few glasses of cheap
wine. I'd run out of the bedroom and throw myself to the living
room floor and start pounding my fists. She'd scoop me up and
deposit me back in my room and hold the door shut so I couldn't
get out. "Relax, Gavin," she'd say. "Fall asleep." I'd shout and cry
for another thirty minutes until exhaustion, and then sleep set in.

Inside my whirl of turmoil, it didn't register with me the load
she was carrying. To make ends meet, Mom had to take on second and third jobs. At different points, she was working as an

assistant buyer in the children's department at I. Magnin four days a week, a bookkeeper in the Financial District once a week, a waitress at Ramona's Mexican restaurant in San Rafael on Friday and Saturday nights, a development director for a Piedmont nonprofit called Aid to Adoption of Special Kids, and a budding real estate agent in the hours that were spare. Mom had to lean on her twin sister, Aunt Anne, to help rear us. My aunt was married to Paul Scherer, who happily took on the role of second father to Hilary and me with a gentle touch that blended humor and wisdom. Uncle Paul had been adopted by a Jewish couple when he was a baby, and he loved the state of Israel and Jewish history as if they ran in his blood. He was a podiatrist who also possessed great skill with hammer, nails, and handsaw. Whenever Mom needed a repair around the house, he came to our rescue.

After Uncle Paul and Aunt Anne had their first son, Michael, and then second son, Jeremy, they weren't always available to rescue us. Hilary and I found ourselves whiling away long hours shooting hoops and hitting tennis balls and baseballs at Funston Park. We were among a gaggle of Marina District waifs who fell under the protective wing of a city recreation director named Frank. I couldn't get enough of Frank, who had an ocean of patience for my quirks. His influence on me was so impactful that years later, when I became a San Francisco supervisor, I dedicated a bench at the playground in his memory. Hilary and I were fortunate to be able to call upon a host of surrogates during our childhood, but there were never enough of them. We were home alone for too many hours on too many days. We raised ourselves on giant bowls of mac and cheese and thought nothing of it. When I first heard the term *latchkey kids* years later, I thought to myself, *Yeah, that was my sister and me.*

It took some epic dawdling to fall behind in the third grade, but I managed to recede far from view at Notre Dame des Victoires, the K–8 school run by French Catholics at the edge of San Francisco's Chinatown. This was no small shame, considering all the Newsoms before me who had graduated from the school speaking fluent French. Being unable to stick it out at Notre Dame meant I wouldn't be walking through the gates of St. Ignatius College Prep, the Jesuit school in the city that my father and his brothers had attended. Mom was afraid I'd see myself as a loser, but she needn't have worried. I'm not sure I saw myself as anything set in stone at that point. She scheduled a visit with our pediatrician, Dr. Brad Cohen, who handed me a lollipop and a diagnosis of "learning disabled." The term was all-encompassing enough to explain my hyperactivity, tantrums, and fear of falling asleep.

We were living in the apartment on Octavia Street where Dad had left us, but it wasn't for long. Over the span of a decade, Mom moved us five times in search of a better house in a better neighborhood with the right schools. First came the two-bedroom flat on Toledo Way with five windows that looked out onto a narrow street of cramped houses filled with second- and third-generation Italian and Irish families like ours. Lucca Deli was right behind us, and when robbers came one night to steal from its till, they used our backyard for their getaway. When one of the families on the block, a mother with three girls, was having trouble paying rent, my mother offered our place as living quarters. The arrangement saved them money and put a little extra cash in Mom's purse. Each of their names began with an *R*, my sister recalls. The girls were Robin, Rachel, and Rebecca. Their moving in required a whole new conception of space. My mother slept on a mattress in the dining room; Hilary and I shared one bedroom, the girls and their mother the other bedroom. How we managed to carve out some semblance of privacy I do not know, but I don't remember it ever being uncomfortable.

Next came the move out of the city and into the suburbs of Marin, at the other end of the Golden Gate Bridge. Mom bought our first house, on Baltimore Avenue in Corte Madera, for forty thousand dollars with a helping hand from Dad. It was a small wooden A-frame with a red door and a white picket fence on a block noisy with kids. The marshland of the bay was on one side of the neighborhood, the peak of Mount Tam, where the sun set, on the other. We were surrounded by redwood canyons. The house came with a real yard, which meant we could have a dog, a springer spaniel we named (what else?) Snoopy. My sister and I were seven and eight, and we finally had our own space after Uncle Paul tore out a wall in the hallway upstairs and built Hilary a cubbyhole big enough to fit a bed.

We made fast friends with the Munson family across the street. They had a daughter our age named Katherine, and she became pals with Hilary and me. Because our mornings were so rushed, with Mom scrambling to get to work, we were Carnation Instant Breakfast kids. This bothered Yvonne Munson, Katherine's mom, to no end. Before we knew it, she was feeding us eggs and bacon and whole-wheat pancakes and making sure we got off to school on time. I can still remember the trepidation I felt walking to school in the fifth grade in a district that ranked among the best in California.

Those children of excellence were the footsteps in front of me. The footsteps behind me belonged to a boy named Jason, otherwise known as the bully of Baltimore Avenue. He was cunning and cruel and possessed a GPS system for kids who were the opposite. He zeroed in on my skinny legs and unruly hair, which did not mind comb or brush. I've managed to erase from my brain nearly all the stunts he pulled on me. Hilary remembers only his telling her this: "If you want to find your brother, look for him hanging on the fence by the threads of his underwear," which strikes me today as one of the all-time great lines of bullydom.

A single tormentor, however, wasn't enough to spoil Corte Madera for me. The Marin sunlight felt like no place I'd ever been. The air had traveled miles over open sea and swept through the canyons with elements of brine, marsh, redwood, mountain, laurel, and poppy. It was an air that called you outside and made you want to build things with your hands. Home alone, I woke up Hilary one morning with an idea to erect a miniature golf course in the backyard and charge the neighbor kids a fee to play. We drew the plans on paper, paced off the four holes, and began clearing lawn and flower bed with shovel and rake. The next day, alone again, we smoothed out the four holes and planted cans and other impediments that a golfer had to work around to put a ball in the hole.

We had a good idea what our mother, who took pride in her manicured garden, would make of it. On her day off from work, seeing for the first time what we had done, she threw a fit. She wasn't the kind to resort to corporal punishment. She resorted to the silent treatment instead. The notion that I was a budding businessman whose first foray into capitalism needed to be nurtured eventually softened her up. Hilary stood behind our split farm door, the top half open, and collected the ticket money and whatever she could wangle for the baked goods. The grand opening of Newsoms' Miniature Golf was a hit.

Apart from my mother, no one attending the Little League games at Joe Wagner Field in Larkspur in the late 1970s would have marked as a future prospect the Newsom kid playing way out in right field for Round Table Pizza. What is seared into my memory is the holy terror of stepping into the batter's box and facing Maurice Bigham, an amazing athlete who went on to become a great high school shortstop. I was one of the only left-handed hitters in the lineup, but this didn't faze Bigham in the least. He struck me out on four pitches my first time up. He struck me out on four pitches my second time up. The third time up I don't believe I ever took the bat off my shoulder. Fastball strike, fastball strike, fastball strike.

Wagner Field was just a couple blocks from our house, and my mother, who had witnessed my frozen stance from the front row, wiped the disappointment from my face, walked me home, grabbed a bucket of balls from the garage, and walked me right back to the field. For the next hour, as the Marin sky went to dusk, my mom, the former San Francisco tennis champion, threw me batting practice. She was a lefty like me and could hurl a baseball even better than my coach. She told me to keep my eye on the ball, swing level, and take the outside pitch the other way—all those pointers that parents can't help shouting at their kids from the aluminum stands. Only years later did it occur to me that batting practice with Tessa wasn't a lesson in how to get a base hit. My mom, who kept a roof over our heads, was teaching me how to persevere.

""""

The drive from Corte Madera to San Francisco across the Golden Gate Bridge took thirty minutes on a good day. The city was near enough that, even as a kid in the thrall of

Mount Tam, I never stopped regarding San Francisco as the place that had shaped the destinies of four generations of Newsoms and would do the same for me. I moved between its flagrant worlds of rich and poor and hardly thought it remarkable. No one on either side of the divide—not those who lived in the stone castles of Nob Hill, not those who slept in the flophouses of the Tenderloin—ever accused me of trespassing. When I crossed over into the Marina District, where my Newsom grandparents lived in what looked to my eyes to be a three-story palace, I did so in the most casual manner. It was a wonder how effortlessly I glided because the two realms of my life, the characters of my mother's world and the characters of my father's world, did not fit together in the least.

The starkness of this crossing must have first occurred to me in the context of our relationship with the Gettys, one of the wealthiest families in the world. As early as seven years old, I had a sense that the Newsoms had been tied to the Gettys for a long time, though I wasn't sure exactly how. Were we distant cousins? Did the two clans sail on the boat together from Hibernia at the shout of California gold? One Christmas season, when Hilary and I were quite young, our father took us shopping at our favorite toy store just off Chestnut Street in San Francisco's Marina. I had no special gift in mind, but Hilary had her heart set on a new pair of pink Barbie high heels that clicked when she walked. Before we turned onto Chestnut, Dad made a detour to pick up his godson, Eugene Paul Getty II, "Paul" to us, who had just arrived in the city after surviving a gruesome kidnapping in Italy that made international news. The boy was seventeen years old, nearly a man, but my father believed that after what he'd been through, an outing to the toy store might be in order.

Paul was waiting for us on the steps of a house, and as we pulled up, Dad admonished us for a second time, "Now, whatever you guys do or say, all I'm asking is that you don't mention Paul's missing ear."

As best I remember, Paul didn't look like the "spoiled brat, rotten child" whose wild party nights had become fodder for the European tabloids. His red hair was curly and touched his back, and he wasn't wearing the tight bell-bottoms and loud unbuttoned shirt that had become his style. He was dressed in a turtleneck and plain pants. Only his fancy sunglasses gave him away. He smiled at Hilary and me in the back seat and climbed in next to Dad.

As we merged into traffic, I could see my father's eyes looking at us in the rearview mirror, which I took to be a third warning to stay quiet about Paul's ear. For a few seconds there was silence, and then Hilary blurted out, "Paul, how many ears do you have?"

Paul, whose sarcasm had gotten him booted out of eight deluxe schools across Europe, couldn't help laughing. "I've got one ear on the side of my head and the other one stuck in my brain."

Dad didn't get upset at Hilary. He was probably too busy admiring Paul's wit. Whatever vacancy was left by Paul's missing right ear must have been covered up by his hair, because I don't recall seeing it gone. Either that or I averted my gaze, which was a wise habit to form when your small aperture on the universe suddenly opened to take in the fantastical comings and goings of the Getty dynasty. It wasn't long before I would become keenly versed in how the Newsoms were connected to the Gettys and what it meant to be an extension of their family.

Young Paul was the son of John Paul Getty Jr. and the nephew of Gordon Peter Getty, two brothers whom my father counted as his closest friends dating back to the 1940s, before they attended St. Ignatius College Prep in the city and then the University of San Francisco. The two brothers were the middle sons of oil magnate Jean Paul Getty, nicknamed "Oklahoma Crude," whose five marriages included one to their mother, Helen Ann Rork, a silent film actress who married five times herself and appeared in movies with Rudolph Valentino.

My dad would tell me that John Paul and Gordon loved their father dearly, but because old man Getty was absent for such long stretches, he was more a mythical figure to his sons than an actual father. Already the richest man in the world, Getty Sr. did not stop grabbing for more. He stretched his empire from the Oklahoma oil fields to a barren patch near the border between Saudi Arabia and Kuwait, where he proceeded to extract sixteen million barrels of crude a year. "The meek shall inherit the earth but not its mineral rights," he was reputed to have said. He hopped from his fifteenth-century castle on the Italian coast to his seventy-two-room mansion in Surrey, England, to his ranch in Malibu. The money he sent to his ex-wives furnished a comfortable but hardly extravagant lifestyle for his children.

As a result, John Paul and Gordon did a lot of their growing up at the three-story Newsom house on Jefferson and Baker Streets, just down from the Palace of Fine Arts in the Marina District. There the Getty boys found a different sort of rearing. My grandfather William "Boss" Newsom and grandma Christine made sure that my father and his five siblings attended Mass every day and went to school with starched collars and cuffs, polished shoes, and packed lunches. When the family sat down at the dinner table on Sunday evenings over a big lamb roast, John

Paul and Gordon would often sit down with them. The Boss, who presided over things with a spirit my father described as "generous and enlightened," led conversations about politics, race, economic disparity, and civilization's ill-treatment of the environment and made clear that at his table, a girl's opinion would be given every bit as much weight as a boy's.

The Getty brothers did not address my grandfather as "Mr. Newsom." They called him "Boss" instead. "Boss, let me ask you a question," Gordon would say. The Boss did not want for his own legend, having run away from home at thirteen (his mother was too bossy, he said) and hopped the rails to Arizona, where he joined a boxcar poker game that ended with one player murdering another. My grandfather took a job with the railroad, learned the construction trade, and returned to San Francisco to build houses atop the landfills of the Marina District. In his middle years, he opened a wholesale flower business with the Zappettini family, who had cornered the market on chrysanthemums ("mums"), which had become required etiquette at mob funerals from San Francisco to Chicago.

The way my dad told it, the Getty boys were practically his sixth and seventh siblings. They venerated my grandfather long after those Sunday salons and never stopped looking upon him as a father figure and role model. When John Paul flew off to Italy in the late 1950s to oversee the family business there, he took a framed photo of the Boss with him. My grandfather then watched with great sadness as the tragedies of the Getty clan unfolded, understanding there was little he could do about it. My father, by contrast, altered the course of his life to provide aid, counsel, and comfort to the Gettys. When misfortune or scandal found one

Getty scion or another, it was Bill Newsom, family consigliere, who flew off in one direction or another to the rescue. At first, he did this out of devotion to his best friends, John Paul and Gordon, but later he would serve the Gettys in an official capacity as one of the lawyers overseeing the family's $4 billion trust.

It pained my father to see John Paul become the first of the siblings to succumb to the disquiet that would trouble far too many Getty men. In Rome, during the 1960s, John Paul found himself separated from his moorings, from San Francisco and his closest buddies and brother Gordon. In no time, it seemed to my father, he had assumed a whole other persona. John Paul grew his hair long, dressed in hipster garb, and showed up at late-night parties with his new pal Mick Jagger. The transformation, splashed across the tabloids of Europe, was hard to behold. His wife, Gail, the debutante daughter of a San Francisco judge, no longer recognized him. In an effort to repair the breach, my father flew to Rome and back in a shuttle diplomacy that failed to bring the two parties together. John Paul and Gail separated and then divorced, and this put a bitter distance between him and his four children, especially his oldest son, redheaded Paul. John Paul was too busy courting Talitha Pol, a Dutch model crowned by the tabloids as "one of the most beautiful women in the world," to mend relations with his kids. He and Talitha married and flew off to Marrakech, where they developed a fondness for heroin.

When a massive overdose took Talitha's life in 1971, a grieving John Paul exiled himself to Wormsley, a 2,700-acre country estate in Buckinghamshire, England, where he hung up the framed photo of the Boss. He became a proud citizen of Britain and then underwent a second transformation into one of England's most storied philanthropists, giving away tens of millions

of dollars to striking miners and needy children and other righteous causes. He befriended Prime Minister Margaret Thatcher
and grew to love the game of cricket, hosting epic matches at his
estate, soaking in the scene with Jagger and playwright Harold
Pinter. His willingness to part with so much of his wealth would
earn him a knighthood from the queen: Sir Paul Getty.

His causes, however, did not extend to his son Paul, who kept
searching for a father figure. The boy had been living in Italy
with his mother, Gail, hanging out with young models and left-
ists, setting fire to his boarding school, and generally earning a
reputation as a world-class misanthrope. Then on a summer night
in 1973, young Paul was walking the deserted streets of Rome at
four in the morning when a big white car pulled up and out
jumped four burly men. One hit him with the butt of a pistol and
the other covered his nose with a chloroform-soaked cloth. Hours
later, when they took off his blindfold, Paul could see that he was
caught in the toe of the boot of Italy, a grim land cursed by ban-
ditry.

So began a five-month ordeal in which some of the Getty
clan, including those who held the purse strings, entertained the
notion that little Paul, the family mutineer, had staged his own
kidnapping. The demanded ransom was $17 million, a pittance
to his grandfather. My father, whose role as consigliere to the
Getty family in times of turmoil came with no salary, jumped
into service. First he flew to England to consult with the boy's
father, John Paul, and then he flew to Rome to consult with the
boy's mother, Gail, whom he'd been close to most of his life. He
thought of calling on Grandpa Getty, ensconced in his castle, but
the old man had already issued a statement to the press: "I don't
believe in paying kidnappers. I have fourteen other grandchildren

and if I pay one penny now, then I'll have fourteen kidnapped grandchildren."

Summer and fall passed with no deal. Each new call from the kidnappers laid down a different demand. The voice on the phone was now insisting on $5 million, "paid in very small notes." My father wasn't sure how to read their dithering. It was either evidence of a gang that couldn't shoot straight or another indication that Paul, a trust fund baby locked out of his trust fund, was in on the stunt. The Italian attorney hired by the family, who'd been consulting with my father, told the kidnappers that $5 million was out of the question. "A friend of the boy's mother is here from America with one hundred thousand dollars," the attorney said. "That's our offer."

"For one hundred thousand dollars," the voice said, "we'll send you a photo of the boy missing an arm or leg." The voice hung up.

Paul would later make the cover of *Rolling Stone* and recount the harrowing details of his captivity. The kidnappers, who were part of the Calabrian Mafia, threw him into a cave and tied him to a stake in the ground. As he lost track of time, he was able to tell from the resolve in their voices that a decision about his fate had finally been made. They untied him, made him face the cave wall, shoved a cloth into his mouth, and told him to bite down hard. They said it wouldn't hurt. They sliced off his right ear and a blood-soaked lock of his hair and put them in a plastic bag accompanied by a ransom note. They mailed the package to one of Italy's biggest dailies and awaited word from the Gettys. What the kidnappers failed to account for was a national mail strike that was postponing deliveries by weeks.

By the time a reporter opened the package, the ear no longer resembled an ear. "This is Paul's first ear," the note read. "If within ten days the family still believes that this is a joke mounted by him, then the other ear will arrive." When the cops showed the ear to Gail, she recognized her son's freckles. My father helped with the logistics of collecting and delivering the $2.9 million in ransom money. As it ended up, the oil tycoon would contribute $2.2 million to free his favorite grandson. This was the maximum amount that was tax-deductible. Paul was let go with a large bandage on his head and hitchhiked his way back to Rome.

Driving to the toy store that day with Paul is among the earliest memories I have of our close relations to the Gettys. My sister and I were far too young to have the least idea of what Paul had lived through, but we sensed that our father was trying to ease his wound. He was just seventeen, a boy who'd been carrying a Mickey Mouse comic book under his arm when the kidnappers stole him from his life. I wish I could recollect something from our roaming the toy aisles, but I can't. Neither can Hilary.

Paul returned to Europe and underwent a series of operations to reconstruct his ear. At eighteen, he married Gisela Martine Zacher, a German film actress who had a child named Anna. This was interpreted as an act of defiance by the oil baron, who apparently did not approve of early marriages for his grandchildren. He promptly wrote Paul out of his will. Paul would later respond to that disinheritance by adopting Anna as his own child in a civil court proceeding presided over by my father. By then, Paul and Gisela had added a son named Balthazar to the mix. Paul found solace in fatherhood and the study of Chinese history, but the past would not let go of him. At age twenty-five, after consuming a mixture of Valium, methadone, and alcohol, he suffered a stroke that left him quadriplegic and nearly blind. Though he could no longer speak except for grunts and moans, he was determined to keep living as full a life as possible. I'd see him out with my father at a North Beach restaurant or at the annual Getty get-together in Lake Tahoe, where he found an inventive way to ski the slopes again. He was able to communicate a whole language with his eyes and show his children the world before dying at the age of fifty-four. My window on the Gettys would serve up many lessons of a realm I could see and touch but never hold, but none was more vivid than Paul's absolute insistence on affirming life no matter the circumstances.

Chapter Three

""

The geographic distance between my father's life and our lives had an impact on my relationship with my paternal grandparents. Our visits with them were few and far between, I'm guessing, because they lived in the Marina District of San Francisco and we lived across the Golden Gate in Corte Madera, and a visit would have required my father's driving in from Tahoe City or Dutch Flat to take us there. The paucity of memories I have of them is surely a consequence of this. Then again, I was nine when Grandpa Newsom died and eleven when Grandma Newsom died, and maybe memories don't plant themselves in children that young, especially a child whose brain was trying to sort out its scrambles. Mom was too busy juggling chores at home and chores at work to act as a conduit. Besides, her relationship with the Newsoms never seemed all that warm, at least by the account of my mother's older sister, Cindy.

Aunt Cindy was a pistol of a woman married to actor Ed Asner, her third go-around, and over the years she took it upon herself to fill in many of my blank spots. When I questioned her about one detail or another, she did not endeavor to find polite words for people or things. I appreciated her blunt honesty, though at times what came out of her mouth made me wince. "Your mother called your grandfather 'Mr. Newsom.' Can you believe that? 'Mr. Newsom.' For Christ's sakes, that was her father-in-law. She was his daughter-in-law. You would have figured that someone in the Newsom family—your father, for one—might have said, 'Tessa, "Mr. Newsom" isn't necessary.' Or, better yet, your grandfather himself would have had the decency to say, 'Tessa, I'm Bill, or how about Poppa to you.'"

It is hard to reconcile Aunt Cindy's severe view of my grandfather with the oral histories of my father and Uncle Brennan and Aunt Barbara. The three siblings detail the delightful foibles of friends and family members, but the stories they tell about their father cast a far more glowing light. They find few, if any, faults in his makeup. Even the tales of his nursing pints of Seagram's 7 they recalled with admiration. The Boss could hold his booze like no one they knew, they said; he would never be caught "in the bag." Under his command, their house was (to use a fifty-cent word) an "agora," my aunt Barbara said. The Boss, a consummate chef, was the one who prepared the Sunday lamb. And it wasn't merely the Getty boys who sat around the table and benefited from his sage mentoring. He did the same with their other friends, boys and girls whose families did not have a lick of wealth. Years later these friends, now grown, would approach my father or one of his siblings at the market or dry cleaner's or at a social gathering and ask, "Do you know what your father did for me?" or say, "You have no idea what it was like to be at your house, what a pleasure it was to be at your house."

In their telling, the Boss was a mathematical genius, open-minded, generous, community spirited, a lover of the Swedish tenor Jussi Björling and a despiser of Senator Joseph McCarthy and his miserable band of Red hunters. He would not join the most blue-blooded social clubs of San Francisco because they forbade Jews. "God, I don't think he knew five Republicans," my father quipped. The front door of my grandparents' house was never locked, and into the entry walked a burlesque of California dreamers.

There was the Hoover vacuum salesman, Mr. Lorenzo, a narcoleptic who, without fail, fell asleep on the couch while demonstrating the sucking power of his latest model. "Sssshhh," my grandma Newsom would whisper to her children, index finger to lip. "Can't you see Mr. Lorenzo is sleeping?" There was Tom Kyne, one of the old Irish types who lived in a downtown hotel. He held the title of the city's "betting commissioner," and if anyone thought this was an official position, they'd be incorrect. Kyne was a bookie and fixer who put up half the money for Pat Brown's first campaign, though Brown probably never knew it, because my grandfather, who raised the money, never told him. If some poor guy died in the streets, Kyne would pay for the funeral. My grandfather was not shy about his affection for Kyne, not even after the Kefauver Committee shut down his bookmaking operation in 1946. He regarded Kyne as a type that had disappeared from the earth. "Solid guy," my father recalled. "Solid. Word was his bond."

Not to be forgotten was the down-and-out stranger with a thickly brocaded Scottish accent who stood on my grandparents' front porch on a very hot day. "Do you think a fellow could get a drink of water here?" the Scotsman asked my young uncle Brennan. The Boss, seated in the living room, overheard the man. "Fine," he said. "Have him come in." So the stranger came in and sat down and was promptly served a glass of water. He finished the drink but the Boss kept proceeding in his utter absorption of the man. He went on and on. "My father entertained the guy for an hour and a half," Brennan recounted. When the man finally departed, Brennan thought his father must have done the immigrant a terrible disservice. "He probably gave the guy the wrong idea about what America was really like: that everybody was like my dad . . . My dad was a very engaging person."

My grandfather Newsom was walking with a cane by the time I have a distinct memory of him. He sat in his throne chair in his parlor and read from a wide collection of dime-store paperbacks, an endless array of cowboy books adorned with western-themed covers that always grabbed my attention. I'd enter his domain, curl up beside his feet, and try to answer the questions he tossed down to me every few pages. "How is school?" was surely one of his inquiries. What was I to tell him? "How is life on the other side of the Bay? Do you miss San Francisco?" I can't imagine he asked me if I missed my father. I tried to describe to him my awe of those bus rides over the Golden Gate to the city and my fascination with the people who would lose all hope and jump off the bridge, down, down into choppy waters of the bay, only to live to tell the story.

He asked if any girl had caught my fancy—I was a boy with a bowl cut and had no such story to tell him—and then he put down the paperback and had me stand up next to his chair. We were now eye to eye. "Where's the dollar bill?" he asked.

I knew the game. It was our one ritual. He reached into his pocket and pulled out a crisp one. "Can you catch it? You gotta be quick, Gavin."

I nodded and positioned my left hand in front of him, with

thumb and index finger stretched out sideways so that only a thin bit of space was between them. It wasn't an easy catch. He didn't dangle the dollar bill above my hand. Most of it was already past my thumb and index finger as he held it there. His own fingers were stained antique yellow from a lifetime of cigarette smoking.

"Ready?" he asked.

"Yes." I nodded.

"Set."

He let go of the dollar, and by a force of gravity I could not reckon it slipped straight between my thumb and finger. I missed it by a whisker. He laughed.

"You're fast, Gavin. But you have to be even faster."

"Try it again," I said, picking up the dollar and handing it back to him.

He let it go, and I missed it a second time and he couldn't stop laughing. I shot him the most determined look and went inside my head to find a zone of concentration. He changed none of his tactics to make the challenge easier. I missed it a third time and came away with the lesson that gravity, like my grandfather growing old, could not be beat. That's when Boss Newsom, taking pity on me, handed me the dollar bill and said, "It's yours." But not quite yet. He grabbed my arm and made me wrestle him for it, a pull that always knocked me backward when he finally let go of the bill.

"You got it," he said, giggling to himself.

We climbed into his old beige Cadillac, windows smoke fogged. The family story was that he had inhaled more King Sano cigarettes—"mildest of the mild," "all that joyous aroma but less nicotine"—than any single person alive. The words on the pack were the product of the tar wars of the 1950s, when cigarette makers were using health claims to sell their deadly cartons. I harangued him to no end, and to no avail, about giving up the habit. He lit up a Pall Mall, his new brand of choice, and drove on to Chestnut Street, the Marina District's main commercial strip, where all our family's favorite haunts hugged the boulevard. There was Lucca Deli, the doughnut shop, the magic store, the toy store where Dad took us shopping with Paul Getty Jr., and O' Sole Mio with its red-and-white checkered tablecloths and pizza that came out of the oven so hot that the cheese slid off if you didn't fold the crust.

As soon as he parked and climbed out of the car, another ritual began. Every half block, my grandfather on his cane encountered another friend or acquaintance or business partner from the old days. They called him "the mayor of Chestnut Street" for good reason. Yes, he had built their neighborhood by piling dirt on top of sinking marina ground, but he was their neighbor above all. And together what a neighborhood they had created, full of Irish and Italian and Jewish success stories, people of climbing wealth who were shedding the old ways by marrying across ethnic lines and embracing what it meant to be a Californian. Or so I gathered in the sunlight of their chatter and from what I've managed to piece together in the years since.

As my grandfather moved from one chance encounter to the next, he needed no map, no crisscross directory, to remember who used to live where. On the corner beside the Spanish consulate was the beautiful house owned by Leno "Fats" Capaccioli, a benign but big-time bookmaker. His son Walter was now a judge, so let's be careful what we say. Next door to my grandparents lived the dapper Simon Goldberg, one of the founders of the Prisunic variety store chain in France. He drove an old Pontiac, and every time Uncle Brennan opened the garage door for him, he handed him a dime. Around the corner was Mr. Birnbaum, who had once threatened to pull down Aunt Barbara's pants and spank her, which sent my grandfather "off the roof." Across the street lived Hugo Carissimo, the chef at the swanky Blue Fox, which looked out to the city's morgue on Merchant Street. The restaurant was owned by Mario Morin from Venice, Italy, but it was Mr. Carissimo who prepared San Francisco's finest meals for a crowd that included Bing Crosby, Frank Sinatra, Joe DiMaggio, and Marilyn Monroe. Joan Crawford stored her own case of vodka there.

Back in the forties, my grandfather had purchased each lot for a thousand dollars and quickly sold each one for two thousand. This return he considered "a fortune," and he pooh-poohed any talk from Aunt Barbara that he would have made a "real fortune" had he held on to the properties a little longer. That day, the two of us standing on the sidewalk of Chestnut Street, I tried to listen to, if not completely absorb, his conversations. He must have glimpsed in me a hint of impatience, because he cut short one conversation and said in the voice of a much younger man, "You want a glazed éclair with almond shavings?" That was *his* favorite pastry. Mine was a chocolate old-fashioned doughnut. We walked into the shop and he let me order for myself, and we wolfed down our confections. I must have made known what I desired next, because the next thing I can recall is him driving in the direction of home and me clutching a Marshall Brodien TV Magic Show kit and a Popeil Pocket Fisherman complete with rod, reel, line, bobber, and hook. These two gifts became my most prized possessions. Looking out through the smoky stain of the window, I could see that he had driven a block past their house and was now parking in front of the Palace of Fine Arts.

"There's a pond with fish here," he said. "You want to catch one?"

I jumped out, and we made our way to the water's edge. I threw in a line and waited and waited. I did not catch a fish. In fact, I fell into the water and thought for sure I was going to drown. But the pond, it turned out, was little more than a mud-hole. The water was maybe three feet deep, a con job. Years later, in my role as mayor, we dredged out that pond, redid it completely, and stocked its waters with real fish.

Back at their house, I studied the rooms with so many antiques and headed for the garden out back. Though every type of vegetable was growing there, I made a beeline for the carrots. I straddled the long row and pulled out a handful and gave them a wash. They were deeply orange and sweet tasting. I climbed the stairs to the second floor, where it struck me that my grandparents slept in separate beds, and then up to the third floor with its own air of mystery. A trove of *Mad* magazines was there waiting for me. At dinner, in the formal dining room, I don't recall my grandfather presiding over the table in any particular fashion. Searching my mind's eye for something more than a fleeting glimpse of my grandma Christine, I can see her, but she flits on the far periphery. Her presence in the house is a shadow out of focus.

My father and his siblings talked very little about their mother. Their easy fondness for their father, it seemed to me, did not extend to my grandmother. She came from a Brennan family of hard drinkers directly out of Ireland. She worked in San Francisco as a secretary for the Pacific Gas & Electric Company and had the stock certificates to prove it. She had married the Boss when she was a teenager and he was in his early thirties, almost the exact same age gap as my mother and father. She carried with her a more stern Irish version of Catholicism than the more relaxed French version embraced by the Newsoms. "My mother was pretty rigid," my father recounted to the oral historian. "Every morning, I had to serve Mass."

With much fondness, Dad then told the story of his father placing a bet on the presidential election of 1948. My grandfather bet "the Greeks" that Truman would defeat Dewey. The odds were five to one in Dewey's favor. He withdrew $13,000 out of their savings account—the equivalent of $165,000 today—and placed the bet at Tom Kyne's joint. By the time the radio declared that Truman had won, it was past midnight. The Boss came rolling home at three in the morning with a few drinks aboard. My father, a fourteen-year-old kid excited by Truman's victory, was awake to greet him. He had never seen his father drunk, he recounted, and he wasn't drunk now. Unlike his mother, his father had a "terrific capacity for drink."

"Billy," my grandfather told my father, "get me my half-pint."

My father brought down a bottle of Seagram's 7 from the cupboard and poured him a drink.

"Look, we did pretty well tonight," my grandfather said. "Is your mother awake?"

"No, she's sound asleep."

"Go up and see."

My father ran up the stairs and confirmed that his mother was "out cold."

"Billy, here," my grandfather said, handing a twenty-dollar bill to my father. He had never seen a twenty spot materialize so easily. "Help me count the money."

It was an ungodly amount, my father said. They counted something like fifty thousand dollars.

"Billy," the Boss said with a conspirator's grin, "your mother doesn't have to know exactly how well I did, all right?"

A week later, my grandfather took a small portion of his winnings and bought my grandmother a new 1948 Cadillac, a beautiful car but not quite the royal-blue Pierce-Arrow convertible he had given her as an engagement gift. She went on believing his blarney, that he had won an astounding six thousand dollars in a bet on Truman and had spent a good bit of it on her Caddy.

Whenever I broached the subject of my grandmother Christine with my aunt Cindy, she pierced her mystery this way: "If you have a difficult time remembering your grandma Newsom, it's for good reason. She wasn't well. She was an alcoholic with six children. That's why her mother from Ireland, Anna Brennan, was such a presence in your father's life."

I can distinctly remember the day in March 1977 that my mother called with the news of Grandpa Newsom's passing. I was home alone eating my mac and cheese. The white phone with the long cord hanging on the white wall rang two times. I picked it up. "I have some bad news," my mother said in a flat voice. "Your grandfather died."

I had never heard those words about someone I loved, and I did not know what to do with the finality of them. I dropped the phone and left it dangling. There was no one home to stop me from pounding my fists into the floor, but the pounding brought no relief. I was all alone with a sorrow I had never felt in my life.

""""

My sister and I did not altogether lose hope that our parents would find a way back to each other. For a brief time in the late 1970s, Dad returned to live and work in San Francisco and would come to the house for holidays and birthdays. Sometimes he'd spend the night. "Oh, I guess Dad's back," I'd tell Hilary, thinking it might lead to something more. Then the next day would come, and he'd be gone again. One evening Rick Barry, the future Hall of Famer who shot his free throws for the Warriors underhand, walked through the door. He was six foot seven, but we didn't know who the heck he was. He and Mom dated, though it never got serious, not like her relationship with Peter, the San Francisco fireman whom she met on the tennis courts at Funston Playground. We heard our father had a "friend" of his own, and during one of the weekends we stayed with him in Tahoe City, we met a lovely woman named Paula. He ended up bringing her to a wedding where family and friends were gathered, and Hilary remembers a look of devastation on Mom's face.

My sense, though, was that Dad was more or less satisfied living a life unattached and that Paula or any other female friend he might find wasn't ever going to become a fixture in our lives. He had his books and he had his forever pals. Many of them he traced back to St. Ignatius College Prep, class of 1951, and to the University of San Francisco. They had become prominent attorneys and prominent businessmen, most of them divorced or never married. The Lonely Hearts Club, they called themselves. John Mallen, Jim Halligan, Lou Felder, Chris Malarkey, Lloyd Fabbri, Art Groza, and my father. I was okay with the notion that my parents would never remarry each other or marry anyone else, which neither of them ever did.

Whether they routinely compared notes on how Hilary and I were faring wasn't made clear to us. Looking back, I'm of the mind that Dad was fine with Mom keeping him in the dark on most domestic matters, including how I was doing in school.

Early on, my teachers recognized the cruelty in giving me my turn to read aloud to the rest of the class. Once I graduated to middle school, the book report became my nemesis. Nothing made me tighten up in the gut more. My English teacher had assigned *Treasure Island* by Robert Louis Stevenson. It was right up my alley, a tale of buccaneers and buried gold. It had action, it had a place remote and mysterious, it had a one-legged pirate disguised as a cook named Long John Silver. It had many words, and many lines, on a page. What was I to do? The book report I turned in ended up being a straight lift of the slick description of *Treasure Island* written on its back cover. I may have changed a half dozen words and replaced them with words of my own. I was no more devious than that. I got a D-minus, and the teacher told me, "We need to talk," though I don't believe we ever did.

My mother tried to help me with my homework, but each day was a hustle for her. She didn't know what to make of my dyslexia. By the time she arrived home from work, she was exhausted. She'd come into my bedroom, open my textbooks, and try to tutor me. I couldn't read; I couldn't spell; I couldn't write. Hilary remembers the lessons always ending the same way: I'd run out of the room screaming that I didn't know what was wrong with my brain.

I can remember one session where Mom grew so concerned over my torment that she closed the lesson book, took a deep breath, and said in the most clear, straightforward manner, "It's okay to be average, Gavin." I understood even back then that this, too, came from her deep reservoir of love for me. But I don't recall crueler words ever said about me. I stayed silent, and she went back into her room and shut the door. I could hear her pour a drink from her Safeway jug of wine.

ıııı

I t did not occur to my father, a decent amateur boxer in his day, that he ought to teach me how to defend myself. Chances are he had no idea I was being picked on. I doubt I ever told him, at least not in a way that was coherent, about my struggles with bullies and books. Confessions of that sort aren't the kind of thing a kid shares when he's looking to give his father reasons to be a bigger part of his life. Besides, in the late 1970s, I had walked out of a theater after watching the movie *Rocky*, feeling as if my life's direction had been reoriented by the story on the screen. A boxer who could barely read, who drank raw eggs from a blender, who pounded his fists into hanging sides of beef, who fashioned a new body with push-ups and sit-ups, who ran up the seventy-two steps of the Philadelphia Museum of Art and lifted his clenched hands above the whole city—it was the *Metamorphoses* for a kid like me.

I returned to the theater again and again; I bought the *Rocky* album and hung the *Rocky* poster in my room. I'd crack three eggs into the blender and drink it down, put on my sweats and tennis shoes, and run from one end of Corte Madera to the other. I took enough quarters from my piggy bank to buy two pairs of Everlast boxing gloves from the sporting goods store. Mom and Uncle Paul built a deck in the backyard that I converted into a ring where I hosted boxing matches between me and my friends. I wasn't a fighter by nature, but I learned how to snap a punch without telegraphing it.

Motion pictures and TV dramas, but oddly not pop or punk music, carried a power that sent me off in new directions.

Unsurprisingly for a home-alone kid, I took in a lot of television. It was *Houdini*, the old Paramount film starring Tony Curtis as the master wizard, that turned me on to magic. The kit of illusions my grandfather had bought me was only my first. Each successive kit promised newer and more complicated tricks, until I was now calling myself "the Great Gavini." At Thanksgiving and Christmas, into the living room of whatever house or mountain cabin held the holiday, Hilary would summon the extended family for the evening's entertainment. Her introduction of me—I wore a hat and an oversize coat and waved a wand—was a veritable drumroll. I exaggerate only a little: "Ladies and gentlemen, it is my honor to present to you, from the redwood canyons of Marin County, where he has been working overtime to master new tricks that he will unveil this evening for the first time, the one and only, ours truly, the Great Gavini." Seated before me with faces glowing were my father and mother, my aunts and uncles, and various cousins from both sides of the family. By this stage of the evening, Dad was drinking port and having fun. Mom was only too delighted to have actual proof that her son was coming out of his shell. My act was twenty minutes front to end, various hidden-card tricks and a grand finale that involved a chemical reaction with water. The applause was generous, though by no means was my performance flawless. Indeed, half my tricks, at least by my measure, failed to land.

My usual practice for dealing with such imperfection was to fixate on every mistake and beat myself up for days on end. But this had begun to change, too, thanks to the patient instruction of my mother's mother, Jean, the once-upon-a-time stage actress known as Trigger, who had been the wife of horticulturist Arthur

Menzies and the daughter of Dr. Thomas Addis. That I was even sticking my head out of my shell was in large part due to Grandma Jean. She lived a monklike existence in a small wooden house in a canyon at the edge of a redwood forest in Marin. Everything about it was simple, spare, precise, immaculate. Not an ounce of excess or ornamentation. It spoke to an entirely different aesthetic than my Newsom grandparents'. The mats on the floor were Japanese style, the kind you'd see for sale at Cost Plus in San Francisco. Arranged here and there, without clutter, were a few pieces of quirky art. Her bathroom, her bedroom, the kitchen, the stove, even the cups in her cupboard, were minimalist. The whole place was Zen-like. The inside became the outside, the outside the inside. It all flowed. Her yard was full of ferns that she planted in a methodical fashion, each one precisely clipped. When she finished shaping them, she placed the clippings in a garbage can that was not the usual metal kind. Her can had an artistic flair, and it was lined just so with plastic.

Because her eyesight had dimmed, she had a hard time spotting spiders and daddy longlegs and various other bugs that had moved from yard to inside. She put a household broom in my hands and asked me to knock down any cobwebs I found. Floor to ceiling, I went hunting. The webs were of a beautiful, intricate construction. They seemed to breathe in and out as the sweep of my broom came near.

"Gavin," she said sharply, "I am giving you permission to take down the webs, but you mustn't ever kill a spider. And whatever bug has been caught in its web, you mustn't kill that either. These tiny creatures are living things just as we are living things. We have no right to cut their time short. Catch the bugs in this jar and take them out into the ferns. They'll make a new place there."

She was talking to her fisherman grandson, who didn't always throw the trout he caught back into the water. "Even the black widows?" I asked.

"Even the black widows," she replied.

That I put this lesson to devoted execution no doubt spoke to my obsessive side. She appreciated this trait, a piece of herself in her grandson, and it eventually allowed her to hand over the fern-manicuring chores to me. She paid me five dollars for my labor, which was a big deal because money always was an issue in our household, and saving a few dollars gave me immense pride. More important, it showed that she trusted my ability to perform such a task, a trust that was an even bigger compliment considering how fastidious she was. When the pruning ended, her lesson began. She brought out big white sheets of construction paper and a box filled with perfectly sharpened pencils of every color. I sat on the floor on a mat and she sat on a chair and watched as I drew one thing and another. Had I been blessed with the gift of art, I might have tried my hand at a portrait of my grandmother, for she was a subject of grace to me. Arthritis had completely misshaped her body. She was still tall and skinny like her father, but she was hunched over with a dowager's hump. Having endured years of struggle with anorexia and bulimia, she was skinny beyond words. She ate only cabbage, as far as I could tell. She wore the same dress every day because it gave her figure a bit of fullness. She had the longest hair, and I wondered if she had ever put a scissor to it. Her habit was to wear it in a bun. But on those occasions when she let her hair down, it literally flowed past her back and down her long legs.

My grandmother must have seemed a frightening stick figure to strangers, and this awareness is likely what caused her to
take her walks at night. I imagined her as a bent, lonely figure in
the shadows, ashamed of how she looked to the world. But to me
she was the most beautiful person. Gazing up at her in her chair,
I could see Trigger Addis, the young actress whose looks were
compared to Katharine Hepburn. I could see the girl who trained
as a nurse in her father's Stanford lab and the young woman, fluent in French, who thumbed her nose at the Red Scare and took
a flight to Soviet Russia and wasn't sure if she'd ever return. She
had aged beyond her years, but at her core she was not dimin-
ished. Her pride was deep. Her love for me was real.

"Gavin, why are you erasing what you draw?"

"Because it's lousy," I said, tossing the pencil back in the box.

"It's not lousy," she said.

"I keep making mistakes."

She lifted herself from the chair and with some struggle sat
down on the mat next to me. She took a closer look.

"What mistake?" she asked.

"This one," I replied.

She grabbed a pencil and began drawing where my mistake
left off.

"Here's a way around your mistake, which is not really a mistake at all," she said. She took the line where I had ended it and
added a zig and a zag and then something that suggested a circle.
"Now keep drawing."

It didn't happen immediately, but back and forth, my pencil to
her pencil, I began to see what she meant. She was teaching me
how to draw beyond the linear. I don't know if she knew I was
dyslexic. But she knew that the disability I suffered from collided

with my need for perfection. She was trying to get me to accept a different version of perfection, a perfection that came through imperfection. She was managing me in a different way from my mother or father. Anything I regarded as a mistake she redefined, showing me that the "mistake" was actually the path to another kind of perfection and maybe even art. Only years later, long after her death, would I look back and see her genius at work. She was trying to disconnect the loop, to break it apart and create a consciousness around my walls. *There is no mistake. Do not tear up the paper. Do not throw the pencil back in the box. Celebrate it, embrace it. The mistake is your expression, Gavin.*

""

I was thirteen years old and tired of hearing my mom complain about money and my dad not coming through. So I finagled a yellow Schwinn bicycle with a big banana seat and thick handlebars and started a paper route. I'd come home after school to this massive stack of newspapers on the stairs leading up to our doorstep. The *Marin Independent Journal.* The *IJ,* we called it. I folded and rubber-banded each one and stuffed them into my canvas pouch embossed with the newspaper's masthead. The pouch had a right side compartment and a left side compartment, and I stuffed the papers into each one and took off down the block and up the hill. The Monday, Tuesday, and Wednesday papers were a breeze. Thursday's was much harder to fold and rubber-band because it was a newspaper fat with grocery ads and other inserts. Some Thursdays the paper was so weighty that when I threw it, the rubber band snapped. A paper with a rubber band about to break can fool you. It throws the same and lands with the same sound on porch or driveway. But after you're down the block and the wind picks up, those unbound papers blow like tumbleweeds all over the place. They get stuck to fences and strewn across grass and flower beds and wrapped around tree trunks.

There was no day that gave a paperboy more fits than a rainy Thursday when no rain had been in the forecast. Unexpected wet days meant that the circulation department had deposited the papers at our house without a supply of plastic wrappings to keep each one dry. These were the days I dreaded. I'd pedal off into a drizzle or a hard rain coming off the Pacific and make my way to scores of houses across an eight-block radius with no choice but to throw the paper anyway. My only hope was to land it in a spot protected from the rain or that my customers would know and care enough to be on the lookout for me and save their paper from a soaking.

These were the days I'd arrive home to a string of complaints from customers who said their *IJ* had blown to the end of the block or was so sodden it had turned to pulp. It was five thirty in the evening by then, time for dinner, time for homework, time for Mom to unwind. The last thing she needed to hear was my pleading about the news of the day being denied to our loyal readers.

"Mom, a quarter of my route needs me to hand deliver them a paper."

"I know. I heard the phone ringing and figured it was either your circulation boss or your customers. This is just the worst time, Gavin. Dinner's in the oven."

"I can't lose this job, Mom." These were magic words to ears that knew all about the need to keep a job.

"Okay," she said, turning down the oven. "Get in the car."

She said almost nothing as I directed her from house to house, but neither did she complain. The windshield wipers moved back and forth, back and forth with friction. The rubber strips needed replacing. I imagine she watched me walk up each driveway, climb the porch, and knock on the door. She must have seen me engage in a moment's conversation with each father or mother as I handed them a dry paper and they smiled in return. I'd like to think she was proud of me, if for no other reason than these deliveries would be remembered on collection day, rewarded with tips that would fill my money bag.

I don't think I ever told my mother what paperboying meant to me. On the days that went well, and those were the majority, I was like pitching legends Juan Marichal or Sandy Koufax. I flung the paper with right arm and left arm. I got so good I could throw even the Thursday paper like a Frisbee—around trees, past dogs, with the wind, against the wind—and never stop pedaling. That was the key. Never stop pedaling. Months in, I found a new throw that took advantage of my natural left side, a slinging action. I would drop my arm slot differently than in baseball, and this gave the newspaper even more movement. No matter the angle at which I approached a house, no matter the angle at which the house sat, I could hit my target.

My route is still burned into my brain. I can trace the hill and flat of it now. On the other side of the tracks, past Joe Wagner Field and up and over the bridge, I can see the front yards and the backyards. I'd ring the *ding-ding-ding* bell on my handlebars. "Hi, Mr. and Mrs. Lear," I'd shout. *Whoosh*, the paper landed right on their porch. "Hello, Janet." *Whoosh*, the paper skidded across the driveway to the small space between the cars. "Hello, Mr. Adams." *Whoosh*, the paper kept going and going until it stopped a foot short of his feet. "Thank you, Gavin." "Hey, Gavin, thanks."

Yes, I was moving fast. My goal was to move at absolute speed without sacrificing absolute precision. Because, as a point of pride, I had become a detail guy. I was not the type who was happy-go-lucky. I was hard on myself. I did not skip a house. When a customer said I skipped their house, I damn well knew I hadn't skipped their house. Perhaps their next-door neighbor who didn't subscribe to the *IJ* had picked it up, enticed by the headline above the fold. Or perhaps the husband had gotten home early, picked it up, read it, and then tossed it away. When his wife inquired of the paper's whereabouts, he pretended not to know. "Where is our *IJ*?" the wife complained to my circulation boss. Because one thing any paperboy will tell you is there's a certain percentage of customers, say 15 percent, who complain no matter what. So I went back, bit my tongue, and delivered the paper a second time.

I was part of a small army of boys out there in the county of Marin, working the streets, delivering the news of the day to people who had climbed inside their echo chambers even back then, who had been driven to the fringes of fear by communism and the dominoes that would topple in Southeast Asia, or by the civil rights movement, or by the Black Panthers of Oakland, and yet these same customers had not yet lost the capacity to believe what they read in the real ink of their own hometown paper. For us paperboys, minimum wage plus tips worked out to $3.50 an hour. I gave everything of myself to the duty—legs, arm, and heart. Once a month, on collection day, I had to get off my bike and go door-to-door, which meant I had to deal with dogs and deal with people who did not pay. They were the 15 percent. The rest of them, our neighbors, took the occasion of my visit to give me an *attaboy*.

This didn't mean that I was safe from my ongoing issue, however. The bully of Baltimore Avenue and his wolf pack kept their eye out for me. My yellow Schwinn was a legend. The yellow of it, the big banana seat, the thickness of the handlebars, it was all so uncool in their eyes. They were dirt bike fanatics, BMX outlaws. They wore arm pads and kneepads and heavy-duty gloves because riding a dirt bike meant courting danger. My Schwinn, a sixties fad, was a ride for dorks. They must have known my route and start time, because one afternoon five or six of them were waiting as I approached the tracks.

"Hey, Newscum, you seem in a hurry," one of them said.

"I am."

"Where you off to?" the bully taunted.

It was obvious where I was off to. The pouch affixed to my bike was filled with newspapers. They blocked my way and closed in, their circle tighter and tighter.

"Where's Hilary? Hilary your twin."

"She's not my twin."

"You two sure seem attached."

"I have to go, man. I have to go. Lots of papers I need to deliver."

Their circle became a noose. The bully drew so close that the next thing I knew I was flying off my bike and the papers spilled onto the road. Many years later, it was easy to see that this was garden-variety intimidation, a torment of the suburban type. They didn't then pile on and punch and kick me. Not a layer of my skin was scratched, not a drop of my blood spilled. Rather, seated on their bikes, they maintained their circle and laughed like hyenas while I picked up every paper and stuffed them back into the pouch. I was prepared for my boxing skills to be called into action, but not one of them moved even an inch closer. Apparently satisfied that they had made their point, off they flew in the other direction, popping wheelies and making skid marks down the hill. It seemed like I could hear their laughter a mile away.

I finished my route and rode home and tried not to say a thing to my mother or sister. But Mom sensed something was bugging me and kept pressing, and I told her it was no big deal, that I'd had another encounter with those punks and handled it my own way.

That my encounter was six on one did not sit well with her. The next afternoon, she came home early from work and summoned me outside, and we marched across the street and four doors down. That's where the bully and his parents resided. I didn't want to be there. I knew it wasn't going to go well. Mom rang the doorbell and the bully answered, and she asked to see his parents, who were now standing in the doorway. Mom was in their faces and I was standing behind her. "This has to end," she told them. They did not invite us in. They did not call their son back to the doorway to pose a single question to him. They chalked it up to boys being boys, which is how I chalked it up. They practically shut the door in her face. On the walk back, I could see that my mother was shaken up. "Why'd you make me do that?" I asked. "It's only going to make things worse." She kept quiet but already she was hatching a plan. Our days on Baltimore Avenue were about to come to an end.

CHAPTER FOUR

""

Among the parental conversations my father managed to dodge was the one on the birds and the bees. During a camping trip with a few of my friends to his cabin in Dutch Flat, an old gold-mining town that sat in the Sierra about 3,500 feet up, it was Uncle Paul and not Dad who showed up to play host and guide. That first night, after he cooked us a great meal, we sat around the table surrounded by thousands of my father's books and began playing poker. The cards and the chips somehow led Uncle Paul, in the most natural way, to talk about men and women and sex. He did not get graphic, but neither did he shy away from all the best details. I believe it was that night, or maybe it was another night, that he demonstrated "safe sex" by tearing open the package of a condom with his teeth and unsheathing the membrane inch by inch over a banana. I went to bed thinking, *Wow, finally I've been taught.* It was one of those incredible moments that does not fade for the rest of your life. Never would my father have been able to pull that off, I thought.

Never. It wasn't until a few years later that I realized I wasn't alone in having a father who shirked such a role, that almost every boy had an Uncle Paul or an older brother or cousin who passed on the lesson.

The transformation I was attempting was accompanied by a growth spurt so freakish that my mother couldn't keep me in tennis shoes. I'd get a new pair, and they'd fit for four or five weeks and then become so tight that my feet would start to bleed. My legs from shin to knee ached so much that I couldn't run or box or swing a bat or shoot a layup. The doctor diagnosed Osgood–Schlatter disease, which sounded terminal but ended up being a swollen tendon in each lower leg that was pulling on bone. My growth plates couldn't keep up with my growth is how I understood it. In case I was inclined to run or jump and cause real damage, the doctor put me in a full leg cast. Whatever street cred I had managed to accrue wasn't going to see me through this phase: a gimpy geek with a bowl cut who couldn't keep the pimples off his face, no matter how many Stridex pads he burned through.

Mom put the house up for sale and looked for a new place with a third bedroom for Hilary. With her Realtor's license, she had an inside track on the better deals and bought a house on Chanticleer Street in Larkspur that wasn't quite a dream but turned a nice profit when she sold it eight months later. One afternoon, she took us on a drive and parked in front of 11 Piedmont Road, a tall Mediterranean Revival–style house that sat on an elevated lot in Larkspur. We thought it was one of those luxury listings she was now entitled to show because she had earned her way into the company's "Million Dollar Sales Club." As we climbed the big steps and the small steps and walked through the front door, she busted out in a grin. "This is our new home," she said. We were standing no more than eight blocks from the house on Baltimore Avenue—it was a two-minute drive away—but this was the land of stepping up. We had made it to another realm, or so it appeared from curbside. Built in 1934 and renovated by the family before us, it had four bedrooms, three bathrooms, 2,300 square feet in all on three levels. Not only did Hilary have a bedroom to herself, but it was "the greatest room of all time," with built-in double bunk beds for sleepovers.

The $100,000 price tag put a weighty mortgage over our heads. Mom was holding down three jobs now, still serving enchiladas and tostada salads on weekend nights at Ramona's, and I had begun to work there, too, busing tables. Because the empty garage was square footage we were not putting to use, Mom decided to rent it out to a man who needed a place to park his collector's car. Because an empty fourth bedroom was an opportunity we could not squander, Mom did her usual. She turned the space into a rental pad for a motley collection of people who came and went. Some of them, like the creepy guitar strummer who showed his bare ass to my sister on his visits to the bathroom, were complete strangers. Others were part of a foreign exchange student program, including a French college student named Gerald, a big guy with a beautiful smile who would become lifelong pals with Hilary. Still others were friends or coworkers who had fallen on hard times, like the paralegal at the law firm where Mom worked who needed a cheaper place to stay for herself and her four-year-old son. The boy was sensitive and wanted a space of his own, so Mom gave up the master bedroom for her coworker and the large master closet for the boy. I watched my mother, as if it were no big deal, pick up and move her belongings into the guest room. She grinned and bore it in such a way that I never suspected there was a price to her sacrifice.

At some point, Stephen Ashby, one of my teammates from the basketball squad at Redwood High School, came to live with us. His family had moved out to California from Chicago, and he was growing up poor with a bunch of siblings in the housing projects of Marin City, right around the time Tupac Shakur and his mother came and went. "Newsom, you don't know how lucky you got it," he kept telling me. I had the sense he regarded our house as a refuge, but I didn't think it was my business to ask why. Later he confided to my mother that his father was locked away in prison and that his home life was grim. Mom listened and did not hesitate to take action. "You're going to live with us from now on," she told him, and he moved into one of the bedrooms upstairs. Not long after, he announced that his mother had given him a new name: *Suliman*, the Muslim version of *Solomon*. If we called him Suli, that was okay, too. Because *Suliman Ashby* sounded at odds, his Mom also changed his last name—to *Akhbar*. Suliman Akhbar. Whether this was accompanied by a deep dive into the Quran I don't remember.

The state of California issued Mom a license to provide foster care, and she used the extra money to take care of Suli's food and clothes. He grew so comfortable living with us that he sometimes forgot the few house rules Mom laid down. One day, I came home from my paper route and smelled something odd as I walked up the stairs. I followed the odor to Suli's bedroom, where four or five of our teammates were lounging in various states of slack and giggle. Suli was sitting upright in the middle of the bed like some shaman, smoking the pipe that Uncle Jim Meeker had brought home to me as a gift from an indigenous tribe in the Southwest. This was the nearest thing I had to a sacred possession. It was hand carved out of fine wood, inlaid with granite, and decorated with eagle feathers, beads, and bear fur. Suli had grabbed it off the fireplace mantle, where I had it on display.

"Suli, what the hell are you doing?" I asked.

"Gavin, we're smoking dope, man. Getting high."

I snatched the pipe out of his hands and ran into the bathroom. I tried cleaning the resin from the bowl, but the stain already had become part of the wood. I must have washed and scrubbed the pipe twenty times before I judged it clean enough to return to the mantle.

"You're not telling your mother, are you?" Suli asked.

"Come on, man, you know me better than that. I just don't want that crap around me or my sister."

*

I discovered in the ninth grade that I was among the youngest students in my class, that my mother, looking for a helping hand, had enrolled me in kindergarten when I was only four and a half years old. Lost in the hurly-burly of high school, I could have used that extra year of maturity and academic support. Too late now. Desperation set in. My classroom deceptions became more artful. Discovering CliffsNotes was a revelation. Who knew writing an essay could be such a prank? Whatever the subject, I'd copy down the CliffsNotes analysis and mix up the themes, thoughts, and sentences just enough that my teachers wouldn't notice my filching. Because these were the preinternet days, there was no fear that a computer program could finger a cheater. I'd go to the library, check out eighteen books on whatever subject had been assigned, and cite the greatest bibliography of anyone. But not a single book did I open.

When language eludes you, identity eludes you, too. You start trying on costumes to see if they'll fit. My sophomore year, a Hollywood script arrived in the mail from Aunt Cindy, who was working for Disney at the time. It was the first episode of a soon-to-be TV series called *Remington Steele*, starring Pierce Brosnan and Stephanie Zimbalist, about a female private eye who opens a detective agency and finds that she needs a front man because who's going to hire a female PI, no matter how qualified? She stumbles upon Steele, a former thief and con man dressed to the nines. The script had plenty of white space. I swallowed it up. I considered it a privilege to be trusted with such Hollywood insider knowledge and told only Hilary and a classmate or two. When the series finally premiered, I was glued to the tube. I became obsessed with Steele, his impeccable dress and perfect rejoinders. I started to copy some of his mannerisms, the wrinkling of his brow being the first. Then I went shopping and found a suit and a classic-fit button-down shirt that looked something like his. I accessorized it with a tie and a clip.

It wasn't enough for me to keep the suit in the closet and wear it on formal occasions. I decided to adopt it as my attire for school. Not every day, mind you, but enough days out of the week to make Remington Steele proud. Of course, I could see that I was alone in my sartorial choice, that there wasn't another kid wearing a suit in all of Redwood High. But I don't believe I was seeking to bring attention to myself, for the simple reason that I was still an introvert. What were my motivations then? Was the suit an expression of what I imagined I wanted to be? Was I trying to be cool in an aberrant way? Or, paradoxically, was I hoping that my attire would be seen as a suit of armor? Some of my schoolmates started calling me El Presidente. The guys on my basketball and baseball teams chalked it up to another one of my quirks. El Lefty. My sister wasn't amused. She attended another school but had started dating one of the soccer players at Redwood. "I have a reputation, Gavin," she explained, dead serious. "Do you have to be such a dork?"

At the mall, she paid me five dollars to try on a pair of Levi's shrink-to-fit jeans. "You've got to stop being an oddball," she pleaded. "Your style needs to change." I tossed back the Levi's and kept wearing my suit, but Hilary had a point. Not long after, roaming the aisles of our local drugstore, I found myself in the hair products section, weighing the relative merits of Dippity-do and Brylcreem. I was tired of my hair not going where I wanted it to go. Something about the translucence of that jar of gel spoke to me. I went home and experimented with the right "hold." I decided to keep my application light so that my new style might pass unnoticed. But Suli, who had seen his share of hair products come and go in his family, knew what I was up to. Heading to school, he caught a glimpse of my new style and grinned. "Looking fine, Newsom."

I liked that Suli lived with us. If he regarded me as a square, he did not make me feel as if I needed to change. As uncool as I might have been, he did not place a contingency on the attention he paid to me. In his own subtle way, he pushed out the boundaries that hemmed me in. It was Suli who grabbed Mom's keys off the kitchen counter one day and taught me how to drive a car. After a long day of school and practice, he'd listen to the dreams I'd weave in the backyard on Piedmont Road.

"We're going to build a basketball court right here where we're standing," I told him.

"Gavin, you blind? You see that slope of ground? Count those four tiers of dirt?"

I had spent the summer digging trenches and planting posts for a local landscaper named Jeff Hicks, who had taught me that any excavation was possible with the right equipment and the right men.

"A court with a floodlight and a backboard made of real glass," I went on. "We could shoot all night."

"Come on. You know glass is for indoors. The weather will make it brittle. One alley-oop and we'll crash the glass."

The next day, I enlisted the support of my mother, who told me there were worse things than turning her backyard into a gathering place for her children and their friends. Dad listened to my outline of the project and agreed to throw in some cash. Then I approached Jeff and asked if he might be willing to lend us his equipment and expertise. Was I prepared to defy gravity? he asked. Was I willing to move a massive amount of earth to make the court level and build a retaining wall that could withstand an earthquake?

I listed the physical attributes of my teammates—Suli, Chris Behm, Larry Joe Bonner, Matt Blair, Mike Lellis, Duane Smith, and his brother Derek—and told him that my mother and my aunt Anne and uncle Paul and cousin Robin, and don't forget Hilary, would pitch in, too.

"Sounds like a crew," Jeff said.

The court rose by the inch and then by the foot, and the day came in late summer when it was time to pour the concrete surface. It cured fast in the sun. We planted two iron poles and then watched Jeff perform a small miracle, buttressing the glass back-board with steel brackets and a solid frame that protected it from the elements and any horseplay. The hoop and net we put up were the real thing. I dribbled, caught white boy's air, and did my best Larry Bird. The bank shot hit solid glass and went in without a rattle. Each of us had scratched our initials in the concrete. It was epic. My mother would tell you the court became the center of my universe. Day or night, she couldn't drag me off it. *Bounce, bounce, bounce, shot . . . Bounce, bounce, bounce, shot.* It drove the neighbors mad. "That goddamn basketball," the man next door would mutter.

""""

Who knows how these things work, but the varied parts of me started to cohere, not unlike Jell-O. I am tempted to say that it happened between my sophomore and junior years, that it was an honest-to-goodness metamorphosis, that I went to bed one kid and woke up another kid, but that would be *Rocky* talking. I do recall how it started. My body began to feel like it belonged to me. At six foot three, I had finally stopped growing. I started to fill out, my shoulders and legs first. Whether at work busing tables or dribbling the ball down the court or catching a pop fly, my body started doing things in space it had never done before. This was no small miracle for a dyslexic endlessly tripped up by the space on the page. And yet that, too, had begun to change.

In those hours spent in the library trying to fool my teachers, I discovered a handful of books, nonfiction always, that had been designed for someone like me—wider spaces, bigger type, paragraphs broken up and punctuated with charts and graphs and sections pulled out and highlighted. I learned that if I marked with a pencil the sentences I found most meaningful, using asterisks and underlines, I could understand what I was reading in the moment and retain the knowledge over the long haul. Weirdly, my disability had blessed me with the gift of an acute memory. The confidence this gave me is not an easy thing to put into words; it reached into all corners of my life. I became the first guy at practice and the last guy to leave. I ran sprints when everyone else was jogging. On the hardwood, it wasn't good enough to scramble for a ball heading out of bounds. I dove for it on both knees.

Coaches and bosses and the patrons at Ramona's Mexican restaurant, where I was working as a busboy, started noticing my extra effort. When I was working for Jeff, furiously digging postholes for a retaining wall on Webster Street in San Francisco, he surveyed my speedy progress and pulled me aside. "Gavin, I think it's time for a raise," he said. My pay went from $6.25 to $7 an hour, a modest bump up even back then, and yet it felt as if Jeff had bestowed upon me something incalculable: his *belief* in me. A customer at the restaurant, a man I had never served before, finished his meal and handed me a twenty-dollar tip. "What you are doing now, keep doing that," he told me. That's all he said before he walked out the door, but I've never forgotten the words. His gesture helped get me through high school.

About that time was when my father's pal Art Groza, a bachelor who belonged to their Lonely Hearts Club, began showing up after practice. "Ready for some BP, Gavin?" He'd been a pitcher in the Oakland A's organization, not quite durable enough to make it to the majors but a legend of some kind in the minor leagues. A big, strapping right-handed fireballer, he set an A's farm system record for consecutive strikeouts—eleven in a row. His curveball was considered top-notch, but the way he pitched to women—well, that's what made Art Groza a legend in the bars and restaurants of North Beach. He was almost a decade younger than my father and the rest of the crew. His hair was perfect, wavy and black, and his skin was never without a tan on account of Art's sailing a boat that he docked in the Marina District. He was a hero to the lonely teenager in me because it didn't appear that his heart was ever lonely, not with a different beautiful woman, some of them half his age, on his arm. He smoked cigars and drove a beat-up convertible Mercedes that he double-parked wherever he went. He was a legend at the Hall of Justice, his parking tickets for one thing and his lawyering for the other. The judges loved Art. The bailiffs loved Art. The court reporters loved Art. The jury loved Art. His wordsmithing was so superb that he was able to get the lightest sentence possible for Brandy Baldwin, the notorious Nob Hill madam. The judge sentenced her to a convent.

"Art, which lady you meeting tonight?" I asked him.

"Chicken Ruth," he replied. Her name was Ruth, and she liked the chicken at Romano's Italian restaurant on Lombard Street.

He had brought with him a bucket of tennis balls cut in half and a broomstick handle. I grabbed the broomstick and Art grabbed the tennis balls, and he marked off some thirty feet from home plate. I had never seen half of a tennis ball come at me. The movement was psychotic. Made a Wiffle ball look completely sane. Darted and danced like a hummingbird.

"Keep your eye steady on it, Gavin. It'll get easier."

It took eight or nine pitches for me to make contact. Once I did, the contact came in spurts. Art was working my hand-eye coordination at another level.

"That's good, kid. Remember, pull the knob of your bat. Swing short to the ball and then long through it. Don't leave your back hip stranded. It's the one violent thing about a baseball swing. Throw your back hip at the ball."

When the accolades for my junior and senior years in baseball and basketball started adding up, it felt as if I were looking down on another me. My buddy Chris Behm and I shared the "Outstanding Athlete" award at Redwood High and made All League in both sports. I managed to bat .435 even under the gaze of Major League Baseball scouts, including one for the Rangers who came to our games to keep tabs on a few of my teammates and me. After one game, he handed me his business card, which I've kept to this day. In basketball, I averaged nineteen points and fourteen rebounds a game, but it was my work ethic and willingness to play through pain that the coaches and athletic director mentioned to the press. "He's a quiet kid. Gavin doesn't play with his mouth," basketball coach Dick Hart said. "In all my thirty-seven years of coaching, I have never had a boy who has played with such consistent pain. After every practice and every game, he has to put ice packs on his legs for relief. Yet I haven't heard him complain once." Athletic Director Phil Roark added, "Some of these guys, you say practice is at three and they come at three fifteen. You call practice at three and Gavin's there before three."

I was not Chris Behm. I was never the phenom. I was never the archetype. Chris was the natural who always had a girlfriend. I didn't have that confidence. He was that guy and I was never that guy. I practiced hard and then had to do another hour after practice. I was a grinder. You can imagine my pride when I landed on the front page of the *Marin Independent Journal*, above the fold, for scoring twenty-three points against powerhouse Drake High School and nearly breaking their winning streak, one of the longest in California high school history. My father was there. As was his habit, he was sitting between two of his pals, John Burton, the political boss and master of profanity, who had just finished his fourth term in Congress and was about to serve in the California Senate, and Joe Cotchett, who would become one of the state's most successful plaintiff's attorneys and sue the pants off PG&E. The cheerleaders at Redwood High rallied our half of the stands with a new yell: "Dippity-do, Dippity-do! Gavin, Gavin, We love you!" I had managed to ditch the Remington Steele suit but not the gelled hairdo.

In the banker's box filled with my grammar school report cards and concerned teacher comments, there's an article from the *San Francisco Examiner* that my father clipped out and gave to his secretary to mail to me. The headline, as headlines are apt to do, reached for the dramatic: REDWOOD'S HOOP LEADER WON'T LET AGONY BENCH HIM. A photograph accompanying the profile shows me standing on the court in my uniform, squirting a bottle of water into my mouth. Reading my quotes, my first public utterances, brings an immediate wince to my face, and then I try to understand the kid I was. "It hurts nearly all the time, and sometimes I think it's getting worse," I told the *Examiner* reporter, explaining the stress fractures in my shins that were an outgrowth of Osgood–Schlatter. "But there's no way I'm giving it up. I love the game too much." The story tried to make the case that I was no mere jock but a scholar, too, noting that my latest report card showed three As and three Bs. "I can't imagine spending all my time on the books," I told the reporter. "It would really be boring. Besides, I really believe athletic competition can help you in so many other ways."

What did my father, the great reader, read in my words? He wrote no note on the newspaper article except a simple instruction to his secretary, who played the role of intermediary between father and son: "Send to Gavin." And yet he had clipped it out with care and pasted it onto a blank sheet of paper, as if preparing it for a scrapbook, one that I would never put together.

""

There was the education Hilary and I received at school and the education we gained by virtue of our relationship with the Gettys, including summer vacations that lifted us out of one reality and plopped us down in another. We climbed aboard private jets and yachts and limos that whisked us to luxury hotels and royal palaces, inducing a shock to our systems that Hilary would later describe as something out of *Cinderella* or *My Fair Lady* when Eliza Doolittle, played by Audrey Hepburn, turns her lowly Cockney accent into high-class English and finds herself hoisted from flower peddler to duchess. We were the guests of Gordon and Ann Getty and companions of their four sons, Peter, Andrew, John, and Billy, a branch of the Getty family that had stayed on in San Francisco.

Gordon considered my father his "best-best friend," and the feeling was mutual. With Dad's assistance, Gordon oversaw the $4 billion family trust on behalf of dozens of Getty descendants, but otherwise he was preoccupied with living the life of an artist lost in his composition of classical music. Gordon was no dilettante. His body of work included scores of choral, orchestral, and piano works and an opera inspired by Shakespeare that he called *Plump Jack*. This is the nickname given to the corpulent Sir John Falstaff, whose comedic antics in three of Shakespeare's plays make him the most endearing of rogues. Gordon, tall and trim and topped by a mop of curly hair, was lovely in his distractions. He got great mileage out of being the absent-minded professor whose capable wife ran the show. Ann had grown up knowing more about tractors than trust funds. The daughter of a Central Valley farmer who raised walnuts and peaches, she studied anthropology and biology at UC Berkeley and took a part-time job at the cosmetics counter at Joseph Magnin near Union Square. This placed her in the orbit of my aunt Barbara Newsom, who had graduated from the San Francisco College for Women and married Ron Pelosi. The two women became dear friends.

How Gordon Getty and Ann Gilbert met is a story my father told many times and always with gusto. It was 1964 and he and Gordon, both still single, were sharing a bottle of wine at their usual haunt, La Rocca's Corner in North Beach. As serendipity would have it, in walked Barbara and Ann. As soon as Gordon set eyes on the farmer's daughter, a striking redhead with a booming laugh, he was smitten. "Bill, she's too tall for you," he told my father. Gordon got off his barstool and immediately introduced himself. "Why don't we play a game, shot for shot," he teased Ann. She wasn't the type to flinch. The bartender lined up the shot glasses and poured whiskey, and Gordon did not leave Ann in the dust. They eloped to Las Vegas that same year and got married on Christmas Day.

At least this was the version of Gordon's wooing of Ann that appeared in the pages of the *San Francisco Chronicle*. My father, who preferred to work in the background and would never take the shine away from Gordon, would almost surely attest to the newspaper's telling. But if you talked to men who were pals of my father and Gordon, preferably over a scotch or two, they'd likely recount a different version of Gordon's snaring of Ann, one that was far less immaculate and credited not Gordon's glibness but my father's charms. They would tell you that Gordon generally had difficulty communicating with the world. In social settings, he would rarely take center stage. Even as people were standing around him and making stabs at conversation, Gordon's eccentric mind was usually somewhere else. He wanted nothing more than to return to the quietude of his study, where he listened to classical music and composed his own scores and read the same great tomes and poems my father read. Their love of literature and opera is how my father built a relationship with Gordon that went beyond their shared childhoods. Dad was one of the few people able to connect Gordon to the outside world. My father had this way of creating a safe space for Gordon to open up. He became Gordon's whisperer, his interpreter and translator, a bridge to their friends, a bridge to Gordon's own children.

In case you think I'm giving my dad too much credit, here's how one close friend of my father and Gordon described their relationship: "Gordon is one of those people who was tuned in to a different channel. Now, his brother Paul was a rounder. Paul lived in this world. Gordon lived in his own world. The one person who could speak to Gordon, who could speak to his heart and his head, was your father. Bill was a world-class storyteller. Gordon couldn't tell a story to save himself. Bill was the one who brought Gordon out of his cerebral head. Bill had this crowd of friends who embraced Gordon for all his eccentricities. And Gordon, in his own inimitable way, found a way to return the favor. He'd invite these guys to go on trips with him. I was lucky to join them a couple times. We flew on the Getty jet, the 'Jetty.' We played rounds of poker until we reached our destination. And there was Gordon in the middle of it all being one of the boys. This was your dad's gift to him."

None of this is to diminish the role of Ann. She ran the house and gave order to their lives. She organized all the family trips, booked the hotels, packed the bags, summoned the limos, paid the tips because Gordon was frugal by nature. His oil-tycoon father, tired of his guests using the phone at his castle in England to make long-distance calls, had yanked it out and put in a pay phone. In the early years of Gordon and Ann's marriage, he tried to camouflage the fact that he was the son of the richest man in the world. He chose to dress plainly and drive an AMC Pacer. But as their four sons came along, legacy exercised its pull. So did Ann.

They moved into a 1914 mansion set atop Pacific Heights with a one-of-a-kind view of the San Francisco Bay. It inhabited a stretch of outer Broadway that became known as "the Gold Coast." Its high-society royals, now led by Ann, worked overtime to give the Brahmins of the East Coast, a generation or two more rooted in their wealth and ways, a run for their money. Ann could match their airs and also puncture them at once. She taught herself interior design, remade the mansion top to bottom, and connected it to a second mansion they had bought next door, which was no easy task because the two behemoths stood at odd angles to each other. She employed a style that the fancy home magazines described as "old-world splendor," mixing French, Venetian, eighteenth-century English, and classical Chinese. The christening of the merged mansions, Italian Renaissance–style and painted pale yellow, was a black-tie affair with eighty invited guests, my father among them, and entertainment provided by opera diva Jessye Norman.

Ann and Gordon were crowned the city's number one social couple. Whenever famed tenor Plácido Domingo came to town, he stayed with them. Hollywood stars who lived in San Francisco jockeyed to marry at Ann and Gordon's mansion. A lavish million-dollar fundraiser for President Clinton was held there. To celebrate the premiere of Gordon's opera, *Plump Jack*, Ann hosted a block party for five hundred guests, serving a French champagne with a lineage that dated back to 1772.

The first time my father took me there, I was no older than eight and thought I had entered a portal to another period and place. I had never set eyes on a butler, and the impeccable butler now standing before us put the fear of God into me. He apparently hailed from original stock. He had served Jean Paul Getty for years with distinction, and after the world's richest man died, he left the Tudor castle in England and came straight to California to serve Gordon and Ann. His outfit wasn't some mere San Francisco butler variety, Dad said. There were fifteen separate pieces he had to assemble in the same order each day. His formality, whether inbred or schooled, was a thing to behold. Not a movement wasted. Not a motion without intent. I was good at capturing accents and manners and would soon try to mimic him. *Nice to see you. May I help you?* But his was a crispness I could not reach. His name was Francis Bullimore, and he had been described by the oil baron as "benevolently despotic." Over the years I would come to admire him as a singular character who literally opened the door for me to another world.

My eyes had a difficult time adjusting to all the rich colors.

Ann, dressed as usual in Levi's, was statuesque and still beautiful with her hair swept back. If you looked at her hands, though, you could see cuts from the hours she spent sewing fabrics and pillows. "I sew until I bleed" was her motto. For each room, she had chosen and placed every piece of art, antique, and fixture, right down to the ornate curtains she made from the plush velvet she had salvaged from the estate of dancer Rudolf Nureyev. On one floor were a lap pool and a small music conservatory where Gordon played his works. On a separate floor, Ann founded and built a preschool to pursue her passion for early childhood development.

""

It was with this same spirit—of composition, renovation, and education—that Ann took on the project of Gavin and Hilary Newsom. Our first summer vacations with the Gettys and their boys, organized by Ann and Dad, were spent fishing and rafting the great rivers of the West, among them the Rogue, the middle fork of the Salmon, and the Colorado. The six of us kids must have shown enough grit that by the third summer we were venturing to a rugged Canadian outpost on the shores of Hudson Bay to study polar bears. Because our wood cabins came without indoor plumbing, we had to find a place outside to relieve ourselves. This was no problem except at night, when the polar bears were roaming the same ground looking for something to eat. My sister suffered from a weak bladder, which meant that Ann had to wake her up in the middle of the night to pee in a bucket. Ann then emptied out the bucket each morning before us boys woke up. This way, Hilary would risk no shame. Ann believed I had been gifted with the eye of a photographer and encouraged me to shoot to my heart's delight as our helicopter hovered over polar bears frolicking on the ice. My camera was a beat-up Pentax MX, but the scene beneath me was so captivating that I required nothing more. Photography became my safe space, a place where I could both observe and create. Dad later blew up two of my pictures and sold them for four hundred dollars each at an auction to benefit his foundation to protect the California mountain lion.

Our mother didn't know what to do with the memories we carted home from our Getty trips. After two or three weeks being gone, it was almost as if we were strangers to her. "So, another grand excursion has come to an end," she'd greet us at the front door. The look on her face was a faraway one. For a day or two, she'd give us the silent treatment, and then we'd all fall back into the form of a life of trying to make ends meet. After enough vacations came and went, a cone of silence took hold.

Hilary didn't tell Mom that Gordon and Ann's houseguest on the Thanksgiving vacation to Barbados was Arthur Miller, the American playwright who'd been married to Marilyn Monroe. We kept hidden our encounters with Luciano Pavarotti, who gave us big bear hugs at Gordon's fiftieth birthday party at the Met and with whom we later shared an intimate dinner at the Getty mansion. This was the same dinner that saw Ann *tsk–tsk* Hilary for forking a petite potato off Dad's plate. In Mom's presence, I didn't let slip how Andrew Getty and I dressed up in James Bond tuxedos and toted toy guns on a yacht that sailed from one famous European port to another. In Venice, we arrived by gondola at the gates of another "fabulous party," this one inside an opulent sixteenth-century palazzo where the debauched face of Jack Nicholson materialized from the crowd. "Well, well," he said, taking all five of us lads in, "if it isn't the Getty boys."

In that moment in Venice, I could not summon my voice. I did not correct his misimpression of who I was. Had I shared this encounter with my mother, she likely would have asked me if deception was something I practiced whenever I hobnobbed with the Gettys. An honest reply would have required a deeper understanding of myself. Answering that question today, I'd be charitable to the kid I was. I'd explain how the close ties between the Gettys and the Newsoms went back three generations, that the younger Gettys all called my father "Uncle Bill," that I even bore some resemblance to the four sons of Gordon and Ann, that passing as a fifth son afforded me the rather pleasant sensation of being subversive.

Fact is, I was always aware of the line that separated us from the Gettys. Not because they went out of their way to make us aware of it but because we, as good Newsoms, paid constant mind to the distinction. We did not reciprocate and call Gordon "Uncle Gordon"; we did not call Ann "Auntie Ann." Hilary had made the mistake once, on a trip in which the first-class section of the plane was occupied by Gettys and Newsoms, of addressing Gordon as "Gordon." He shot back a look of reproach. "I'm Mr. Getty," he said. She was eight or nine and ran crying to the lap of my father, and he wiped away her tears and brushed back her hair. Back then, I did not understand my father's silence. It appeared to me a swallowing of pride, one more abrogation of fatherly duty.

By the time we became teenagers, Gordon would soften a great deal, insisting that we call him by his first name. Hilary would grow so close to the Gettys that her children would call Gordon "Uncle Gordon" and Ann by her nickname, "Manga." But the trespass of being too comfortable in the presence of inherited wealth was a lesson my sister and I learned early—and did not have to learn twice. Because we inhabited a lower station, we did not possess the luxury of presumption.

When I think of the end of my adolescence, I invariably return to the last two family vacations we took with the Gettys in the mid-1980s, both epic but in very different ways. East Africa was sold to us as a no-joke safari that would deepen our knowledge of the human species and the animal kingdom. Ann, a student of prehistory, had gone so far as to set up a tour with the renowned British paleoanthropologist Mary Leakey. We landed in Nairobi and explored the city and a sprawling shantytown on its outskirts. It was reputed to be the world's biggest slum, a half million people living in squalor. The whole place felt short-tempered. Teenagers no older than me were clutching AK-47s. Families of eight and ten members sidestepped the narrow paths filled with raw sewage and hurried inside one-room mud huts that smelled of smoke from the cooking fires.

A few days later, we took off for the hinterlands, traversing plains that went on forever. Our guide had instructed Gordon and Ann to bring bags of toothpaste and stacks of *People* magazine, which were hard to come by in East Africa, and this is what he used to bribe our way past checkpoints. Crossing into Tanzania, we drove north to a cratered landscape that had been the top of a volcano before blowing its lid more than two million years before. It was now an immense grassland—home to black rhinos, water buffalo, leopards, zebras, warthogs, wildebeests, gazelles, and the densest population of lions in the world. From camp to camp, sunrise to sunset, the light and landscape just blew me away. I kept snapping photos, including one of Ann hugging a captive leopard about to be returned to the wild. A pair of hot air balloons awaited us at the next camp. We climbed aboard, the adults drinking champagne and the kids sipping sodas, and sailed over the great Serengeti.

Mary Leakey, a sturdy woman with a helmet of gray hair and a fat Dutch stogie sticking out of her mouth, greeted us in the volcanic beds of northern Tanzania. She and her husband, Louis, had been digging there since the 1930s, hunting for the stone tools and bones of "Adam and Eve's ancestors." No one had funded their work more than the Gettys. Gordon was board chairman of the Leakey Foundation and Ann had been a fellow since 1973. Louis had died the year before, but that hadn't stopped Madame Leakey from continuing the work.

She stood in front of us at an excavation site known as Laetoli and, in her cut-glass English accent, posed the most foundational of questions: "Who are we and where did we come from? What does it mean to be human?" She then led us to the crack in the sediment where only a decade earlier she had unearthed the fossilized fragments of twenty-three of our ancestors. As I understood it, their top halves were ape and their bottom halves were human, which had enabled them to walk upright. Here before me were the actual footprints of human lineage that dated back 3.7 million years, a missing link in our being.

""""

Hilary and I took one last childhood trip with the Gettys, a vacation to Spain. The king and queen, Juan Carlos and Sofía, were hosting a coming-out party for their daughter Cristina. Gordon and Ann and the boys were invited as special guests, which meant that Hilary and I were invited, too. Ann, as usual, took charge of things. Hilary was summoned to Neiman Marcus. I got called to Wilkes Bashford, the San Francisco clothier made famous by Willie Brown. The luxury store fronted Sutter Street with an awning that was San Francisco Giants orange.

I took the elevator to the menswear floor, and there was Wilkes Bashford, a small, trim man in his early fifties with a balding pate and a clipped gray mustache. He was nattily dressed and holding a black-and-tan dachshund. He apparently knew my father from the weekly 1:11 p.m. lunches that brought together Bashford, Willie Brown, and *San Francisco Chronicle* legend Herb Caen at Le Central, where they rolled boss dice for the check. "Gavin Newsom, I presume," he said with a warm smile. "Let's get started, young man." Per Ann's instructions, he said, I would need a lunch outfit and a dinner outfit for each of the eight days we'd be staying in Spain. "Clothes appropriate to meet a king," he kept repeating.

He gently ushered me from one expensive rack to the next expensive rack, blazers and double-breasted suits by Brioni that cost thousands of dollars apiece, though he did his best to hide the price tags from me. Across the fabric he moved his polished hands as if they were instruments of fine detection. What they detected was perfection. Monday, Tuesday, Wednesday, Thursday, Friday, Saturday, Sunday—he had the whole trip and its evenings of spectacle in his head. The alteration man appeared from the back with chalk and pins and marked each suit. Mr. Bashford then quickened his pace, because now was the easy and fun stuff I'd be wearing in the light of day: the plaids of Valentino, the solid bolds of Ralph Lauren, the pastels and linens of Versace. In the mirror, it looked as if I were about to walk onto the set of

Miami Vice. My Adam's apple felt stuck. "Fits you to a T," he said. "Now, let's head this way for the evening shoes and a pair of loafers. And let's not forget that suitcase."

No one cared how much it cost. Not Ann, not Gordon, surely not Bashford. I cannot claim that I walked out of the store that day with a sense of guilt or entitlement or even a feeling of self-loathing, thinking I was one of the charity cases of the Getty philanthropic arm. I walked out understanding that this was the split personality of my life. We flew to Spain in "the Jetty," the 727 the Gettys had bought from Revlon's Ron Perelman, who had decorated it with rifle racks and carpet designed to look as if you were peering down on a wild game preserve. A line of limousines greeted us upon our arrival, with Ann standing beside the lead limo holding a stack of cash. One by one she called us forward, first her sons and then my sister and me. She peeled off six crisp hundred-dollar bills and pressed them into my hand. "This is your spending money," she said. "Have fun with it." I had no business taking it. I did not want to take it. But I did.

The eight days came and went with so many gestures of prostration on the part of hotel staff and the king's court that I began to see there was a price to being rich. The way people treated you was completely fraudulent. No one held you to task; no one called BS on your wants. Ann had a business partner named Alecko Papamarkou, a New York investment banker and high-society maven, whose Greek accent was so thick it seemed to be a put-on. Alecko accompanied Peter, Andrew, John, Billy, and me to several events, introducing us to those assembled as "these beautiful boys from California." At the coming-out party, a couple wanted to know which Getty I was, and I told them I wasn't a Getty, I was a Newsom. I immediately felt a retraction in their body language. They shut down and stopped wasting their time on me and focused on the four brothers. I can't say this caused me any psychic pain, because I regarded my entire presence there as an adventure, a chance to watch and study people, a peek into absurdity.

One of the nights, I was handed a choice seat at the Madrid performance of David Bowie's Glass Spider Tour. I wasn't a fan yet, but when I saw him dressed in black-widow red and floating down from the rafters as if on a string of web, I thought it was cool. The next night, sitting with the king's nieces and nephews in a private movie room watching Pink Floyd's *The Wall*, someone next to me rolled half a dozen joints and generously passed them around. I had gotten through my first nineteen years without ingesting a mind-altering drug—so rigid that even my father poked fun at me—and I wasn't going to start then. I used the excuse of not caring much for the movie to head back to my room at the Ritz Hotel. This was our Madrid trip in a nutshell.

Back at home, a large Giants-orange box arrived at our doorstep a week before Christmas. My mom, who had a hunch what it was and who had sent it, called me into the living room. She did the same with Hilary when the box from Neiman Marcus arrived. "I'm sure Ann got you something wonderful for Christmas," she said in a voice that tried for enthusiasm but fell short. Because this wasn't the first time such Getty holiday gifts had come to our home, we knew the drill. Whatever clothes Ann had bought us, no matter how much we liked them, we pretended to take issue with the style or color or size. This gave Mom a chance to return the gifts and use the credit—it was an eye-popping amount—to shop for Christmas last minute. She hung stockings on the fireplace and stuffed them with art supplies and coins, toothpaste and deodorant from Walgreens. She placed boxes under the tree that were precisely the same boxes from Wilkes Bashford and Nieman Marcus, only the clothes inside were different. Our mother had chosen them. They were gifts from her to us.

CHAPTER FIVE

....

S anta Clara University had no business taking a chance on
me. My high school grades were all over the place, and I
scored lousy on the SAT, three hours of dyslexic torture.
And yet here was the head coach of the Broncos baseball team, in
the late spring of 1985, sitting in the living room across from me
and my beaming mother. She took a coach's pride in my "sweet
swing from the left side," the stroke I had fashioned in the mold
of Will Clark, the Giants first baseman whose video I had played
over and over. I could hit for average, and I could hit for power,
and if my left arm found a wild streak now and then, it was no big
deal, because Santa Clara wasn't recruiting me as a pitcher but as
a first baseman. "Gavin, it's late in the process, so we can only
offer you a partial scholarship at this point," the coach said. I was
nothing but grateful. I'd been resigned to a stint at the local community college, and now a four-year school, just far enough away
from home that it would feel like independence, was willing to
give me a shot.

I skipped college dorm life and moved straight into the Alameda, a converted Motel 6 that offered the luxury of a private bathroom for each apartment. One of my roommates was an Oklahoma kid named Craig who, thankfully, did not wear Sooner State politics on his sleeve. He was a serious student and we got along well. My freshman year I met Becky, a Santa Clara girl who was attending the university, and we became boyfriend and girlfriend, my first relationship. Becky could see me straining to hold up academics and baseball and was more than encouraging. I had developed an odd numbness in the fingers of my left hand, and it wasn't easy taking notes, much less flinging a baseball. Because I was playing first base, I told her, I didn't need a cannon for an arm. But every throw at practice was causing me discomfort. At night, I was losing sleep from the pain. Then one day at practice, during a routine drill, I heard my arm pop. Each time I moved it, something inside clicked.

"Tough news," the orthopedic surgeon said. "It's the ulnar nerve in your elbow. If you want to play baseball again, you're going to need surgery." At that moment, I might have recognized the folly of a comeback, but I opted for surgery and a long mending. That's how my freshman season ended. Becky's mom not only talked me through the lows of my rehab but cooked for me nearly every day. My arm got stronger but not strong enough. I was having trouble throwing from first base to second base on a double play, and I couldn't fully extend my bat through the ball to hit with power. The head coach could barely look me in the eye. Baseball had always been an escape for me. When the world brought confusion, baseball's lines and distances and logic brought sense. The discord between my eyes and brain disappeared when it was a ball coming at me. In my most doubting times, the self-confidence I felt in the batter's box and out in the field was a rare calm. Hitting the ball on the nose and watching it fly over the fence was a sublime feeling, mostly because you couldn't explain how it happened. It took both maximum effort and no effort at all. You did not feel in that instant that you swung very hard. And yet the sound off the bat was a different sound, a knock that filled the park. It would not be easy to part from that sound. All through summer before my sophomore year, I played long-toss and hit in the cages to prepare for winter ball ahead. I was seeing the ball well and my swing felt fluid again, but my arm never came around. I saw no choice but to hang up my cleats for good.

Feeling adrift, I threw myself into the upper-division courses of my political science major. As improbable as it sounded, given the Bs and Cs I was earning, law school was my goal. The idea of spending a semester abroad intrigued me, and I came up with a plan to take art history classes at the Monte Mario International School in Rome. I figured if art history wasn't a good fit, I'd at least have four months to visit friends and travel cheaply on a Eurail pass, and maybe even sort out who I was and where I was headed.

The hit-and-miss diary I kept that semester is written in the language of a transformative experience. Art history became a subject that I actually excelled in. The visual aspect of it spoke to my dyslexia in a way that no other subject had. It was a profound feeling. Not only could I see what my professors were describing, but I was able to add my own language to it. The breadth of Rome—its architecture and art, paintings, frescoes, sculptures, mosaics, pottery, the beauty the Italians had lifted from ancient Greece, the beauty they had created on their own—came alive to me. Even the damn textbook for our main course captivated me.

Maybe it was the typesetting, maybe it was the illustrations—the frescoes of Giotto from the dawn of the Renaissance, the intense dark and light from the angry hand of Caravaggio—but I pored over it. I had never derived such contentment from a book. It clicked; my mind worked.

I took the train to Siena, three hours north of Rome, and watched the annual Palio, "the world's most insane horse race," which featured ten village riders from ten different neighborhoods, a communal festival that dated back to the seventeenth century. Then I boarded the Eurail and headed to Greece, Hungary, Poland, and Czechoslovakia—so many places that my passport ran out of room to stamp them all. I had a hundred chance meetings. Strangers became friends; friends became intimates. Crossing into Poland, I proceeded through the beautiful countryside until the train tracks met the gates of Auschwitz. The architecture of the concentration camp—bricks and barbed wire, walls of shoes and suitcases that never found the road out—was a creation of mankind I did not have the language to measure. I walked out of its horror and into the ferment that was Warsaw, Poland, in the 1980s. The nonviolent movement known as Solidarity had been engaging in a revolt of labor strikes and hunger strikes for a decade. Students my age were marching and protesting. I had no idea that the Iron Curtain was about to come down and the Cold War as we knew it was ending.

The train took me back to Italy, where my father and some of his Lonely Hearts Club pals were waiting for me in Rome. I showed them all over the city, pointed out the rococo style of the 135 Spanish Steps and gave them a tour of the Pantheon. My dad knew the streets. I knew the art. We had meals that stretched late into the night. We talked about everything. He could see that I was a different person. I could see that he was a different person. Italy, he confided, was where he felt most comfortable in the world. Had he been given a chance to do his life over again, he said, this is where he would have landed and tried to make a life out of literature.

I returned to Santa Clara, only to discover that my girlfriend, Becky, had fallen in love with my roommate, Craig. I'd had no inkling of a spark between them. Because of my time in Europe, the months of distance, it wasn't exactly heartbreak. Becky and Craig made a great couple and would go on to marry. I found an apartment closer to campus and tried to wrap my brain around a statistics class that stood between me and graduation. I failed it once and then failed it again. Finally I made an appointment with my adviser. Stats aren't about numbers, I told him. If it were about numbers, I'd have sailed through it. The concepts that underlie it, all these relational things going on, just scramble my brain.

"Are you dyslexic?" he asked.

"Yes."

"Well, why didn't you tell me that?"

A college education at a Jesuit school had apparently progressed to the point that dyslexia was now part of the lexicon of disabilities that merited leeway. He signed a waiver, and I was handed my diploma. This led to a conversation with my father in which he presented a lawyerly case that law school might frustrate my brain the same way stats had. "You've got a good head on your shoulders, Gavin. And you've never been afraid of hard work," he said. "Don't look to me for your example. Look to my father. He had a brain for business and a heart for politics. He lived a good life. Maybe he's your path forward."

꙳

I took a job delivering orthotic inserts to people with fallen arches and hammertoes. Pro Lab Orthotics, which reached across the Bay Area, was my uncle Paul's company. He didn't pay by the hour but by the number of inserts I delivered each day. This meant that if I hustled and pursued the quickest route from point A to point B, I could work a half day and get paid for a full one. Every shortcut in the book, from Marin City to Palo Alto, I memorized in no time. I didn't regard my car-to-door service as anything special, but customers were calling up my uncle, saying they'd never had a delivery boy who showed such speed and politeness.

I was living with my mother again, an arrangement we both understood to be temporary. Hilary was off to college at Georgetown University, and Mom had rented out our house in Larkspur and moved back to San Francisco. This placed her closer to her paralegal job and closer to the University of San Francisco, where she was earning a bachelor's degree in social science. We were proud of her. I was sleeping in her spare bedroom, though sleep ranked at the bottom of my list. At Mom's suggestion, I started attending real estate classes at Anthony Schools of San Francisco Peninsula and helping stage open houses for her Realtor friends when my deliveries for Uncle Paul were done. I breezed through the course at Anthony and aced the three-hour licensing exam. It could not have been designed more perfectly for me: multiple-choice questions that required little more than memorizing my notes.

My father said it was time to pay a call to Walter Shorenstein, lord of the Financial District, who had known my grandfather, Boss Newsom, back in the day. Shorenstein had his hands in half the city's real estate transactions, Dad said, and might have a lead or two for me. During the previous two summers, I had worked as a janitor at various buildings downtown, including an iconic neo-Gothic tower at 235 Montgomery Street owned by Shorenstein. He had a reputation for being gruff and obsessive, a man who would show up out of nowhere to perform detailed inspections of his properties. Though there were sightings of Shorenstein by other janitors, I had never laid eyes on him.

I put on a coat and tie and arrived early for my appointment. Mr. Shorenstein, a short block of a man with a ruddy face, was huffing and puffing. "You the Newsom kid? Your grandfather was a great man, a great Democrat. I loved him. But what in the hell am I supposed to do with you?"

I was quite sure I didn't want him to do anything with me. I was a newly minted real estate agent who was there for a little old-school advice. I'm not sure why I didn't have the guts to tell him that. Maybe because he was yelling at me. "What do we do? What do we do with you?" He barked at his secretary to get Stan Roualdes, his top man, on the line. "Stan, this Newsom kid is here. He looks good in a suit, but where the hell can we put him?"

Stan told me to report, bright and early the next Monday, to 235 Montgomery Street—the Russ Tower, he called it. I walked out so discombobulated that I failed to mention I knew the building well. I had a new job, I told my mother, but what was it? I woke up early, put on the same outfit, and took the 30 Stockton bus to the tower, where a man named Craig Edwards, Shorenstein's building manager, was waiting for me. He stubbed out one cigarette, only to light up another. The coffee in his cup he mainlined. I stood there waiting to be called to duty, but he had no idea where to put me. "Kid, what are we going to do with you?"

He dispatched me to the boiler room to see if the janitors were up to no good. He had no idea that I had spent part of two summers in the same basement as a janitor myself, awaiting nightly assignment to one of the floors in the tower. I walked in, only to be greeted by the same faces. Several of my old workmates did double takes.

"Gavin, is that you? What the hell are you doing here?"

"Apparently, I'm working for Mr. Shorenstein. Apparently, I'm your new boss," I said, hugging one and then the other.

It had taken me two years, and a college degree, to land back in the same spot. I was making a salary now, twenty-two thousand dollars a year, but if you worked it out by the hour, I was bringing home less pay than I had for my nights as a janitor.

I was soon splitting rent with Andrew Getty in an upscale apartment on Baker Street, close enough to the Russian consulate that we'd sit and study its weird comings and goings. Andrew and I were the same age and good friends. He had attended film school at USC and was trying to get Hollywood to green-light one of his "cheesy horror movie" scripts. His mom, Ann, was about to start renovating the Getty compound again and approached Andrew and me with an offer. She would provide us two rooms in the mansion, rent free, in return for our keeping an eye on the contractors and handling the shipments of artwork that arrived regularly from Sotheby's. We'd have been fools to say no. I set up my bed next to the "Turkish room," and whenever a piece of art pertaining to the Ottoman Empire came through the

service door, I placed it against the wall where it would be arranged or hung. This was the extent of my duties.

Living the bachelor life alongside tens of millions of dollars in
rare paintings and sculptures simply became one more crazy jux-
taposition. On Sunday mornings, Ann would sometimes surprise
me with a visit, finding boxes of pizza and empty beer bottles
strewn about among the gilded pieces of antiquity. I'd be wiping
sleep from my eyes when she gave me her grin. "And you're the
one running the cleaning crews at the Shorenstein Company?"
Gordon never checked up on us, and that was fine with Andrew,
who struggled more than his brothers to find ways to reach his
dad. Andrew had a quirky brain, a genius for visual recall that
was almost savantlike. When he was younger and found himself
overstimulated by a flood of images, he would flap his hands in a
ritual of "stimming." He was the sweetest guy and always concerned about his friends, and you never doubted that he was
rooting for you. He regarded my job as a dead end and kept counseling me to leave it. "You're better than that, Gavin."

The job may have been an underutilization of my skills, but I
learned a great deal from watching Mr. Shorenstein. His obses-
sion with detail was such an all-encompassing force that the security guards at one building would walkie-talkie the security
guards at another building: "Mr. S is heading in your direction.
Should be arriving in five minutes." Five minutes was hardly
enough time for me and the janitorial crew to make sure there
wasn't a piece of litter on the sidewalk or a dust ball on the lobby
floor. If we thought we'd pass inspection, we were badly mis-
taken. Craig Edwards would accompany Mr. S to his office, only
for the old man to find the tiniest of scratches in the elevator's
bronze plating. Without saying a word, he'd twist the lapel on

Craig's jacket. A janitor would be dispatched to buff out the scratch before Mr. S left for his next building.

Craig served as more than my shield. Between gulps of coffee and puffs of smoke, he taught me about the folly of what he called "the human condition." He gave me a 51 out of 60 on my first evaluation, describing me as "bright and personable with no apparent weaknesses and a great future," though apparently not at the Shorenstein Company. "You've been here nine months, kid," he told me. "Enough time for me to tell you that you're not a nine-to-five kind of person. Get out of here before the old man decides to give you a promotion."

""

It was the early 1990s, and Big Tech was about to make its first metamorphic rise in Silicon Valley. At the age of twenty-four, I still saw myself as a neophyte and wondered how I might find my place in such a frenetic world. I wasn't necessarily seeking a guru, but there on the TV screen I found Tony Robbins, the self-help evangelist with the mighty jaw and mighty hands. I bought his motivational tapes and played them on Andrew's Walkman. His voice was mighty, too, a bass made deeper by a benign tumor on his pituitary gland. After a week or two of listening, his preaching found ground inside my head.

"Your past does not equal your future."

"You have to make the shift from being a consumer in the economy to becoming an owner—and you do it by becoming an investor."

"There's the business you're in, and the business you're becoming."

"The secret to living is giving."

As I understood it then, Robbins was dispensing some variant of neurolinguistic programming, which offered a fix for those suffering phobias, depression, low self-esteem, self-sabotage, and tied tongues. The fix was not only easy but practically instantaneous: Find a person who embodies all the outward traits of personality, bearing, charisma, language, and power lacking in yourself. Study that person. Copy that person. The borrowed traits may fit awkwardly at first, but don't fret. You'll be surprised how fast the pose becomes you, and you the pose. If the chosen model happened to be Robbins himself, all the easier, because he had written more than one bestseller—*Awaken the Giant Within*, *Unlimited Power*—that personalized the process of personal transmutation.

Skeptics were dismissing the "Robbins Success System" as outright cant, the creed of a new pop psychology. But Robbins had been a janitor in a high-rise building in Glendale only a decade before, and the examples he brought to the page, of people constantly underaiming their potential, reminded me of me. So I took some of the principles and jargon that made sense to me— *stretch goals, inspiration and desperation both lead to a path*—and put them to work.

My father, who scoffed at such nonsense, thought I could use a little schooling of the Pat Kelley kind. She was the "blond bombshell" whose legend had been told to me in various versions by members of the Lonely Hearts Club. That she was Irish and could drink any man under the table was only part of it. She had made a fortune and lost a fortune, her rise and fall and rise again chronicled with genuine affection in the columns of Herb Caen. She'd been a single mother in 1962, earning a meager wage at

Allstate Insurance, when she strode into the boss's office and asked to be promoted to manager. She was told that no woman had ever climbed to such a rank, and she would not be the first. She quit right there. No income. No savings. No child support. She talked her way into a job at EF Hutton and was sent to New York for training. There were one hundred men in the room and one Pat Kelley. As the first female stockbroker in San Francisco, she became a star at Hutton. When she quit to go into real estate, she happened to catch the front end of the condo conversion craze. With her new wealth, she opened a wine store, a gourmet grocery, a culinary school, and two cafés known for never serving an uninspired meal.

Dad and I found her on her fourth act, this one as the grande dame of the Balboa Cafe, one of the longest-running saloons in San Francisco, which still featured its original mahogany bar. She and famed chef Jeremiah Tower had teamed up with Doyle Moon and Jack "Slick" Hobday and turned the Balboa into a leading light of California cuisine, a place where, in the words of one customer, "straight, gay, young, old, millennial, techie, socialite, politician, single or with your family, rich, poor, or just a plain old sports fan, were welcomed inside with open arms." The arms belonged to Pat, who played hostess and just about everything else inside the elongated space at Fillmore and Greenwich in the Marina District.

Dad and I took a corner table and both ordered the signature Balboa Burger with its hard-soft baguette and pickled red onions. Pat sat down with us, her shift over, drinking a martini named the Double Pat Kelley. She asked how my job was going and laughed when I told her that I didn't see much of a future in being employee number 892 at Walter Shorenstein. Dad ordered a bottle of Rafanelli zinfandel, one of his favorites, and he and Pat started talking cheap reds, middling reds, expensive reds.

"You should have seen Pat's wine store just around the corner from here, on Union Street," Dad said. "She started with wine, added some food, and had the best cheeses in the whole city."

"It's an empty storefront now," Pat said.

"Up and down Union, it's the same unfortunate story," he said.

"If I was a younger woman, I'd build it all over again," she said.

I went home that night stuck on an idea. The early techies were starting to move into the suburbs surrounding San Francisco. Flush with disposable income, they were heading to Napa and Sonoma for their getaways. Among the niceties they wanted to learn more about was pairing excellent wines with excellent food. And like everyone else, they were looking for a bargain. I canvassed San Francisco thinking I might find a business that was serving such a need. But as far as I could tell, the democratization of fine wines wasn't a concept in operation at any shop or bar or restaurant in the city in the early 1990s.

My father and I kept going back to the Balboa to visit with Pat. I shared with her my idea of starting a wine store that wasn't the discount rack at Price Club but wasn't some precious shop that catered to the initiated either. It would offer great selections at competitive prices and educate customers on the virtues of different varietals and how they best paired with food. If the store did well ("There's the business you're in, and the business you're becoming"), the next step would be a café that would serve the same wines with scarcely a markup. A bottle of cabernet selling for twenty dollars at the store would sell for twenty-three dollars at the café.

Pat wondered if I fully grasped the rebellion I was proposing.

You'll piss off the best restaurateurs in the city, who sell that same Cab for $45 a bottle, she said. To mess with convention even more, I said, the café would offer the highest-end wines—bottles that sold for $100 to $150 apiece—by the single glass. Regular folk would now be able to taste what they never could afford to taste before.

She knew I didn't have any money to push the concept forward. My father said he'd be willing to kick in an undetermined amount. You should take the idea to your cousins the Mohuns and the Pelosis, Pat suggested. And why not the Burtons and other politicos? And while you're at it, you might want to share the idea with Gordon and Andrew and Billy Getty. In the event I needed her counsel and connections, she'd be more than happy to get involved, she said.

I hugged Pat and headed straight to a new bar and restaurant called the Paragon, where my friend Keith Belling was one of the owners. I asked Keith if he might assist me in writing a formal business plan. He reached into a drawer, xeroxed his plan for the Paragon, and gave it to me as a template. Before I knew it, Andrew was in and so was Billy and my cousin Paul Mohun and a Pelosi or two. Pat then pointed me in the direction of an antique store across the street from the Balboa Cafe. It was going out of business, she said, and if I could grab the lease, it would make a perfect location for a wine store.

Problem was, the other three corners were each occupied by a business selling liquor. Residents would almost certainly oppose a fourth such establishment. I went door-to-door putting my best spin on it. We wouldn't be a bar, and we wouldn't be a liquor store. None of our customers would be shouting at the moon at two in the morning. My proselytizing managed to win over some of the residents, but that was only the start of it. I had to sign the lease even though I hadn't yet secured city approval or acquired a state liquor license, which would be difficult to come by and far from cheap.

Strolling the sidewalk along Fillmore one afternoon, I noticed an odd bit of language on the old Coca-Cola sign affixed to the Balboa Cafe. OFF SALE LIQUORS, it read. The café had two liquor licenses, it turned out, and one of them allowed for the sale of beer and wine off premises. I asked Pat to find out if the owners ever made use of this second license. Not only didn't they use it, she said, but they were willing to sell it to us. We had raised $174,000 from fifteen friends and family to kick-start the business. We couldn't afford to spend it all on a liquor license. Unbelievably, Pat was able to finagle a deal that met our budget.

Our idea had quickly turned into something real. I quit my job at the Shorenstein company, to the delight of Craig Edwards, who was such a supporter that he helped me negotiate the lease at the wine store. I was launching my first business in the same Marina District where my grandfather had built his first homes.

Word spread in the neighborhood, known as "the Triangle," of our lease and liquor license. The news aggravated residents, who in turn aggravated city hall. If Boss Newsom once held sway over city teams inspecting his housing construction, the same blind eye would not be afforded to his grandson. Getting my permits should have been a walk in the park. The building had recently undergone a major remodel approved by the city. And yet the inspectors seemed to relish nothing more than to fight me on every trifling change. It became so ridiculous that the Health Department insisted I install a special sink for mops that would require an elaborate system of copper pipes. It was going to cost me thousands of dollars. I had no need for mops, I told them. Wall to wall, the floor would be carpeted. Wine was a food, they countered. If you're going to be serving food, you need to have a sink for mops. None of my appeals to logic made a dent, so I took on the city's bureaucracy. Andrew and Billy recommended patience. For more than a year, I exhibited all the patience in the world, only for city hall to prevail.

Andrew thought the time had come to make a pitch to his father. I understood that he would not be the one to ask his dad to become one of our investors. Gordon controlled the trust that would distribute the money to the next generation of Gettys, but his children, nephews, and nieces would have to wait until he died to gain full access to it. Gordon watched over this money with the utmost fiduciary responsibility. When it came to asking him for any smaller sums of his own money along the way, the Getty scions weren't always sure how to approach Gordon. Indeed, when they needed to be rescued from a financial jam, say a car that had broken down, they often went to "Uncle Bill," my father. The irony, of course, was that Dad was overseeing one of the Getty family trusts. The double irony was that he did not have the extra cash to make his own children's lives appreciably easier, but he did find ways to make good for the Getty kids.

As I approached the meeting with Gordon, I also understood that my father would not be assuming the task of asking his best friend to reach into his pocket to become one of our investors. That request was mine alone to make. I cannot say I drove to the Getty house that day without apprehension. I was no longer a kid traveling to Tanzania on his dime. I was twenty-four years old and looking to enter into a business relationship with one of the richest men in America. Gordon had no office atop a tower, like

Shorenstein. Andrew and I found him in his workspace on the bottom floor of the mansion, distracted by Liszt and whatever composition he was creating at that moment. His hair was a ravel of curls, and he was wearing a button-down shirt, slacks, and an old Members Only jacket.

"All righty, boys, what can I do for you?" he said.

I did not start where Andrew thought I would. I began with Sir John Falstaff, Shakespeare's grog-swilling Plump Jack, who was not only the inspiration and title for Gordon's two-act opera but also a two-foot-tall statue in his office. The figure, like the character, had a quality of mocking old-world stuffiness and celebrating life's absurdity. To me, its tongue in cheek expressed the same temperament that was behind the wine store. Weeks earlier, meeting with our designers, LeavittWeaver, we had envisioned Falstaff as our signage, design, logo, and feel. PlumpJack Wines, we would call ourselves. If this sounded like flattery to Gordon's ear, I was willing to take the risk. But now, sitting across from him, the words, my words, didn't come out right.

"The wine store," I blurted. "It's finally coming together."

"Now you're talking!" he roared. "Be authentic. Be creative. Be bold. If it fails, so be it."

"Yes, sir," I said. "We're thinking of naming the business PlumpJack."

He looked at me slightly bemused. Maybe he thought I was pulling his leg.

"I'm serious," I said. "PlumpJack. One word."

He pounded the desk with his fist. "I love it, man."

"That's great," I said.

Andrew was smiling. I was smiling. Perhaps we were smiling too freely.

"I'm not your huckleberry," he said. We weren't sure what the idiom meant. "You should know that I'm not subsidizing this thing. But I'd be willing to do whatever the next guy is doing."

Andrew told him we had seven or eight investors at fifteen grand each.

"No more, no less," Gordon said. "I'll talk to Ann, and she'll make sure a check is sent."

As we said our goodbyes and headed toward the door, he told us we had forgotten something: the statue of Plump Jack. "This is yours," he said. "Good luck." Not since that stranger at Ramona's restaurant had handed me a twenty-dollar tip and told me to keep doing what I was doing had I felt such a purpose. I thanked him again.

It wasn't an easy walk back to the car. No matter which way I held Plump Jack, he was heavy. On the drive back to the Triangle in Cow Hollow, I kept checking on the jolly old fat man. Like a Buddha, I gave him his own space inside the wine store, right there on the counter beside the cash register.

""""

Andrew was spending more time in LA, and his movie scripts were becoming darker. After three or four screenplays that went nowhere, he began to grow distant. I didn't see it back then—indeed, it would take me years to recognize the deterioration—but torment had begun to envelop him. He was talking about a new screenplay that had attracted enough financing and strong actors that his break in Hollywood was about to happen. The film, *The Evil Within*, would end up taking fifteen years to finish, but Andrew would not live to see its premiere. He had begun to dabble in drugs to quiet himself and would eventually take it too far. I asked our mutual friends about ways to reach him, but Andrew was living the life of a recluse in a historic mansion in the Hollywood Hills. He didn't want to be rescued.

As Andrew receded deeper into his own world, his brother Billy and I grew closer. The youngest of the Getty boys, Billy liked to recite arcane facts and figures from San Francisco's past and was captivated by the subject of wine and its making and selling and pairing with food. We spent many hours discussing the vision for PlumpJack, and he was a constant source of ideas, sending me articles from wine magazines and copies of menus and wine lists from restaurants around the country. Given how far back our two clans went, it made sense to make Billy a bigger part of the venture. He understood it was going to be an uphill climb. My battles with city hall, the red tape that kept us from opening for a year and a half, meant the business was woefully undercapitalized. Yes, we had cash from our investors, but we couldn't afford any employees. I was the wine buyer, accountant, marketing man, guy behind the register, janitor, delivery boy. No matter where you lived in San Francisco, it was our pledge that we would deliver wine to your doorstep for free. Nine p.m. on a Friday night, I'd get a call from Potrero Hill for a middling bottle of pinot and head out across the canyons of San Francisco to find the address. The transaction hardly paid for the gas, but I'd spend a minute or two at the door chitchatting with the customer. I met hundreds of new people this way, people who became our regulars.

Whenever the list of tasks became too much for me, Billy was there to help out. We leaned on Pat Kelley without shame. She figured out hours in the evening to help me with the bookwork, and on weekends she took over the floor so I could make the bigger deliveries. I rarely took a day off and, frankly, I didn't want one. Having so little capital ended up being a perk. It forced us to innovate and become more entrepreneurial and capable. I never counted the hours I worked because it didn't feel like work. Nonstop became a devotion, a zone where dyslexia had no purchase.

For a time, it didn't look like we would make it. There was one day where our sales amounted to a bottle of chardonnay for twelve dollars, and that was a purchase made by my father. The heat of a San Francisco summer, by which I mean the month of October, saw temperatures rise past ninety degrees, and we had no air-conditioning unit to turn on. The morning sun blasting through the windows started to warm the wine. I frantically drove up through Santa Rosa trying to find a large portable cooler, but every Home Depot had sold out of them. When I returned to the store, it was so hot inside the building that the bottles were starting to bleed. Wine was running through the corks and down the labels. By the time the heat wave passed, we had lost a quarter of our inventory but gained a valuable lesson.

Desperation became innovation. We took out a line of credit and officially went into debt. This allowed us to remodel the storefront with awnings and install an AC unit. I was able to hire an employee and devote my time to doing whatever it took to get people to walk through our door. I cased the more successful wine stores in the city to see what they were doing better and put up new signage comparing our prices to theirs. I walked every block in the neighborhood passing out flyers that pledged a money-back guarantee. We tasted every wine and proudly sold only those we could back up with our own pithy reviews. Billy and I even persuaded the cast of the American Conservatory

Theater to come to the store on Valentine's Day to perform *Romeo and Juliet*, offering free PlumpJack condoms with every bottle of champagne sold. My father was not amused; Gordon loved it.

Business picked up and I was able to save enough money for a small down payment on a flat in the Marina District that passed my mother's inspection. About that time, I met a young woman, Mary Kelley Phleger, who had a distinguished pedigree and deep roots in San Francisco. Her father's father, one of the founding members of a prominent law firm, had been a prosecutor at the Nuremberg trials and U.S. delegate to the United Nations. Her late father, Atherton, had been a lawyer and member of the Wells Fargo Bank board. Kelley not only was part Irish and held a degree in fine arts from Cal Berkeley, but she also came with an enthusiastic thumbs-up from Ann Getty, who had taken it upon herself to curate the right girlfriend for me. Like Ann, Kelley was pretty and nearly six feet tall and not afraid to get her hands dirty. She was teaching elementary school and in her off hours helping me with gift baskets at the wine store.

As for my suitability as a partner, my focus would become less on Kelley than on growing the business. Two years after launching the wine store, we opened PlumpJack Cafe half a block away and made good on the threat to pair excellent wines with excellent food and not sell a bottle at the usual 200 percent markup. Our wine store–to–café pipeline gave us enough vertical integration to serve our diners the finest wines at prices too good to be true. We offered some of the best cabs, pinots, and zins in the world and poured them by the glass. Pat was right, of course. Our model ended up pissing off every restaurateur in town and more than a few wineries in Napa and Sonoma whose tasting rooms couldn't match our prices—for *their* wines.

The line of patrons outside the café kept lengthening, and then one of the city's most respected food critics weighed in with a rave review about our "extraordinary" main courses and excellent but reasonably priced wines. The years of struggle started to fade; we began to grow in a way I had not imagined. Near Lake Tahoe, we opened a new PlumpJack Cafe at the old Squaw Valley Inn, where so much Newsom history had played out. With Pat Kelley's lead, we purchased the Balboa Cafe in San Francisco and opened a second one in Olympic Valley. It would take several years, but our portfolio would expand to include four wineries, two boutique hotels, seven restaurants and bars, and two retail clothing stores. We had seven hundred employees, including my mom, who worked for a time as controller, and my sister, Hilary, and cousin Jeremy Scherer, who later became copresidents.

Along the way, *The New York Times* heralded our arrival with an article on the Balboa Cafe headlined (wouldn't you know it) "Where the Gettys Hold Court à la Falstaff." There was Billy, soft-spoken and ponytailed, dressed in a sweater and sport coat, sounding a bit defensive about his life of privilege. "This is in no way a vanity investment," he said, describing his stake in Plump-Jack. "The questions always come like this: 'Do you drive a Mercedes? Do you get your hair done at such and such?' That's beside the point. We provide 360 people with jobs." And there was me still trying to get comfortable in my skin, depicted in a manner that would soon become its own stereotype: "A charismatic figure, with slicked-back dark hair and a voice that seems perpetually hoarse, not from cigars or liquor but from nonstop talking." Barely out of my twenties, the writer noted, I had already mastered a politician's gestures—placing my arm "conspiratorially on a listener's shoulder, punching the air to make a point." Reading the piece years later, I can also see that I came off a little full of myself, explaining that we had acquired the iconic Balboa, a watering hole with seventy-five seats for meals, "because we're standard-bearers." What my dyslexic brain actually meant to say was we were "stewards." As high-minded as that might have sounded in a hit-and-run story about two youthful restaurateurs caught in a hip scene of their making, I saw our mission as more than transactional, more than a bottom line. Whether a vineyard or a business as storied as the Squaw Valley Inn, we were managers of authentic places entrusted to our care.

I had spent months conceiving and producing a handbook— "PlumpJack's Core Ideology and Random Notes," I called it—that we handed out to each employee. I took quotes from Churchill and Michelangelo and even Wayne Gretzky to try to impart the notion that we weren't in the business of commerce so much as we were in the business of building personal relationships with our customers. The grafting of such an ideal wasn't always smooth. My day-to-day management of PlumpJack was a constant lesson in humility. I didn't want our staff to walk in fear of me. I wanted them to challenge my assumptions and add their own innovations to the mix. Toward that goal, I decided to give out a yearly award to the employee who took the biggest risk, only to land flat on his or her face. A Failure Award that all but forgot the failure and honored the chancing of an unconventional idea, the daring of an innovation. The first recipient of the Failure Award was a genuine story that my father might have told, except it belonged to me. Our Squaw Valley Inn was surrounded by ponds, and every summer the ponds gave hatch to the worst swarms of mosquitoes. We had spent millions of dollars remodeling the hotel, but it still had no central cooling. In the evenings, the staff would open the doors and windows to let in the breeze. Riding the breeze, naturally, were the mosquitoes. Our night clerk was fed up with the choice between stifling heat and stifling bugs and came up with a solution. Problem was, he didn't tell Ludo, our touchy engineer. Ludo called me one night fit to be tied.

"This is a disaster!" he shouted.

"What's going on?" I calmly inquired.

"There's eyeballs and carcasses, bones and fins, all over the inn."

"What are you talking about?"

"That damn night clerk. The son of a beech."

"What did he do?"

"He bought catfish."

"Catfish. For what? Dinner?"

"No, he bought live catfish by the dozens and planted them in the ponds. To eat the baby mosquitoes."

"Okay."

"And the raccoons came. They fished out the catfish and ate the meat and scattered everything else. Bones, bones. Heads and tails. The hotel, inside and out, is a goddamn mess."

I couldn't stop laughing. We had treated the raccoons of Olympic Village to a feeding frenzy. Looking to repeat their gluttony, they were sticking around for the next batch of catfish. There wouldn't be a next batch, but I did give the night clerk a bonus and our first annual Failure Award.

I told the catfish story at San Francisco's venerable Commonwealth Club. Billy Getty and I had been invited to address the members on how we had turned PlumpJack into more than a wine store: restaurants, wineries, and hotels. We had built an actual brand, or at least that was the theme of my first public speech.

Billy talked for a bit, and I must have rambled on for a good thirty minutes about the Failure Award and what we were trying to foster among our employees and customers. I kept using the words *culture* and *relationships* and could see some of the audience members' eyes glazing over. So I switched course. I recalled one slow night at the wine store when a sharply dressed young man walked through the door with a tense look on his face. He wanted to know where the cold champagne was located, and I pointed him to the right chiller. He must have stood there for fifteen minutes pulling bottles out of the cold and mulling over their labels. His indecision was causing him more grief, I could see, and I was about to walk on over when he grabbed another bottle and showed it to me.

"Is this a good one?" he asked.

"Yes," I said, "it's a good one."

"Are you sure?"

"Yeah, I think you're going to be happy with it."

It wasn't a cheap champagne, but neither was it very expensive. I put the bottle in a gift bag, and he drove off. An hour or so passed, and I was about to close up when the young man walked through the door again. My first thought was *Oh no, buyer's remorse. He's here to tell me the champagne was a flop.* But he was wearing a grin and so was the young woman beside him. "It was a great champagne," he said. "I came back to thank you and to introduce you to my fiancée." This was the story he hadn't told me, the one that explained what brought him to our store in the first place and why he'd spent so much time agonizing over his choice of champagne. He had taken the love of his life to the Palace of Fine Arts, not a mile from the store, and asked for her hand in marriage. When she said yes, he popped the cork and they toasted their first toast. I told his fiancée it was a pleasure to meet her, gave him a congratulatory clap on the shoulder, and watched the two of them walk back into the night. *How decent was that?* I thought. A customer had returned to the store on the most memorable night of his life to tell me that what had taken place between him and me wasn't a transaction at all. He wanted me to know that I was part of this moment, their lives coming together. At the Commonwealth Club that evening and at almost every public telling of the champagne bottle story since, I found myself getting emotional.

''''

We kept innovating and PlumpJack kept growing. From his initial 5.7 percent share, Gordon continued to invest more money until he had a sizable stake in several of our businesses. When the *San Francisco Chronicle* asked him why he had chosen to invest with me, he said the answer was elementary. "I've put in more money because of the success of my first investments with him." While Gordon wasn't the type to play tycoon and second-guess my business decisions, he was far from a passive investor. Whenever I came to him with a new idea, his response was always the same: "Don't ever shy away from taking a risk. If you're going to make an error, make it on the bold side."

Gordon, Billy, and I were having dinner one evening at the Balboa Cafe when the subject of musty corks tainting fine wines came up. It was 1996 or '97, and the problem seemed to be getting worse. I told them that 5 percent of our sales at the wine store were being returned because of cork taint; it was a growing issue and costing us money.

At that moment, we lifted our glasses and awaited the dazzle of a bottle of Paul Hobbs cabernet.

"Can you believe it?" Billy said. "It's corked."

"It's corked," I said.

Billy was shaking his head at a fine wine turned sour. "What are the chances?"

Gordon was lost in thought. "All righty, boys," he said. "Here's my crackpot idea. All wines at our winery should be screw-top. All the wines, boys."

Corks had been the preferred method of sealing wines for centuries. Corks were part of wine's mystique. "Come on," I said. "A screw top on a hundred-dollar bottle of reserve cabernet?"

"Why not?" Gordon replied. What was the argument in favor of cork except that it had been around for so long? Why not turn tradition on its head?

I went home thinking that screw tops were for Boone's Farm Strawberry Hill. But the more I consulted with experts, the less crazy the idea seemed. We would have to redesign our bottle. We would have to customize our own screw top. This would require a higher grade of tin and an inserted wafer to make the fit tighter and keep out the air. It wouldn't be cheap, but it aligned with our whole irreverent reason for being.

To hedge our bets, John Conover, our general manager at PlumpJack Winery, suggested to Gordon that we do half our bottles with screw tops and half with corks. We could sell our PlumpJack Reserve, our best cabernet, in a wooden box with both choices. Let the drinker decide if there was a difference. "I love it," Gordon said. "Let's shake things up."

And that's pretty much what happened. Robert Parker had already launched us with a great review, ninety-five points for the reserve. But it was Robert Mondavi, the incomparable vintner who had almost single-handedly convinced the world of the high quality of Napa Valley wines, who anointed us. The day we introduced our screw tops to the public, Gordon, Billy, John, and I were walking into the main tent at the Napa Valley Wine Auction at the Meadowood Resort when Mr. Mondavi was walking out. He stopped us with a wide smile on his big, craggy face. "Better you guys than me," he said, which was his way of tipping his hat to the daring of our move. In time, he would put screw tops on his own varietals.

Entrepreneurship had been my first calling. Few pursuits in life had given me more satisfaction than starting and growing my own business. But even as PlumpJack took on another dimension, I had no desire to become a mogul. I was casting about for some other role—not the political kingmaker played by my grandfather Newsom or the patron saint of lost causes that had my father invariably going to bat for one underdog and another, but a path that took me deeper into the city and its influence on the West.

CHAPTER SIX

⁗

I n 1996, I got a call from an aide to Mayor Willie Brown, who was one of our regulars at PlumpJack Cafe. I had co-hosted a fundraiser at the wine store as a favor to Willie and also walked precincts for him.

"The mayor wants to appoint you to the city's Film Commission. What do you say?"

The idea of public service intrigued me, and it took me only a moment to say yes.

A few weeks later, I made my way to city hall for the swearing-in ceremony with thirty or forty other appointees. As Mayor Brown went down the list, I could feel my heart pounding the closer he got to me, the newest member of the Film Commission. "And Gavin Newsom. Welcome to your seat as the next chair of the Parking and Traffic Commission," Willie said. Parking and Traffic? The chair? What role did the chair play? Was this Willie's idea of a joke? In a blink, he swore me in, and then a reporter from channel four had me cornered.

"Congratulations. What's your vision for Parking and Traffic?" she asked.

"Vision?" I stammered, and laughed. I blurted out something about paying my outstanding tickets and dashed out the door.

The next day, I bought a copy of *Robert's Rules of Order.* At my first few meetings as chair, I literally read from the script, but it didn't take long for me to commit every rule to memory. I learned the blunt art of running a decent meeting and not being heavy-handed about it. I learned that even a commission on parking and traffic, lowly as its duties seemed, held the capacity to make workers' lives better, if only the government's bureaucracy could be made to listen. Meeting after meeting, the members of SEIU Local 790, many of them Black women, walked up to the podium to tell their stories. These were the meter maids who came into public view mostly when they pulled out their ticket books. Who knew—certainly not me—the day-in-and-day-out abuses they were made to endure for simply doing their jobs? They were shouted at and spit on, called the *N*-word, even shot at with BBs and pellets. What the public too often did not see were the untold acts of kindness and decency they performed to help drivers out of so many jams. The flat tires they fixed, the ambulances they summoned, the fits of road rage they calmed, the hands they held of women going into labor right there in the back seat.

With nowhere else to turn, they were pleading with the commission for respect and protection, not easy fixes for a governmental body at the very bottom of the hierarchy. The title *meter maid* was part of the denigration, we reasoned. So we pushed for a change so that they were now known as "parking control officers" and began handing out a monthly award to underscore their good deeds. I'll never forget the joy on the face of one young gentleman, not long on the job, who stood up to receive his Officer of the Month award. It was hardly a ceremony, but there was his prideful mother, sitting near the front row, crying. In the same manner as the wine store, we weren't just moving through an item on the agenda. It was about people.

Before I finished my first year as chair of the commission, Mayor Brown approached me with an even more unusual offer. Would I be interested in filling a vacancy on the San Francisco Board of Supervisors? I was a political greenhorn with scarcely the credentials to warrant such consideration, and the question occurred to me: Why was Willie choosing me except that he knew my father and was privy to my more or less competent performance on the Parking and Traffic Commission? I might have been inclined to say yes right then, but this was a step in a far more serious direction, one whose potential perils my father knew much about. We were having a meal at the Balboa when I told Dad of Willie's offer. I'm sure he provided me wise counsel, delved into the complications of juggling a political life with a multipronged business, but that's not what I recall. What sticks with me is how he literally glowed with pride. He did not need to tell me that we came from an extended clan that numbered forty-six attorneys and one genuine power broker but never a politician, which he considered a high enough calling that he had run for the San Francisco Board of Supervisors himself in 1967, the year of my birth, only to lose.

The next day I called Willie and told him I was in. When the occasion came again for the mayor to explain my selection to the public in January 1997, Willie did so by telling another joke: "Let me introduce Gavin Newsom, my affirmative action pick." The line got a laugh, but it was, in fact, true. The eleven-member board included a gay white male, a Latina lesbian, a Jewish lesbian, a Latino male, a Black reverend, and two Chinese Americans, one of each gender. Not only was I the youngest member of the board, but I was the only straight white male. ODD MAN IN, read the headline in the *Los Angeles Times*. It was certainly more artful than the screaming headline in the local *Examiner*: BOARD GETS A STRAIGHT WHITE MALE.

Only twenty years earlier, Harvey Milk had become the first prominent openly gay elected official in the country when he joined the board of supervisors. Those who kept alive his mission weren't sure how to regard my appointment. I hadn't campaigned. I wasn't elected. My selection was seen by some in the community as a throwback to the days when white male businessmen didn't even have to pretend to share power in the city. "Newsom has a pedigree," Jeff Sheehy, president of the Harvey Milk Lesbian/Gay/Bisexual Democratic Club, told the *Times*. "He's smart and charming and he's working hard, but it's obvious why he is where he is. . . . You have to regret that he couldn't answer specific questions. He's a fourth-generation San Franciscan. Doesn't he know what's going on in the city he lives in? If he can't transcend that background and show that he understands what it's like to wait 45 minutes for a bus then he's not going to do well. I like Gavin, but he needs to have some positions."

I was attempting to do that very thing, to stake out an unambiguous position, on the day of my swearing-in when I appeared on Ross McGowan's morning show on Fox Channel Two. It was bright and early in the city, and McGowan didn't waste time getting to one of the most contentious issues facing the board of supervisors. What did I think about the $100 million in revenue bonds that would soon be appearing on the ballot, a measure to build a new $525 million stadium and mall complex to keep the DeBartolo family and the 49ers from fleeing the city and quite possibly the state?

I did not pause before answering. My answer gave no space for equivocation. What did I know about wiggle room? I was a businessman who thought it logical that before the citizenry voted on such an expenditure, we needed to see the fine print of an actual deal with the development company. To hold a vote before such a deal had been struck seemed a classic case of putting cart before horse. It might have occurred to me in that moment that the man directing the cart was Mayor Brown himself, who not only had appointed me to the board but was passionately committed to keeping the 49ers in San Francisco, cost be damned. Instead, I walked right into the question, blithely telling McGowan that "I wouldn't be able to support the project unless I saw the business plans first. As of now, there isn't a business plan."

Whatever early version of a cell phone I was carrying began to light up on my drive home. The first caller was John Burton, a California state senator and boss of one of the state's most powerful political machines. He was a confidant to Mayor Brown and a pal of my father.

"What the fuck did you just do?" He sounded like a disappointed father. "What the fuck did you say about the 49ers?"

"McGowan caught me off guard," I muttered. "I should have expected the question. My answer made sense to me."

"You have to clean this up with Willie. He's waiting for you at city hall."

"I'm going to be seeing him later at the swearing-in."

"I don't give a fuck about the swearing-in. You need to see him now."

I didn't know it then, but it was Burton who had suggested to Willie that he appoint me to the vacant supervisor's seat. Burton had vouched for me. I headed straight to city hall, only to be told that the mayor had a busy day and would see me when he could. I must have sat for an hour in a waiting room turned shrine to the man and myth that was Willie. Staring down at me from every conceivable angle were paintings of Willie by famous artists and framed portraits of Willie on the cover of national magazines.

When I was finally allowed into his chamber, he had the oddest smile on his face. "You don't know how excited I am to be swearing you in tonight."

I let out my breath, only to inhale Willie's fire. "If you want to make it in this business, you have to know how this works. I appointed you. You did not get elected by the people. You did not receive a single vote. Except for mine. You knew my position on this matter. If not, you should have known."

What I said in reply was something along the lines of "Yes, sir."

He kept on going. He was in filibuster mode. "Until you run your own campaign, until you walk your first precinct, until you have to decide between some sacred principle and a five-hundred-dollar donation from a silk stocking whose next deal is already on your agenda, you don't know. You do not know."

In the absence of such knowledge, he was saying, the only truth was my loyalty to him. Now, I shouldn't mistake that loyalty for fealty in the face of corruption. That was a different request, he noted, one that he would never make of me. This deal, though, was righteous. It would keep home the 49ers, the first major league sports franchise in San Francisco history. With a nod, I told him that I understood. Lesson over, he guided me to the door.

"I'll see you later at your swearing-in."

I walked outside and dialed John Burton's number. "I'm not cut out for this. I'm a businessman. What the hell am I doing in politics?"

"Fuck you!" he shouted. "Your old man's swearing you in."

And later that day the Honorable William Newsom III swore me in. He kept his smile restrained, but anyone in that room who knew father and son could see that this was a big moment for him and me.

Thus began, to the everlasting disappointment of my mother and the everlasting satisfaction of my father, my life as a San Francisco politician. An effusive Mayor Brown introduced the twenty-nine-year-old me as "part of the future generation of leaders of this great city." I introduced myself as a "social liberal and fiscal watchdog" whose business acumen would balance out a board that sometimes tilted too far left. My moderation reflected the people I would end up representing, the citizens of the second district, home to three generations of Newsoms: Pacific Heights, the Marina, Cow Hollow, Sea Cliff, and Laurel Heights, which boasted the city's strongest concentration of Republicans and, not surprisingly, its highest income levels.

As for the $100 million in revenue bonds to help the 49ers build a new stadium near Candlestick Park, I wasted no time making my new position known. With or without the development details, I would be voting "yes" to place the measure on the ballot. Mayor Brown was kind enough to explain my change of heart to reporters. "These are rookie mistakes," he told them. "It's not a matter of him changing his position. It's a matter of fully understanding the facts."

In June 1997, voters passed the bond measure by the slimmest of margins, 50.1 percent, only to see the actual deal never come together for precisely the reasons I had feared. The numbers simply didn't pencil out. Willie's pleas notwithstanding, and despite my own grueling efforts when I became mayor, the storied 49ers would leave our city. Their departure would not be as dramatic as, say, the Colts fleeing Baltimore under the cover of darkness and moving six hundred miles east to Indianapolis. The red-and-gold would land forty-five minutes down the road in Silicon Valley. They'd play in a new stadium built for them in Santa Clara but remain, for branding purposes, the San Francisco 49ers.

I stayed true to my pledge to steer left on issues of poverty and inequality and find the middle on the economy and taxes. I pushed for more construction of housing projects through public-private partnerships and for stiffer penalties against landlords who flouted rent-control laws. I visited every park in the city and compiled a long list of improvements that we made happen through the passage of a countywide bond. I became a persistent voice on sentencing disparities between those arrested for using powdered cocaine and those busted for using crack, a contradiction in the law that was helping fill our state prisons with more poor people of color.

Nowhere on my agenda in 1998 was a plan to tackle the deplorable state of taxicabs in San Francisco, though I knew well how dismal the service had become from the experiences of my restaurant patrons. Mayor Brown asked me to show up to a "little town hall" he was hosting to address the matter, and when I opened the door of the hall, I could hear the groaning of a thousand people. Angry cabbies, angry customers, a frustrated but determined Willie pledging to overhaul the entire system. At meeting's end, he announced the formation of a task force that would have ninety days to come up with a list of recommendations. The task force, he told the crowd, would be headed by Supervisor Gavin Newsom. From the front of the hall, Willie's naughty eyes found where I was sitting. He nodded at me. What could I do but nod back?

I lost count of how many neighborhood meetings I presided over during those three months I ran Willie's taxicab task force. The job called on me to do a lot of public speaking, which at first put me in a state of dread, my hands drenched in sweat. Speaking to a crowd was not unlike the fear I felt in third grade reading to my classmates. The constant shifting of my eyes from words on paper to faces in the audience dizzied my brain, so I learned to memorize my talking points and best lines an hour before the meeting and wing it from there. This is how I discovered one of the secret powers of dyslexia. I could read a room with the best of them. I'd walk in and immediately size up the faces, mood, and manners. On the spot, if pressed, I was able to come up with new talking points and one-liners. If the mood I read was foul, I'd start out with humor. If the mood was no-nonsense, I'd get right to the meat of things. If the mood was anxious, I'd find something of comfort to riff on. I learned that an audience didn't mind occasional hiccups of speech, as long as you looked them in the eye. Indeed, if you were too seamless, they began to regard you as silver-tongued, which was no better than being regarded as silver-spooned.

When my ninety days were up, the task force brought to the ballot an initiative that established a new taxicab commission, which ushered in broad reforms that changed the state of the industry. I was credited with returning civility to the movement of people throughout the city, no small feat. How was I to know that the whole thing would be undone in a matter of a decade by the likes of something called Uber? Of the five supervisors Willie had appointed to the board during his time as mayor, only two of us went on to win an actual term at the ballot box. Willie said I was beginning to get the hang of politics, and I had to concede there was a powerful and mysterious attraction to seeing an idea turn into policy with the heft of government behind it. Watching a head of steam build and carry along a righteous issue might have been politics' purest intoxicant, though winning an election with a well-executed campaign wasn't half bad either.

I imagined this was why my father had run for office twice and why, even after his defeat in both instances, he continued to be one of the keenest observers and storytellers of San Francisco politics. At least half the jawing of the Lonely Hearts Club concerned his reads on the current state of politics. As if playing a parlor game, the boys turned old men were now studying my moves and conjecturing where I might—and damn well should—strike next. If I joined them at Moose's, I knew I was in for a whole beautiful night of it. Steadily, politics was becoming the medium by which my father and I were building a fuller relationship, and it gave me no small satisfaction.

On issues of poverty and inequality, I did not always please the Left. To the dismay of homeless advocates and the homeless themselves, I sponsored a voter initiative, Proposition N, otherwise known as "Care Not Cash." It would take a portion of each general assistance payment to a homeless person and apply it to their housing and drug and mental health treatment. The initiative gave rise to accusations that I was robbing the city's most deprived of the only sense of dignity they had left—to decide for themselves what to do with their assistance checks. I argued that the growing camps of the unsheltered on our city streets called for a wholly different approach. Proposition N passed in 2002 with 60 percent of the vote, burnishing my credentials for a run at higher office and bringing home the lesson that it was better to be aligned with the people than with the pundits.

My climbing the ladder of city politics did not please my mother. As my bookkeeper and accountant, she had seen first-hand how devoted I was to running PlumpJack and the joy it gave me. She had been born to San Francisco, knew well its vindictive side, and understood how the political aspirations of my father had played a part in ending their marriage. She watched the society crowd, whose wealth went back to the Gold Rush or some other California extraction, turn its gaze my way at fundraisers. Was I wearing gel in my hair, they wondered? Who was that latest girlfriend at my side? Was she a third-generation or fifth-generation Californian? My mother did not want that world for me: the shrewd marriages of tall husbands and tall wives that kept each year's Cotillion Debutante Ball stocked with children of the same; the gritted teeth behind the social smiles; the spectator sport of who was in and who was out based on so-and-so's dinner party guest list.

My mother believed that my obsessive drive as a businessman and now my resolute leap into politics were a response to my childhood. I was trying to solve the riddle of my identity, the question put there by my learning disability and the vastly different worlds that she and my father had presented to me. As I grew up trying to grasp which of these worlds, if either, suited me best, she had worried about the persona I was constructing to cover up what she considered a crack at my core. If my remaking was skim plaster, she feared, it would crumble. It would not hold me into adulthood.

This is not something she ever told me straight up. Digging into the compensations of my psychology would have required a different mode of communication, a different language, from the give-and-take we shared. Instead, I surmised my mother's concerns for me through hints and clues of feelings she dropped to me or my sister or maybe my aunts. Mom conducted her life mostly as a thing to be concealed. In her early fifties, it became clear to me that she was involved in a relationship, but she never said a word about it. Why is she dressed up in her tennis outfit? Why is she packing for the weekend? Where is she going? Who is he? I never asked. I didn't want to intrude on her private life. Truth is, I didn't want to know the details. She wasn't looking for me to be curious. She didn't want the conversation and neither did I. Had we talked about the man she was seeing, had their relationship been out in the open, I likely would have told her that I was happy for her. After years of carrying the weight of multiple jobs and two children, she deserved to find some joy.

I can't say that I was any more diligent in keeping her abreast of the goings-on in my life. By then I had moved out of the flat in the Marina District and broken up with my longtime girlfriend, Kelley Phleger, who couldn't figure out my intentions. I had trouble figuring them out myself. We were at a birthday party for Willie Brown when in walked the *Miami Vice* actor Don Johnson. He had a new TV series, *Nash Bridges*, set in San Francisco, and this put him in the Getty orbit. He had been married four times, twice to actress Melanie Griffith, and apparently was unattached, because he made a beeline for Kelley. Shortly afterward, we broke it off and she and Johnson became an item and then tied the knot at Ann and Gordon's mansion.

I was working my usual crazy hours, which had Billy Getty

concerned. "Gavin, you're going to burn out," he kept telling me. "You need to take a break." He suggested a vacation to Hawaii, which sounded like a great idea if only the timing were better. At that moment, Billy and I were hustling a few real estate deals. Raised by a mother who moved us from house to house and was a Realtor in her spare time, I had developed a decent eye for slightly run-down properties in the more exclusive parts of the city. I suggested to Billy that there was no reason our partnership couldn't extend to flipping a house or two. He loved the idea. I had saved some money from my salary at PlumpJack, and Billy was able to draw upon an investment fund his father had set up for him. We bought a fixer-upper in Pacific Heights and planned a complete remodel with the addition of a third floor. We agreed that I would live there and oversee the job, hiring the same designers who had redone PlumpJack's wine store and café and the Squaw Valley Inn.

On his own, Billy then threw himself into a 5,500-square-foot space on the top floor of a building in Russian Hill. His vision, which did not suffer from a shortfall of grandness, was to turn the entire space into a penthouse that would exploit the spectacular view and "show off the city." The remodel was a costly one, and Billy had to be careful not to run through the money Gordon had given him to undertake the project. He wanted to know what I thought of the idea of asking his father for a new infusion of cash to finish it. Of course, Billy wasn't comfortable making the ask himself. No son of Gordon Getty was. "You know my father," he said. "Would you mind asking him on my behalf?" I was the son of Bill Newsom, one of the few men in the world who could routinely find the channel to reach Gordon Getty. Billy believed I held the same power. I agreed to give it a try.

Walking into Gordon's office, I had none of the nervousness of before. We'd been partners in PlumpJack for several years, and his investment in the business was making him more money than he had ever expected. I knew because I was the one who delivered the checks to him four times a year. Though the amount was fairly modest at first, each check brought a smile of delight to his face. Wine had joined music to give him two passions. So I proceeded to make an enthusiastic case for Billy's penthouse project, and Gordon could think of no good reason to say no. Billy was relieved.

When it came time to finally plan our vacation to Hawaii, Billy told me he was thinking of asking his girlfriend to join us. "You should bring along someone, too," he said. I had no steady girlfriend at the time and mentioned the possibility of inviting Kimberly Guilfoyle, a San Francisco native who was working as a prosecutor in Los Angeles. Billy knew her well. In fact, they had dated for a time. Kimberly and I had shared long conversations about San Francisco and its politics. I liked that she was passionate about her job, and I found her attractive.

"She's smart and fun," I told Billy.

He thought about it for a moment. "You and Kimberly might make a good pair," he said. "But I'm warning you. Be careful."

Off to Maui the four of us went.

''''

Remodel finished, Billy sold the Russian Hill penthouse for $15 million, the highest price ever paid for a co-op in the city. He had fallen in love with Vanessa "Nessie" Jarman, a San Francisco socialite. As such things happen, Billy and Vanessa had known each other since he was fourteen and she was twelve and they found themselves walking together, two tall and lanky figures, on the path to school. All these years later, they made a beautiful couple, and I was more than honored to play the part of best man, a role that included working alongside my friend Stanlee Gatti, San Francisco's preeminent wedding planner.

On a flawless June afternoon in 1999, the bride rode sidesaddle on a speckled horse into her Renaissance-themed wedding at Maria Manetti Farrow's villa in Napa Valley. Vanessa wore real jewels in her blond hair and a diamond bracelet from Billy, who helped her down from the horse in a show of old-fashioned chivalry. I stood beside Billy as my father conducted the ceremony with perfect notes of wit, dignity, and grace. This was his comfort zone. Gordon sang a beautiful Welsh song and Stanlee read a poem by E. E. Cummings. The whole day was seamless, and there were enough Gettys and Browns and Pelosis and Newsoms with smiles on their faces for the next day's headline to read A FAIRY-TALE WEDDING.

When the newlyweds returned from their two-week honeymoon in Bali, I could see that something had changed in their dealings with me. Among the matters troubling Vanessa were business ties between Billy and me that concerned both PlumpJack and the house we co-owned on Pacific Avenue. She questioned why the house was not listed for sale, and I reminded her that our plans for the property had been clear from the outset. I was living there and paying my half of the expenses and overseeing a complete remodel, which was a sizable job. Vanessa was of the mind that the real estate market was too hot for me to keep residing there. Soon after, she and Billy forced the sale of the house—we split a tidy profit—and I went looking for another place to live.

Vanessa and Billy then enlisted an East Coast attorney named Zapruder, the son of the man who had famously filmed JFK's assassination, and initiated a forensic audit of PlumpJack. I didn't know what a forensic audit was, but it sounded serious. In a phone call with Zapruder, he made his intention plain. He wanted to make sure that each partnership agreement, more than a dozen in all, had advanced and protected Billy's interests. He wanted proof that I wasn't benefiting at Billy's expense. His insinuation infuriated me. This was going to get tangled, I knew, and the last thing Gordon needed was to be dragged into our troubles. He had his own complications he was now dealing with, namely newspaper headlines that revealed he was father to a second family—three young daughters living quietly with their mother in Los Angeles. Gordon's love for the girls was no secret to me. My father had shared with me the many trips he was taking to Los Angeles to work out an arrangement by which Gordon would make them part of the family trust. Over time, Ann and the boys would embrace them as well.

Now the local *Chronicle* was snooping around about "a bitter falling out between toast-of-the-town buddies Billy Getty and San Francisco Supervisor Gavin Newsom." The dogged reporting duo of Phil Matier and Andrew Ross found Gordon at the PlumpJack Hotel outside Lake Tahoe. "I believe 100 percent in Gavin," he told them. "When he is accused of wrongdoing, I'm on his side." As much as I was gratified to have Gordon's confidence, the last thing I wanted was our business affairs to come down to a choice between Billy and me. The forensic audit showed nothing inappropriate about the operations at Plump-Jack, and Gordon saw no other solution than to buy out Billy's entire interest in the business. This is how Billy and I parted ways. Whenever we found ourselves at the same social events, including birthday parties for Ann or Gordon, I always believed the warmth between us would rekindle and we'd find ourselves back to being pals. Alas, it never happened. My loss of Billy as a friend became one of the great holes in my life.

The way I tended to tell the story to myself—the story I just told you—lacked the virtue of seeing fully my own hand in the matter. In the years before our rift, Billy and I had been flying to various places on "trust-related matters," on the lookout for good investments that he could then take back to his father.

Before one trip, Billy turned to me and said, "Hey, the trust can pay you for your time."

"You don't need to pay me anything," I said. "I enjoy doing this, and I'm learning a lot."

"No," he replied, "you should be compensated for your time. It's not a lot of money, but it's something."

What Billy was proposing was not unlike the arrangement that Gordon had worked out with my father a few decades before. Not only did I find his offer alluring, but it seemed like I was honoring some spoken, or perhaps unspoken, tradition. I was the next-generation Newsom now called to duty on behalf of the Gettys, and what harm could come from saying "Yes"? I assured myself that my father had found a way to be both his own man and a Getty man. The years he was a judge, he took no pay for his Getty services. He accompanied Gordon and Ann on trips around the world; he lived a millionaire's lifestyle. He was "Uncle Bill" to all the Getty children and nephews and nieces and cousins, even if it meant that Hilary and I, his own children, were sometimes the last items on his list. The years he was off the bench, as both a younger man and an older man, he took a modest salary for his Getty work.

I thought I could do the same with Billy and be without any encumbrances. It was simple enough. I would play middleman between Gordon and Billy, the translator, à la my father. If this sucked me further into the Getty vortex, I would be able to handle it. What I did not see, was too blind and naive to see, was the irredeemable line I was crossing. I certainly did not foresee the trust that it would cost me. I never considered the possibility that Billy and Vanessa's reliance on me would turn into resentment. Or that my deeper entry into the Getty world would rob me of my own hard-earned story, a theft that would become one of the very reasons for writing this book.

In my life as a husband, father, and politician, the Getty connection would cloud and distort many things. In the eyes of the press, I was forever the "golden boy" whose daddy had prospered because of his ties to the Gettys and now the son was simply following suit. It was all too easy for journalists to paint me as the "fifth son" of Gordon and Ann Getty, born with the same silver spoon. Ann and Gordon had said it publicly enough times themselves: "Gavin is like a son to us." Over the years I would play my own part in serving up the red meat—campaign contributions from San Francisco's elite, my routine presence at society events, my own wedding reception at the Getty mansion—to the press's hungry narrative of "the pampered one." Caricature was one of the time-honored and well-deserved outcomes of being a politician. Touché. And yet the press's one-dimensional portrait of me pissed me off because I knew the way I grew up, the struggles my mother had to endure, the hard times that made my life a duality that never seemed to get its due, a duality I would spend years trying to comprehend.

''''

During the vacation in Hawaii months earlier, I made a deeper connection with Kimberly Guilfoyle as we shared stories about our parents and childhood. Her father, Anthony "Tony" Guilfoyle, had come to San Francisco, a place he called "God's half acre," from Ennis, County Clare, Ireland, and took up work in the construction trades in middle management at PG&E. Her mother, Mercedes, a native of Puerto Rico who taught special education, had died of leukemia when Kimberly was eleven years old. Her devoted father became all things to Kimberly. She graduated from Mercy High School in San Francisco, the University of California, Davis, and earned her law degree from the University of San Francisco.

She was about to leave the district attorney's office in Los Angeles and return home as a prosecutor. I liked that she was opinionated and ambitious and had a deep streak of loyalty to family and friends and to our city. As a bonus, I enjoyed hanging out with her father, who understood the politics of San Francisco on every level. Our get-togethers with my family seemed to go fairly well. My mother gave the general impression of liking Kimberly, but I couldn't tell for sure. My sister, Hilary, blessed with a discerning eye, saw the signs of trouble ahead but kept mostly mum. Only years later did Hilary share with me her first impressions of Kimberly: "She was smart, quite smart, but not my type of gal. She was a little over-the-top. Overdone style. She was never not put together, but understatement was not one of her attributes.

She needed to command a room. She needed to own a room. All eyes on her. She came from a good family. Her father was a very decent man. And Kimberly was a fierce prosecutor. She took her job seriously and was good at it. But her need for attention and love could not be met. I saw a lot of adoration from her to you, Gavin. But less from you to her."

I might have caught the signs, telltale as they were, but I was already making plans to run for mayor, plans that did not please my mother. "Get out of politics," she told me. "Get out before it's too late." I had rarely heard my mother's voice so emphatic. She had been diagnosed with cancer in 1998, a tumor that had been growing in her breast for as long as seven years and had now spread to her lymph nodes. She had skipped her mammograms. It was an aggressive type of cell, the prognosis did not look good, and I fell into a deep funk. My way of dealing with her illness was to spend even more hours at work, seeing to the chores at PlumpJack and serving my constituents as supervisor. I had become quite skilled at repressing my feelings, and Kimberly allowed me this emotional distance, in part because she was so busy trying to make her mark at the DA's office in San Francisco. She was hungry to climb the ladder and be respected. We at least had that much in common.

One night, perhaps eight or nine months into our relationship, I sat alone in one of our PlumpJack delivery trucks and contemplated whether marrying Kimberly was the right thing to do. Did I love her? Did she love me? By morning, no sleep, I had come to a decision. I was a member of the San Francisco Board of Supervisors and my mother was sick with cancer and I was going to pursue my father's dream and run for mayor. I would stay with Kimberly whether it was the right choice or the wrong one. I would go through all the motions until the motions led me right up to the altar.

Tessa Newsom managed to put on a good smile for our exchange of vows at St. Ignatius Church on the campus of the University of San Francisco and then the big reception at Ann and Gordon's mansion. My mother was of the mind that the marriage between Kimberly and me would not last, but she chose to hide those feelings from me. She was worried that I had brought a kind of passivity into the relationship, a "go along to get along" that was itself a devil's bargain. In exchange for being allowed to work the marathon hours that my compulsion to master details required, I would be laid-back, if not altogether disengaged, in my role as husband. Kimberly was too busy trying to prove all doubters wrong to recognize the shortcomings in our relationship. This was the fear my mother confided to others and what my sister feared as well.

Mom kept working seven days a week at PlumpJack and doing her knitting and rummaging flea markets for antiques. Tony Guilfoyle kept bringing over his pots of special chicken soup that he said would "kill the cancer cells twice as fast as the chemo." Mom even took her first girls' trip to Italy and India with Ann and Hilary and my aunt Barbara, a vacation paid for by the Gettys that my prideful mother accepted because Ann could not have been more down-to-earth about it.

Then in early 2002, the chemotherapy treatments stopped working, and X-rays showed that the cancer had spread throughout Mom's body. As it moved deeper into her bones, the pain became unbearable. That spring, Mom was determined not to suffer anymore or, more to the point, not to make her children further witness her suffering. She planned her own assisted suicide, right down to the doses of morphine that would stop her breathing. She called and left a message on my voicemail, sounding only slightly miffed that I had not talked to her for a week. The hard truth is I was hiding from her, hiding from myself. "Gavin, if you want to see me, you should probably do so before Thursday. Because that's going to be my last day on earth." The clipped British accent she would sometimes put on for reasons never made clear to us was gone. She was lying in her bed at her small apartment in Pacific Heights, surrounded by the people who loved and admired her most: me and Hilary and Dad, several of our aunts and uncles, and Ann and Gordon. Kimberly wasn't there. She had visited a day earlier, only to have my mother scold her about things she'd seen in our marriage. Kimberly left in tears. Mom had finally found a voice, it seemed.

Before the dose was administered, she asked us to leave the room for a moment so she could be alone with our father. He would never tell us what they had said to each other, except that she had asked him if she could be buried at the cemetery near our family cabin in Dutch Flat. When Hilary and I came back into the room, Mom had a picture of the two of us, ages six and five, propped up on her chest. "My works of art," she said.

I felt in that moment an anger for what life had dealt her. She had grown up with a mother who was clinically anorexic and a father whose devotion to breeding flowers could not quiet the haunting of his prisoner of war years. Our mother had endured a childhood of enough dysfunction that it must have seemed a perfect promise, at the age of eighteen, to be given the chance to marry into what she presumed was a more stable family, only to find a sort of Irish curse in a husband who was far from malignant but removed enough that he could not provide her with the emotional and material comforts she needed. She had lived a whole adult life of unceasing motion, trying to provide those comforts to herself and her children.

I was standing at Mom's left, holding one of her hands, and Hilary was standing at her right, holding the other hand. Her breathing was beginning to labor, but it would not go shallow. "When is this morphine going to work?" she asked. "These poor kids shouldn't have to witness this." Kids? I was thirty-four and my sister was thirty-three. Hilary could not bear it, and I told her it was okay to wait in the other room. Had I known better, I might have followed my sister out the bedroom door, for what came next was a look on my mother's face that will never leave my mind. There was no peace that blanketed her. She gasped and took a last breath, and I kept holding on to her hand tighter and tighter and sobbing. I placed my head next to hers, just the two of us now. Hilary remained in the living room with Dad and the others. The photo of her works of imperfect art lay flat on her chest. She had stopped moving. The mother who had taught me how to grind away, who showed me the meaning of fortitude, was dead at fifty-five.

Years later, wedged between the books in my father's library at Dutch Flat, we would find a letter he had written to my mother the night of her death. He told her he would honor her request and bury her at Dutch Flat because that's where she belonged. He told her he would never forget the sacrifices she had made to raise "our two beautiful children." He told her he was sorry that he did not endeavor enough to make their marriage work, and that he loved her and would love her always.

CHAPTER SEVEN

""

T he accidental politician was not always patient. Knowing that Willie Brown was about to term out in 2004, I began taking steps to run for mayor of San Francisco. The field was packed with compelling candidates, including Angela Alioto, daughter of legendary Mayor Joseph Alioto, and Tom Ammiano, a gay political icon who had nearly defeated Brown. I was polling fourth but campaigning hard, zipping around town in a GM EV1, "the first mass-produced electrical vehicle of the modern era," though it had a habit of turning gutless whenever I needed to climb the hills of San Francisco. Drivers to my right and left would laugh at me. I felt like a kid in an old wooden go-cart race, waiting for the downhill.

That's how I found myself in a runoff with a Green Party candidate named Matt Gonzalez. A graduate of Columbia University with a law degree from Stanford, Gonzalez was a genius at connecting with people's fears. He pinned on me the label of pampered prince, and it stuck. The press ate it up, none more than the *San Francisco Chronicle*, whose editor, Phil Bronstein, brought an astute persistence to the task of deconstructing me. Bronstein had done time in Peru, the Middle East, El Salvador, and the Philippines as a foreign correspondent and had good reason to think of himself as worldly. He cut a dashing figure, too, with his black leather jacket, black hair, graying mustache, and goatee. Indeed, his ego was healthy enough that he was married to actress Sharon Stone. My issue with Bronstein was his paper's coverage of the campaign, which I found exceedingly myopic. In story after story, the question never varied: Who is Gavin Newsom and why have the Gettys taken such an interest in him?

My campaign people were anticipating the inevitable piece on Gonzalez, who'd been selling himself as a progressive sleeping on borrowed couches when in fact he had grown up in a life of Texas privilege, the pampered son of a tobacco company executive. Bronstein sent word that he knew about Gonzalez's past and his reporters were tracking down the details. Two days before the vote, the story on Gonzalez finally hit the front page. It wasn't exactly a gotcha, but the reporter revealed enough details of Gonzalez's cosseted life that readers could see the hypocrisy of his going after me for my supposedly privileged upbringing.

I managed to defeat Gonzalez by six percentage points, becoming at age thirty-six the youngest mayor of San Francisco in more than a century. It was enough of a mandate that I didn't have to grovel to get things done. At the top of my agenda was homelessness, but before I could really dig in, a problem inside the San Francisco Police Department reared its ugly head. As a businessman and supervisor, I had enjoyed a strong rapport with law enforcement; the police unions had backed my run for mayor.

But racism inside the force was a fester that Willie Brown, in his two terms as mayor, hadn't seen a way to fix.

I was holding my first official meeting with my department heads when a young Black man burst through the doors of the conference room and began to shout. I had no idea who he was, but he was all moxie. He addressed us as if his arrival were overdue. "If you're serious about anything," he bellowed, "you need to be deadly serious about getting to the bottom of police abuse of Black people living in Bayview–Hunters Point." I did not attempt to interrupt him. It took only a half minute for him to command the room. *Damn, this guy's good*, I thought to myself. *Damn, he's got the whole room in rapt attention.* His name was Van Jones, the same Van Jones who would later become a fixture on CNN. When he finished, I assured him that police reform was on my radar. "I'm holding you to it, Newsom," he said.

Before leaving office, Mayor Brown had installed a new chief of police, Alex Fagan, whose thirty years in the department had been distinguished by numerous displays of valor. He had helped rescue three dozen men from a fire at a gay bathhouse in the 1970s and a few years later swum out into the bay to save a suicidal woman from drowning. But Fagan had a hard time shutting off his motor. The more alcohol he consumed, the worse his violent side showed. He became physical with one California Highway Patrol officer, threatened another, and got into a drunken brawl at a hotel outside Phoenix. His conduct gave me no choice but to find another police chief. The department was already one of the most ethnically and racially diverse in the country, and I thought the time had come to go even further. I decided to replace Fagan with Heather Fong, the first female to head the

SFPD and the second police chief of Chinese descent. Fong's selection, I would soon learn, did not sit well with a considerable number of our men in blue.

Some of the rank and file, most of them white, began to push back on Fong's commitment to reform. I told them they might do better if they focused instead on the department's dismal rate of solving murders. It stood at half the average for major U.S. cities. As a goad, I started showing up at murder scenes, careful not to interfere with the police work but letting the cops know I was keeping watch. Then a video of uniformed San Francisco officers performing a series of vile skits arrived in our mail. Becca Prowda, one of my first assistants and loyal to the core, was waving it in my face. "You have to watch this. Right now! Stop everything you're doing," she said.

I went into my office, shut the door, and slid the tape into the player. I watched until my stomach began to turn. One skit ridiculed Chinese people with cruel images and slurs, including a racist trope directed at Chief Fong, whom the officers referred to as "Feather Fong." Another skit showed a white police officer in Bayview–Hunters Point directing his finger at a Black teenager. "You see that kid over there?" the officer said. "Well, he's ignorant and uneducated and he's going to be dead by the time he's nineteen." The image then cut to a mock commercial for Pepto Bismol, only the label read BAYVIEW BISMOL: USE AS NEEDED FOR SCREAMING BLACK MALES.

For me, Bayview–Hunters Point wasn't just some place on the seven-mile-by-seven-mile map of San Francisco. It carried a telling history. Along its waterfront in 1938, the city evicted a community of Chinese shrimpers with just forty-eight hours' notice. The Chinese had to go because the U.S. Navy was coming to

Bayview–Hunters Point to build giant warships out of steel that would be made here, too. This coincided with the years of the Great Migration, when tens of thousands of Black people, fleeing the Jim Crow South, landed in Bayview–Hunters Point to work the shipyards and live in houses they could call their own. But as soon as the war effort ended, hard times set in. The shipyards shuttered. Public housing projects rose. The community was defined as a ghetto. Johnson's War on Poverty became another broken promise.

When I first showed up to Hunters Point as a San Francisco supervisor in the early 2000s, the gangs and their drug dealing were already making a scene. Longtime residents, some of them living in middle-class homes, had no patience for politicians, white or Black, who deigned to visit only at election time. I walked over to the basketball court at the corner of West Point and Middle Point, where a game was about to begin. Bullet holes were shot through the backboards. There were no nets, just rims, and the lights had been shot out, too. Holes pocked the playing surface, so that dribbling up court required a ball handler with skill. Even though I was wearing my dress shoes, I got a nod to join in. I might have made a fool of myself, but the stroke doesn't just leave you, not after all those countless hours shooting with Suli on the basketball court we built at 11 Piedmont Road. "You still got it, old man," one of the young players from the projects joshed me. "But you ain't real. You're a ghost. You'll be gone until the next election."

After my election as mayor, I took a busload of department heads and senior staff to show them the broken court, the broken park, the broken streets, the broken Muni bus stops. We would not be one more administration that would fail Bayview–Hunters

Point, I told them. We ended up razing the projects and building new public housing through a program called Hope SF. Any time I lost my way, not sure why I was doing what I was doing, I'd head to the court at West Point and Middle Point and find my bearings.

The racist tape produced by the crew of cops had simply found the wrong mayor. I called Reverend Amos Brown, pastor of the Third Baptist Church, who had sat beside me on the board of supervisors and was a figure of moral authority in San Francisco. "Can you come on over? I need to show you something." He took a seat next to mine, and we watched it together. The look on his face was troubled but he didn't flinch. He was a son of Jackson, Mississippi, and I imagined he had seen far worse in his day. He agreed that the video was too incendiary to be shown to the public. Nothing edifying would come of it. At the same time, he said, I had no choice but to reveal its existence.

We stood together at the press conference—indeed, he led it—and instead of pointing fingers at anyone, the reverend calmed the nerves of everyone. In the weeks and months that followed, I forced the captain of the officers in question to retire. As I moved in deeper, the union chief resisted the need for any real housecleaning. He argued that the video might have been in poor taste, but it was simply cops letting off steam. No racist offense was intended. None should be taken. Boys will be boys.

It struck me as a fundamentally different problem. San Francisco, as liberal and progressive as it was, had allowed the formation of an institution that was contrary to the ideals it espoused. The Dems who ran the city—generation after generation of Irish, Italians, and Germans—had allowed the department to go its own way for no greater reason than they had a father or brother or son who wore the badge of the SFPD. The first Newsom of San Francisco was just such a cop. As for the reform that was required now, it wasn't enough to simply remove the top brass and hire a new team faithful to the vision of Chief Fong, which I did. I had to root out all layers of the malignancy, a job that would outlast me and require the intervention of the state and feds.

""

On January 20, 2004, I took a seat in the gallery of the House of Representatives to hear President Bush deliver his State of the Union address. The seat came courtesy of House Minority Leader Nancy Pelosi. Ten months earlier, Bush had made the decision to invade Iraq after his administration's historic campaign of lies convinced the American people that Saddam Hussein possessed weapons of mass destruction. We would not extricate ourselves from that costly conflict for another seventeen years. Much of his speech that night was a further attempt to sell to the nation the justification for his war. "Had we failed to act, the dictator's weapons of mass destruction programs would continue to this day," Bush said. He characterized the Patriot Act, which had unleashed a new magnitude of spying on American citizens, as "one of those essential tools" in the war on terror.

The rest of his speech was standard fare, ho-hum really, until he reached a section near the end about American values and the need for us to "work together to counter the negative influences of the culture and to send the right messages to our children." He said he was troubled by activist judges in activist states who were threatening to undo the Defense of Marriage Act signed into law by his predecessor, President Bill Clinton. We had to "defend the sanctity of marriage" as the union of one man and one woman, he said. If need be, he would seek a constitutional amendment to ban same-sex marriage.

As I was leaving the chamber, a middle-aged couple next to me was talking about how pleased they were that their president was finally confronting the "homosexual agenda." The word *homosexual* came out of their mouths bent by contempt. I was supposed to head downstairs for a reception with Congresswoman Pelosi and a delegation of California Democrats, but I needed a breath of fresh air. Outside the capitol, I kept walking and muttering to myself. "These are my people Bush is attacking. My constituents. My staff. My closest advisers." In the cold and dark of Washington, I called one of my aides back in San Francisco and pledged that I was "going to do something about it" as soon as I returned home.

The law in our state was no different from the law in every other state. Same-sex unions could not be recognized by the local assessor-recorder's office. They were illegal. As I explained to aides my willingness to now defy that law, I held up a copy of the California Constitution. In Article I, the first section promises that "all people are by nature free and independent and have inalienable rights." Among these rights are pursuing and obtaining "safety, happiness and privacy." It was not until section 7.5 that these rights were then abridged: "Only a marriage between a man and a woman is valid or recognized in California." This not only contradicted the first section but was discriminatory on its face.

My top staff didn't disagree with my reading, but almost to a person they were opposed to my taking on the issue. Steve Kawa, my chief of staff, a gay Bostonian whose accent cut through all nonsense, pulled me aside and spoke from his heart. His father had renounced him for being gay, and he wanted nothing more than to live in an America where homophobia was no longer the norm. But swinging open the doors to the city clerk's office and inviting gay men and lesbian women to the marriage altar was political suicide, he argued. We were new to office, for one thing. And polls showed that less than one third of Californians supported gay marriage.

The "go it slow" admonition was the mother's milk of Democratic politics. In the endless battle for the hearts and minds of moderates, it seemed the only feasible way for a Democrat to get elected and govern. But this was San Francisco, and we were talking about equal protection under the law for a class of people whose ostracism by family, friends, and community had brought them to San Francisco in the first place. If not here, where? Eric Jaye, one of my campaign consultants, could see my quandary. I was caught between my conscience and the sound political advice of the people closest to me. We had several late-night conversations on the phone. "What the fuck are you doing here? Why did we work so hard to win if you can't do something bold?" he asked. "This is a short life, Gavin. Your time as a politician to get things done is just a blip."

I thought back to my model for the wine store. The entire purpose was to turn the staid on its head and create a new reality. I called Joyce Newstat, my policy director, who was also gay. "We need to do this," I told her. She could hear in my voice that I had made up my mind. "Okay, but we can't afford to take a wrong step," she said. "Gays and lesbians have a history of being blindsided, and you don't want to become part of that narrative. Give me a week or two to reach out to the community." Joyce sat down with Kate Kendell, the brilliant executive director of the National

Center for Lesbian Rights, based in San Francisco. "Who is this guy?" Kendell wondered. "He can't just come waltzing in here and upset the delicate balance we've taken years to achieve." Joyce told her I couldn't be talked out of it, that it had become internalized after I had gone to Washington and heard the words of bigotry ring out in the capitol. "Well, okay. But if he's going to do it, he has to do it right," Kendell said. She directed her attorneys at the center to work with our team on fashioning a plan.

I then went to Mabel Teng, my former colleague on the board of supervisors who was now the assessor-recorder of San Francisco. I asked her what complications would be presented to her official duties if we allowed same-sex marriages at city hall. Mabel, who began her career in politics as an activist with Jesse Jackson's Rainbow Coalition, did not surprise me with her reply. "It would be no problem at all, Mayor." The marriage of a man and a man, or a woman and a woman, would require hardly any change to the paperwork. Rather than "man and wife," they would show up in her computer as "Applicant One" and "Applicant Two."

Alarmed by my plans, my father and Uncle Brennan and their close friend Joe Cotchett—each one steeped in law and politics but only Joe standing six foot four and a former Special Forces paratrooper—attempted a last-minute intervention. They lured me to the Balboa Cafe for dinner and wine. They weren't the kind to beat around the bush. Did I realize that I was about to torpedo my political career?

Joe got right in my face. "Why are you doing this, Gavin?"

"I'll tell you why I'm doing this," I said defiantly. "Because it's the right thing to do."

I could not have given him a more simple and true answer, and it seemed to hit Joe, who had built his career out of representing the underdog, right in the gut.

"Okay," he said in a different voice. "Then let's do it."

With that, my father and uncle went quiet. Not another word was said about it. I left there that night thinking that even my Newsom kin, the ones who had my best interests at heart, could get it wrong from time to time. While I was open to skepticism and second-guessing, indeed I welcomed such a process, in the end I had to trust my own gut. On the matter of civil rights for all Californians, there was no turning back. As for big Joe Cotchett, he ended up joining the ranks of lawyers fighting for the legal right to same-sex marriage.

⁗

On February 12, 2004, my thirty-sixth day in office, in walked Phyllis Ann Lyon and Dorothy "Del" Martin. They had fallen in love in 1952 while working for the same magazine in Seattle and moved to Castro Street in San Francisco on Valentine's Day the following year. They wanted to consecrate on paper what they had consecrated with their lives for the past fifty-two years. Though their ceremony at city hall was just down from my office, I did not attend because I wanted the cameras to be focused on them. In the documentary *Pursuit of Equality*, directed by my brother-in-law Geoff Callan, I can hear the crack in Mabel Teng's voice when she says, "We are making history today." Teng continued for the next twenty-eight days to defy state law and marry 4,035 couples. We married the famous, such as Rosie O'Donnell and her spouse Kelli Carpenter, and we married regular folks who came from as far away as Texas. We married members of my staff: Steve Kawa and his spouse, Dan Henkle, and Joyce Newstat and her spouse, Susan Lowenberg.

Inside the ornate rotunda, evangelicals from around the country came to sing their protest. "The mayor of this city is acting in defiance of God's law," one member of Repent America declared, raising his Bible. But others came to show support. A gay man who had traveled his own long distance to get there said he had been sitting on the sidelines for too many years. "This is my march to Selma," he said. Local flower vendors pulled up to the curb and handed out free bouquets to couples standing in line. Jewelers sold out of wedding bands.

I could hear from my office, sometimes at a clip of every sixty seconds, throngs of people cheering another couple emerging from city hall as newlyweds. I wanted so much to soak in the scene myself, if just for a few minutes, but my presence only would have emboldened the protesters. By day six, I couldn't resist and stepped out my door and down the hall and into the crowd. Who were these couples getting death threats for deciding to join their lives? They were teachers and nurses and grocery clerks and transit drivers. I hadn't gotten very deep into the crowd when I felt a tug on my jacket and looked down to find a beautiful little girl, no more than eight or nine, smiling at me. "I'm sorry," I said. "I didn't see you." I bent down, and she gave me a great hug. "Thank you," she said. "Thank you for giving me two mommies." I hugged her right back and started to tear up. The emotion must have been welling up for days, because it started to pour out, so much so that I had to immediately return to my office.

Governor Arnold Schwarzenegger could keep quiet for only

so long. "It is time for the city to stop traveling down this dangerous path of ignoring the rule of law," he said. State attorney general Bill Lockyer, an Oakland native whose heart was with us but
who had no other choice legally, filed a petition asking the California Supreme Court to issue a writ of mandate to stop marriage
licenses from being given to couples not man and wife. The
"Winter of Love," as it was dubbed, was shut down by the court
in the spring. The marriage license belonging to Del Martin and
Phyllis Ann Lyon, along with several thousand others, was declared null and void. "Del is eighty-three years old, and I am
seventy-nine," Phyllis said. "After being together for more than
fifty years, it is a terrible blow to have the rights and protections
of marriage taken away from us. At our age, we do not have the
luxury of time."

My pushing the matter forward had made members of the
Democratic elite uncomfortable. The Democratic National Con-
vention, held in Boston that year, could not find a two-minute
spot for me in its long list of speakers. On a trip to San Francisco,
then-senator Barack Obama, agreeable to "civil unions" for gays
and lesbians but not yet to marriage, kept a mile's distance between himself and me. When we found ourselves at the same
fundraiser hosted by Willie Brown, Obama told Willie he wanted
no picture taken of the two of us. The snub bothered Willie
enough that he later shared the story with the press. (Obama
would eventually see the wisdom of legalizing gay marriage and
do for the nation what we had done for San Francisco.) My own
senator and political mentor, Dianne Feinstein, was not pleased
by my stance. She said my actions on gay marriage had stoked the
fear of right-wing America and helped defeat John Kerry. This

was odd, because on Election Day we were having lunch at Moose's in North Beach and she did not utter even a hint of dissent. To top it off, Barney Frank, one of the first openly gay people in Congress and a man I respected immensely, said I was a naive attention seeker who had imperiled the cause of same-sex marriage.

It would take another four years, but California's supreme court, in May 2008, would finally rule that equal protection under state law afforded gay couples the same right to marriage as straight couples. Surprisingly, the 4–3 vote saw Ron George, the conservative chief justice, side with the majority and author the opinion. His unexpected vote, he later explained, was a simple matter of doing right by the law and having an office with the right view. The court's ornate building happened to face Civic Center Plaza; George had been greatly moved by the thousands of gay people outside his window celebrating their marriages during the Winter of Love.

Sadly, the matter would not rest there. A few months later, the Knights of Columbus would team up with the Latter-day Saints to spend tens of millions of dollars to back Proposition 8, a state constitutional amendment to again outlaw same-sex marriages in California. It would pass in November 2008 by a margin of 52 percent to 48 percent, and the state supreme court, citing the will of the people, would uphold it. A headline in *Newsweek* proclaimed, SF MAYOR GAVIN NEWSOM RISKS CAREER ON GAY MARRIAGE. The writer noted that "Newsom has become a joke to Democratic insiders, a man whose bright national future ended before it began." The ban would remain in effect for another decade, until the U.S. Supreme Court overturned it and later declared that same-sex couples across the nation would at last enjoy a constitutional right to marry. Del would not live to see that day. Phyllis would welcome it as a final victory.

""""

I saw something in those marriages that I did not see in my own. Three days after I had been sworn in as mayor, Kimberly flew to New York to start a new job as a host for Court TV. She was on a career path that would take her to Fox News and into circles of right-wing politics that could not have contrasted more with the world in which we were raised. Her father, Anthony, must have wondered what had gotten into his girl. He and I never discussed it. He became one of my staunchest supporters and schooled me on whom I could trust and whom I could never turn my back on. It pained him to see our marriage suffering; I know because it showed in his eyes. He would have been right to blame it on the striving that had consumed the both of us, but the mismatch of our marriage went far deeper than that.

I gave only a little of myself to Kimberly. Instead of regretting this, I kept wishing I could have given a lot more to my dying mother. I had chosen to see Mom's pathos and the way she had choreographed her death—*Thursday will be my final day on earth*—as a way out for me. Nothing in my power could change the course she had charted. I was off the hook. She was dying and I chose to spend those days and weeks at work, distancing myself from her reality. It was the same in my marriage. Kimberly packing her bags and walking out the door for New York became one more convenience. I was better when I was alone. She'd fly back and we'd go into pretend mode for a week or two, the mayor and the First Lady. This was never more true than in the summer of

2004, when Kimberly and Ann conspired to lure *Harper's Bazaar* to the Getty mansion for a photo shoot on the "new Kennedys." Guess who that might be.

I was dressed in a tuxedo, and the crew directed me to lie down next to Kimberly on Ann's Oriental carpet. It was supposed to be a gag shot, a whim of Ann's, but to my embarrassment it turned up as part of the eight-page glossy spread. The critics mocked it, but none more than me. When the magazine came out, my sister was aghast. She would later tell me that my lax assent to the photo was part of a familiar pattern. "In your workspace, you don't let anyone push you around. But in your private sphere, you have a pattern of letting the women in your life dictate your movements—actions that come back to bite you. You're kind of emotionally distant that way, or at least you were before you met and married Jen. That *Harper's Bazaar* spread was case in point. Ann was there directing it. Kimberly was there. So you went along with it. Had I been there, I would have told you, 'Get your ass off the floor. You're the mayor of San Francisco. That's not a good look.'"

The fairy tale of the new Kennedys was not to be. The distance between Kimberly and me became a breach, and the breach widened into a chasm that could not be repaired. When it was time to part after four years of marriage, we parted about as amicably as two people could. I then proceeded to plunge into my second act of bachelorhood, which I did not handle with discernment. In my off hours, I thought of myself as a single guy who happened to be the mayor. Had my head been on straight, I would have seen it was the other way around. After a twelve-hour day at work, the single guy showed up at the restaurant bar, ordered a glass of wine, chatted with an old customer, chatted with a new friend, ordered another glass of wine, ordered takeout, went home, and woke up the next morning believing the night before had been a private matter. Instead, the mayor went to work and heard all about it from his aides. *That date of yours used to be the girlfriend of a Silicon Valley mogul.* Or *That date of yours, the dark and seductive actress Sofia Milos, is a Scientologist trying to recruit you to the flock.*

When I accompanied Sofia to the annual dinner of the Citizens Commission on Human Rights, a group cofounded by the Church of Scientology, *Chronicle* columnists Phil Matier and Andy Ross all but accused me of abandoning my faith. "My gosh, folks, relax," I told the press. "I'm a practicing Irish Catholic. I'm not a Scientologist, and I couldn't tell you two things about it." When I took Sofia to a Sunday meal at Ann and Gordon's house, Gordon did something he had never done before. He went down to his study and wrote me a personal note, in pen, that arrived at my apartment a few days later. "I'm very concerned what's going on between you and this woman. I don't think she's right for you." A few weeks later, Sofia and I went our separate ways.

""""

The boys of tech were hardly titans back then. There was Steve and Sergey and Larry and Reed and Marc. There was Craig from Craigslist and Ev and Biz from Twitter and a South African named Elon who was sleeping in an office and showering at the YMCA and sharing a single computer with his brother when he first arrived on the scene. We began our maturations at the same time and in the same place, the spawning ground that was San Francisco in the late 1990s and early 2000s.

We began with the same mentality of nothing to lose. When we first started running into each other at dinner parties and birthday bashes, they had maybe enough money to swing a mortgage and a short vacation or two a year. They were, as we say now, "prerevenue." I watched them ascend. I watched them break norms and then break industries. I watched them fail dramatically and then rise again to reshape the world in their own vision, even if the rest of us didn't know what light and grievous dark that vision was taking us to.

I was there the evening Steve Jobs, at a cocktail party in the penthouse suite of the Fairmont Hotel, made a gesture of "come on over" to Sergey Brin, Larry Page, and me. I was the only one in the room dressed in suit and tie. Sergey and Larry were wearing T-shirts. I want to say that Steve was dressed in his blue jeans and black mock turtleneck. He had, as was later noted, something up his sleeve, though it was actually in his pocket. As we walked on over, he gathered us around him and pulled out a sleek device that none of us had ever seen before, a solid piece of glass with no keyboard that could be held in one hand. It had apps, as he called them, that your fingers could manipulate and turn from one function to another. The device was about to go public. We were transfixed. He swiped the screen and we said, "Whoa." He let each of us swipe it, and I repeated, "Whoa." We were quite aware that he was sharing something akin to a state secret, something that was proprietary in the fullest meaning of the word, something that might even make him a billionaire many times over. But Steve didn't seem to give a damn about any of that. He simply wanted us to understand how its inner workings worked. He wanted to share the creativity that had gone into its elegant design and maybe engage in a bit of showmanship. The old art history student in me wondered if what was taking place in San Francisco at the turn of a new century was perhaps the same spirit of Florence on the eve of the Renaissance. It wasn't much later that Sergey and Larry had assembled their own Android version of the smartphone that would share many of the same bells and whistles.

Seeing how nimble they were and how entrenched and plodding city and state bureaucracy was, I gained more than a few lessons from my friends in tech. Sergey and Larry had conquered the internet by starting out with a fanciful notion and enough code to give it a go. To believe that the city of San Francisco could solve its problems by sticking to the same old vision would be to miss the magic that was tech. In one respect, the internet was just another iteration of what California had been doing since its invention. In another respect, it was an extraction of a far different magnitude, one that wasn't mining gold or water or soil but the neural networks and attention spans and social spaces that made us human beings. As mayor, could I find a way to incorporate tech's ethos of busting up outmoded structures without blowing apart the world?

I was having great fun learning about political capital, how to save it and how to spend it. My staff and I agreed that it was time to make good on my campaign promise to take on the city's growing homeless problem. I started with the approaches of the mayors before me, which were all over the map. In fairness to them, the dimensions of the crisis were not of their making. No liberal bias was required to put forward the case that the one man most responsible for the rise of homelessness in America was California's own sunny Ronald Reagan. In 1981, his first year as president, he gutted Jimmy Carter's model Mental Health

Systems Act, which had committed the federal government, for the first time, to take a prominent role in the care of the mentally ill. It had earmarked nearly $800 million to California and other states for local communities to establish their own mental health facilities.

The need for such an approach had been made urgent by the nation's embrace of "deinstitutionalization," a wholesale emptying of state hospitals across the country and the relocation of mentally ill onto the streets and sidewalks of San Francisco, Los Angeles, and other big cities. But instead of funding President Carter's epic reform, Reagan spent the money on more military arms and a tax cut for businesses and the wealthy. Then he turned around and slashed federal funding for affordable housing and public housing, telling cities and towns that sheltering the poor was their burden alone.

Mayor Dianne Feinstein didn't know what to make of the trickle of street people living out of shopping carts in downtown San Francisco in the mid-1980s. Like other big-city mayors, she opened a smattering of temporary shelters and offered a cot and a sandwich to the down-and-out. What Feinstein didn't figure on was a doubling of housing prices in the Bay Area between 1984 and 1990, the trickle of homeless turning into a river.

Mayor Art Agnos put forward an approach he considered a model for the nation. San Francisco would open two large centers offering mental health assessments, counseling, job training, beds, and food. It was a grand vision in search of grand funding, which never arrived. Next came Mayor Frank Jordan, the former police chief, with a get-tough approach that used force to clear homeless from the streets. The cops were issuing a thousand citations a month to those flouting San Francisco's new vagrancy law.

Welfare payments redirected to housing vouchers weren't enough for the homeless to cover the rising costs of a room in the city. Six thousand people were now living on the streets.

Willie Brown, seeing the one-term fate of mayors unable to solve the homeless crisis, kept flogging the issue until it won him a landslide victory in 1995. He pledged to bring in outside government funding to expand social services and develop a regional plan with nearby cities. It was the right idea, but the money again fell short. The ebb and flow of the problem wore him down. Brown ended up riding the dot-com boom, gentrifying once-affordable neighborhoods across the city and fueling skyrocketing rents. The boom only landed more San Franciscans on the streets. As he surveyed the scene from the vantage of his second term, Brown declared that homelessness was a problem "that may not be solvable."

The task was now mine. During my stint on the board of supervisors, I had pored over scholarly studies on homelessness and visited New York, Chicago, and Seattle to see for myself the best practices used in other cities. Back home, I walked for hours through the Mission and Tenderloin districts, encountering men and women whose wages did not cover the cost of housing or who were in the grip of mental illness and refusing to live in shelters that banned their dogs and their drink. I got to know many of them by name and story. They were my people, my constituents.

As supervisor, I had championed the Care Not Cash measure, which took more than 80 percent of an individual's county welfare check and redirected it to the cost of their housing. I then pushed to outlaw the most aggressive forms of panhandling near ATMs and on public transit. Homeless advocates and other supporters of mine were not pleased and staged protests in front of my house. They spray-painted my garage door and dumped trash in my yard. Their disappointment in me kept on. So did my belief that the best approach to reducing homelessness was one that utilized both carrot and stick.

President George W. Bush was offering hundreds of millions of dollars in federal grants for cities embarking on ten-year plans to end homelessness. The money helped cover the rent for hundreds of single rooms at hotels throughout San Francisco. It wasn't only housing we were offering but twenty-four-hour clinics and mental health counseling. Word had spread that San Francisco's safety net was far better than the safety nets of other cities in the West. New Joads began migrating to our city. In response, we conceived Homeward Bound, a program that provided bus tickets to thousands of homeless whose family or friends in other cities and states were willing to take them in.

In the fall of 2004, I found Cynthia Abrams standing in front of a liquor store on a grimy corner in the Tenderloin. She was hunched over two milk crates filled with her possessions, and though she was turned away from me and I could not see her face, I could tell she was crying.

"How are you doing?" I asked, placing my arm around her shoulders.

"I'm tired of being on the streets," she said.

She told me she was a crack addict and an alcoholic and feared she would end up a victim of homicide like so many other street people who called the Tenderloin home. I persuaded her to walk with me one block to the city-leased Hotel Pierre, where we were launching a new program called Project Homeless Connect. Instead of asking homeless residents to show up for appointments at one or more government agencies, we were taking our desks, computers, and sign-up forms to the streets. As I led Abrams into the cramped lobby of the hotel—one of our "linkage stations"— she could see a half dozen social service and health care workers helping others like her. They were signing up for general assistance, doctor and dentist appointments, methadone treatments, haircuts, eye exams, and beds in shelters or hotel rooms.

Trent Rhorer, director of human services, and Alex Tourk, my deputy chief of staff, had spent months coordinating the separate functions of several city agencies into a unified outreach. It didn't sink in completely at the time, but we were designing a system for serving homeless unlike any other in the U.S. Indeed, Project Homeless Connect would soon become a model for cities across the country.

Trent saw me guiding Abrams to one of our stations and did a double take. She was the same woman he had tried to assist weeks earlier when he found her distraught in a city park at four in the morning. There was no need for me to wonder what Trent was doing in a city park at such a benighted hour. This was the devotion my staff was bringing to the cause. I sat down next to Abrams as she told her woeful tale to a social worker. Given her confused state, she would not have managed without the smooth transition from one service to the next. One-stop shopping, we called it, bureaucrats without the bureaucracy. At last she was able to access the help she needed.

My first year in office, the population of homeless in San Francisco dropped by an astonishing 30 percent. Few, if any cities, could boast the same. We truly believed we had found a way to address one of the most intractable problems of postindustrial

America. We did not rest on the success of that first year. We got smarter and better. We figured out who our homeless were, which allowed us to determine how best to help them. One third were mentally ill and most at risk of a permanent life on the streets; one third had come from outside the city or the state; nearly half of these outsiders were youth, and many were gays and lesbians who no longer felt welcome back home. It was distressing to see how significantly race presented itself as a factor. San Francisco was a city with a 6 percent Black population. And yet nearly one third of our homeless were Black.

We were fully expecting another big drop in the population, but then everything flattened out. Over the next five years, the overall number of homeless in San Francisco never dropped below six thousand. This did not mean we did not assist another few thousand off the streets each year. We did. But for every hundred who found their way to stable housing, a new contingent of sixty, seventy, or eighty found their way onto the streets. The causes were manifold: the economic dislocations of the Great Recession, the concentration of unbelievable amounts of wealth into fewer hands, a shortage of affordable housing, rising rents, rising drug and alcohol abuse. Sadly, the stressors would only grow worse. Over the next decade, San Francisco would experience the greatest increase in wealth disparity of any city in America. In the blink of an eye, the rent for a two-bedroom apartment in the Mission District would rise from $1,900 a month to $3,200 a month to $5,000 a month.

Perversely, the success of our plan had become its perceived failure. The more we did for the homeless, the more we found ourselves facing new homeless who needed us to do more. As I kept tinkering to find the right combination of programs that might put a further dent in the problem, I began to think of our task as a parable. In Kobo Abe's arresting novel that became the film *Woman in the Dunes*, a wind keeps burying a woman's home in sand. To stay ahead of the drifts, she must shovel out each day what the night blows in. Her life is the same endeavor day after day. Buckets of sand removed; buckets of sand returned. "Are you shoveling to survive or surviving to shovel?" she is asked.

A local reporter covering the homeless beat asked me about the Sisyphean nature of our task. The answer I gave sounded a lot like Willie Brown. You can provide housing to thousands of people and, for each of them, homelessness is over. But for the city, it's not. New people are always coming in, suffering through the down cycles of America and their lives. Homelessness is the manifestation of our complete, abject failure as a society. We'll never solve it at city hall alone. And yet we did not relinquish our efforts. We would end up reducing street homelessness by 40 percent during my years as mayor. We would move 12,391 homeless people into permanent housing or back with their families.

""

San Francisco's ruffian start, and its early bouts of nativism, had given way to a place of live and let live. Yet one had to be careful not to misread the city's laid-backness. It was not a burg easily pushed around. It was tough, could smell BS from a mile away, and had absolutely no fear of taking the less-trodden path.

As mayor, I marveled at the city's pluck, its exuberant embrace of "Baghdad by the Bay," the moniker coined by Herb Caen to capture its zest for experiment and exotica. If I had a bent toward finding solutions that were novel, San Francisco only fed my inclination. It helped that my staff was full of locals just as obsessed and impatient as I was. I had inherited Jared Blumenfeld, our director of the Department of Environment, from Willie Brown. He'd grown up in a rural village outside Cambridge, England, went to Berkeley Law, and trained to be a human rights attorney. Then it occurred to him that a community's right to clean water and clean air was the ultimate human right.

Jared was sitting in my office, just back from a trip to the United Kingdom, when he mentioned that he had shared an illuminating conversation with the Irish minister of the environment. Did I know that Ireland taxed plastic grocery and shopping bags? I did not, but the idea immediately intrigued me. In San Francisco, we were running through two hundred million petroleum-based bags each year. They were littering our streets, littering our bay and the Pacific, choking marine life, and disrupting the endocrine systems in all of us. It was 2006–2007, time for our progressive city to declare war on plastic, too.

We reached out to the powerful grocery store chains and their unions. "You guys are good team players," I told them. "Why don't we work together to substantially reduce plastic shopping bags?" They seemed wonderfully amenable. We shook hands on a compromise to replace the old bags with biodegradable ones made of corn. But no sooner had we finished a joint press conference announcing the deal than the grocery chains ran to their lobbyists in Sacramento with a scheme to scuttle it. The lobbyists pressured the state legislature to pass a bill, disguised as consumer friendly, that prohibited grocers from charging customers for the eco-friendly bags. The chains thought they had sneaked one past us: they could now cry financial burden—"We're not allowed to pass on costs to the public"—and back out of the deal.

This became one of my first real lessons in the power and gall of a corporate lobby. Chatter over drinks and handshakes meant nothing when their bottom line was on the line. How to respond? My next step wasn't sneaky or subtle. We turned San Francisco into the first city in the nation to ban plastic shopping bags altogether. Municipalities up and down the state came aboard. We banned Styrofoam and required paper bags to contain more and more recycled material. Duro Bag, the largest manufacturer of grocery bags in the world, changed the specs on its bags to meet San Francisco's new standard.

The EPA under George W. Bush couldn't rid itself of the onus of environmental protection fast enough. The White House had no intention of signing the Kyoto Protocol on global warming, for one thing. A 7 percent reduction in greenhouse gases from 1990 levels, achieved over the next decade, was judged injurious to capitalism. In the face of such indifference, how could a single city make a difference? I started working with Greg Nickels, the farseeing mayor of Seattle, who regarded global warming as a local issue first. He led and I jumped aboard as more than six hundred U.S. cities pledged to cut their greenhouse gas emissions by amounts roughly equal to those set forth in the rejected Kyoto Protocol. No city in North America had ever hosted World Environment Day, and San Francisco turned the international event into a weeklong gathering under the banner of "Green Cities: Where the Future Lives." More than one hundred mayors from across the country attended and added their own signatures to the protocol. Al Gore presented a slideshow that would spawn his monumental movie, *An Inconvenient Truth*, before a huge crowd. "We can't ignore it. We can't put our heads in the sand," Gore said. "Is it only terrorists we're worried about? Is that the only threat worth our attention?"

We set out to prove the deniers of global warming wrong. The Green Economy did not hurt big business, as they contended, but instead created a whole new ecosystem of jobs. San Francisco became the first municipality in the country to go into the composting business. Our city vehicles now included a fleet of electric cars with EV charging stations. We piloted buses that ran on a new B20 fuel, a blend of old diesel and biodiesel. By cobbling together one program and another, we reduced San Francisco's greenhouse gas emissions by 7 percent.

No surprise that the attention we were receiving as the "most sustainable city in the nation" did not please every power broker in town. The sourness on the face of *Chronicle* editor Phil Bronstein was especially hard to miss. Bronstein knew where I lived and what day the refuse company emptied the trash on my block. One night, according to our sources at the paper, he sent a reporter with a flashlight to my front curb to examine the contents of my garbage can. Was I hiding telltale eggshells and coffee grounds that belonged instead in the compost bin? Was I an eco-phony? No story about my trash ever ran, but Bronstein was now fixated on a new hunt. Where might he find a lock of my hair to do a DNA test? He was convinced that if he could just lay his hands on a strand, it would be the first step in proving, once and for all, that my father wasn't William Alfred Newsom but Gordon Peter Getty.

Chapter Eight

""

Outside city hall, during off-hours, my sister could see a connection sparking between me and Ruby Rippey-Tourk, one of my staffers, before even I could. Ruby was drinking too much and so was I. Her marriage was frayed and mine was over. Hilary, who'd had my back all my life, was now in my face. "Gavin, are you insane? Do you need to be reminded that Ruby is married to Alex, your deputy chief of staff?" I assured Hilary that Ruby and I were friends. Nothing more. Not long after, at a social gathering, Hilary noticed Ruby hanging a bit too close to me and pulled her aside. "What are you thinking, Ruby? Gavin may be single, but you're not. You're married to a great guy." Ruby's voice cracked as she replied, "You're absolutely right, Hilary."

A few months later, Ruby was among a group of staffers who came to my apartment for a party. She was the last to leave. It was the stupidest and also briefest of affairs. A year later, to her credit, Ruby decided to come clean to her twelve-step group. I came clean to Hilary and to Alex Tourk. Then I stood before the cameras at city hall, took a deep breath and spoke without equivocation. "Everything you've heard and read is true. And I'm deeply sorry about that. I've hurt someone I care deeply about, Alex Tourk, and his friends and family, and that is something I have to live with." With the benefit of time and reflection, it would become clear to me that what I had done was not just a transgression that tore at friendships and staff. It was the worst betrayal of my life.

In such a moment of damage control, the imperative that consumes the elected official is the act of contrition. More than anything it is a political gesture. How many times have we seen it? The politician caught in a lie coming clean to his public with his grim-faced wife standing resolutely, or not so resolutely, at his side. I was that guy, only I had no wife fixed beside me. Only my sister, whom I had told emphatically not to be there, was standing nearby. Her presence was a calming factor. She knew more than anyone what my explanation had left out. She knew the work I now had to do to get right with myself and the past. I was a best-practices freak when it came to business and governance, but I didn't know where to start when it came to me. And so I began with the most obvious. I stopped drinking at the insistence of Mimi Silbert, a family friend and the dynamo behind Delancey Street, a rehab center in the city that operated something like a kibbutz. Using shared work as a guiding ethic, the center had changed the lives of ten thousand ex-felons, gangbangers, prostitutes, dope fiends, and drunks, as Mimi boldly told you herself. I wasn't there for a twelve-step treatment program; that wasn't her thing. God never came up. Only the foolishness of man. At our first session, in early 2007, she tore into me. Was I willing, over the next days, weeks, and months, to lay myself bare? "Your entire explanation doesn't hold water," she told me. "You're not some single guy. You're the goddamn mayor. You're thirty-nine years old. And what the fuck are you doing getting involved with a staff member?"

I saw her twice a week for six months and then on occasion after that. I put up the usual defenses and she knocked them down one by one. She made me understand things about myself that I'd spent so many years running from: the child trying to make sense of dyslexia and divorce; the gangly outcast who wore a suit to school; the jock who shot baskets day and night and swung a bat until his palms blistered; the young entrepreneur who found language in dictionaries and self-help books; the fool who rushed into a marriage he could not explain to his mother, or himself; the single mayor who could not fathom all the flattery he was receiving and decided to subvert himself with an act of self-sabotage. Don't dismiss it as psychobabble, she told me. I was a classic case. "Your feelings, your emotions—you need to go a level deeper, Gavin." Silbert wasn't sure if I had a problem with alcohol, but she said her digging into me would tell her soon enough. "If and when I decide you can have a drink, I'll let you know." Like my mother, she considered thin plaster a lousy way to fix a crack. I would never reach where I needed to go, she admonished, if I didn't peer deeper inside myself. After eighteen months of grilling me, she told me I was all right. "What do you mean by 'all right?'" I asked. "You're good," she said. "You don't have a drinking problem. You can start drinking your fucking wine again. But I'm not going to stop watching your ass."

....

I wasn't trying to get off easy. I wasn't looking to blame my lineage for the way I interacted with the world. But I couldn't very well puzzle out myself without puzzling out who and what had come before me. What explained the demons that cut me off from family and friends and found such comfort, such purpose, in isolation? The insults that stuck to my core? The crazy work ethic that turned into my get-evens? The expensive shoes and suits and posh parties and lavish weddings that offered me entry into a highborn world that the Newsoms and Menzies always brushed up against but never had the keys to unlock? Before my image had been curated and projected onto the screen by the packaging of politics, I was some combination of genes and upbringings whose imprint I struggled to deduce. I had my mother and father as flesh and blood, my grandparents as smoky, indistinct figures, and their parents as only a legend or two. Who were they, truly? I began to tunnel backward, the questions more lucid in my head. I might have stopped at the first painful revelation, but my obsessive gear kicked in and I kept on boring deeper into the past.

I spent hours and hours with my aunt Cindy, my mother's older sister, who resided in Los Angeles. If Mom and her twin, Aunt Anne, lived to recede into the world, Aunt Cindy, six years older, traveled through life on a mission to bulldoze whatever stood in her way. She had begun her career in entertainment in the early 1960s working for WOR in New York, booking big names for its radio and TV shows. A lifelong leftist who led marches to ban the bomb, she became an agent in Hollywood and then a producer of movies. *Sister Act* with Whoopi Goldberg and *Gypsy* with Bette Midler were among her better-known credits. She'd had three marriages, the last to Ed Asner, none of them walks in the park. As a narrator, Aunt Cindy did not blanch. She had no filter. You entered her realm knowing you were going to be told stories that no other member of the family would be willing to tell. In other words, you went in understanding that some damage to your notion of things, some alteration, was going to take place.

"There's abuse and there's abuse," she began. "Your parents did not physically or psychologically torment you. My gosh, no. But you were a child with a disability, a scrambled brain, who required a certain touch. And neither of them possessed that touch or worked to gain that touch. Their failure to even seek out the right professional help for you left you on an island all alone. That's a kind of abuse. Abuse by omission."

"Mom had this passivity. It could drive me nuts," I told Aunt Cindy. "And Dad, for all his accomplishments, had it too. Not in his professional life. But as a father. And look at me in my personal relationships."

"You can't imagine what I saw growing up in the Addis-Menzies family," she said. "My mother, your grandmother, lived by a code of secrets and silences."

"Grandma Jean was my one rock when I was a kid," I said. "Those art lessons in her tiny house in the redwoods. She taught me a different way to regard myself."

"Yes, she was a gigantic force in many ways. A fetching young woman who went off to Russia, became one of the Reds and then a stage actress. Trigger Addis. She lived two lives. The first one filled with daring. The second one trying to conceal the consequences of that daring. As much as she tried, the secrets came out one by one."

The transmitting of those family secrets from Aunt Cindy to me took place over many months, and even years, and in many different locales: Los Angeles, Brentwood, Studio City, Westwood, San Francisco, Marin, and Dutch Flat. We chatted in person and on the phone and texted. Her emails to me were stream of consciousness and often epic in length. She was an entertaining correspondent. She wrote in the King's English and impolite vernacular. Never once did I get the impression she was holding back. Her portraits of my mother's side of the family—complicated, even tragic people—were sometimes too fixed, too cut-and-dried, too severe. They were difficult to bear, and whenever a part of me wanted to write them off as caricature, I consulted with Aunt Anne. Anne possessed a passivity like my mother, and she found Cindy's personality too puncturing. And yet their recollections were remarkably similar. Anne took issue with Cindy's sometimes sharp language but almost never with her details.

The two sisters depicted the tiny redwood house on Stanyan Street, above Golden Gate Park and across from Mount Sutro Forest, in the same horrifying light. It was, for each of them, a house of terror. There was a desk where my mother and Anne would sit and wait for my grandmother Jean, a fabulous cook, to finish preparing dinner. One night, when my mother and Anne were seven and Cindy was thirteen, the middle drawer of the desk was partly opened. Anne saw a document inside and reached in and grabbed it. It was Cindy's birth record or some similar document. It listed the name of her biological father. Not Arthur Menzies, the horticulturalist she called Daddy, but Milton Weiner, a poor Jew from Brooklyn whose family had immigrated from Russia. This was the first of the secrets to be revealed. My grandmother Jean had met Milton at some leftist meeting when they were in their early twenties. He was educated at Harvard, Princeton, and UC Berkeley and must have seemed like he had a promising future. Only after they married did my grandmother discover that Milton had no interest in working. He wanted to sit around all day and talk politics. My grandmother and Milton divorced after a year or two. As a result, Cindy scarcely knew her biological father.

That night, when Anne opened the desk drawer and saw that Cindy had a different last name, she asked her mother why. It was a child's question. Innocent. Cindy wasn't home at the time, and my grandmother ran over and shut the drawer and slapped Anne in the face. "It's none of your business," she told her. The family never spoke of it again. "Don't stand out." "Be quiet." "Nothing here shall be spoken on the outside." These were the rules of the house set down by my grandparents. No adult friends or kid friends ever walked through the door. It was as if they were living in hiding.

As I pieced together the story of my maternal family, the trail led back to an entirely respectable beginning, to Grandma Jean's father, Dr. Thomas Addis, a tall and distinguished Scotsman who had been doing groundbreaking work on hemophilia at the University of Edinburgh in 1911 when a letter from California arrived. It was written by the dean of the medical school at Stanford University, Dr. Ray Lyman Wilbur. He was starting up a Stanford Hospital, not on campus but on Clay Street in San Francisco's Fillmore District. It would focus on research, and he wanted Dr. Addis to come west as one of his first recruits. My great-grandfather jumped at the chance to have his own clinical laboratory there. Dr. Wilbur, a prominent eugenicist, would end up becoming the third president of Stanford University, a post he held from 1916 to 1943 and left only to run the Department of the Interior for his pal President Herbert Hoover. For years, he gave my great-grandfather the leeway to operate his lab and treat patients as he saw fit.

Great-grandpa Thomas met my great-grandma Elesa, a nurse, on the tennis courts at Stanford. She was a descendant of the Partridge family, who had come from England to California during the Gold Rush and started one of the first newspapers in San Francisco. They had been around long enough, and with enough distinction, to be considered patricians. The men in the Partridge family were mostly doctors who attended Stanford. One brother, an engineer, was instrumental in building the Golden Gate Bridge. My great-grandmother couldn't go to college because she was a woman, but she had the best of finishing school, learning manners and how to dance and then coming out at a debutante ball.

Great-grandma Elesa had been trained as a dietitian and worked right beside my great-grandfather. From the age of three on, Aunt Cindy grew up in their lab. She described it as a big old barn with one section devoted to research and another section filled with sick patients in hospital beds. Most of them were suffering from Bright's disease. It was considered incurable, and they'd come from all over the country to be treated by Dr. Addis. Poppa, as Aunt Cindy called him, was their last hope. He was incredibly gentle with them. He spoke barely above a whisper. He had done years of research with lab mice to come up with a minutely calibrated diet that quieted the disease. Linus Pauling, the Nobel laureate, was one of those he actually cured. Pauling wrote much about my great-grandfather in one of his books. They were such close friends that Aunt Cindy would spend nights at the Pauling house in Pasadena when she was a kid.

My great-grandfather had died twenty years before I was born. Great-grandma Elesa had lived as a widow for another twenty-five years. I had one very faint memory of her. I must have been five or six, and my mother took me to visit her at the old folks' home in San Francisco. I didn't know anything about old people or where they went when they could no longer care for themselves. I remember being freaked out by the place. The air had a weight to it. She had the whitest hair. I wanted to go home. And then out came the lemon drops and the Pepperidge Farm Milano Milk Chocolate cookies, and I settled down. In her youth, my aunts told me, Great-grandma Elesa was elegant-looking, tall and thin, and she dressed magnificently. A lot of her clothes she knitted herself. They hardly ever saw her without a pair of knitting needles in her hands. My mother took after her in that way.

The empathy my great-grandparents showed their patients was extended to the oppressed and the poor. Elesa had been an early-days suffragist, protesting on the front lines for a woman's right to vote. Thomas Addis fought for fair wages and fair housing and civil rights for Black people. He thumbed his nose at the Red Scare and the commie-sleuthing antics of the House Un-American Activities Committee, which had its offspring in the California legislature. At a time when HUAC was printing handbooks on how to identify hidden commies plotting the nation's demise—best to corner them the way you cornered a rat—my great-grandfather was a proud fellow traveler, if not an actual member of the party. He had organized a group of international doctors to aid the antifascist guerrillas in Spain. In the hills of the East Bay, where certain houses were lit with red lanterns, he attended meetings with professors, most of them Jewish, from UC Berkeley and other schools. Not long after, the FBI began tracking him.

"The Addis family was no enemy of the country, I'll tell you that," Aunt Cindy said. "But they were not about to sit by and watch America squander its promise."

One of my cousins was able to locate FBI documents stored in archives that backed up Aunt Cindy's account of my great-grandfather's dealings. In a letter dated January 26, 1942, FBI agents in the San Francisco office wrote to FBI director J. Edgar Hoover about an "internal security" matter involving Dr. Thomas Addis, Dr. J. Robert Oppenheimer, and Professors Haakon Chevalier and Alexander Kaun. "The above individuals represent, in the opinion of this office, a group which is inimical to the welfare of this country." The agents then detailed the activities of each man.

"DR. THOMAS ADDIS has his name on the sponsorship list of perhaps more Communist Party front organizations than any other individual in this area. . . . DR. J. ROBERT OPPENHEIMER, professor of physics at University of California and born in New York City, has been more discreet in exhibiting his Party connections and sympathies but they, nevertheless, are known to exist. Upon at least one occasion, OPPENHEIMER donated $100 to the Communist Party. He is referred to by known high Party members as 'the big shot.' . . . The widely separated professional fields of these individuals could not be a basis for this close association, and it is undoubtedly due to their mutual interest in a common field, namely, Communism."

Director Hoover wrote back two weeks later, telling his West Coast agents to lay off Dr. Addis and Dr. Oppenheimer for now.

As for Professor Chevalier and Professor Kaun, "appropriate requests have been made to secure authorization for the desired surveillance."

Months later, Dr. Oppenheimer would be called upon by President Franklin Delano Roosevelt to head the Manhattan Project. He would make it a point to sever his ties to Dr. Addis and others who had come under the eye of the FBI. My great-grandfather never held this against Oppenheimer, though he fought fiercely against the development of the nuclear bomb, as did Linus Pauling, who toured the country warning of its evils. Not long after, my great-grandfather was removed from his lab. He and Great-grandma Elesa relocated to Los Angeles. This is where he would die in 1949 and where his wife would burn thousands of pages of his letters and papers.

"He was lying on the sofa near death," Aunt Cindy recalled. "I was nine, and my grandmother would stop knitting and take another pile of my grandfather's papers to the incinerator. I stayed there for the summer, and the whole time my grandmother was burning and burning. When I finally asked her why, she said, 'Because these are Poppa's papers and they must go with him.' Even at that age, I figured his papers were too dangerous politically. There were certain secrets that had to go up in smoke."

My grandma Jean was nothing if not her father's daughter. His passions became her passions; his fights became her fights. If he was reading R. G. Collingwood, the British philosopher and historian, she was reading Collingwood. His politics explain why she became a Red. She had all the advantages of San Francisco privilege and rejected them. She turned into a true bohemian, a beatnik before beatniks were a thing. She skipped out on a chance to go to college at Stanford. Instead, at the age of eighteen, she headed to Russia to learn Russian and study acting under Stanislavski. This was in the mid-1930s. The early days of the Soviet Union. It seemed like a movie to me. There was a detour on the way as she stopped off in New York City and took Russian language courses for a year.

To pay for the lessons, Grandma Jean worked as a maid for the Mirsky family, Russian Jews who lived on the Upper West Side. Dr. Addis had done research with Dr. Mirsky. My grandmother Jean didn't enjoy the housecleaning chores because Mrs. Mirsky had hundreds of little tchotchkes, each one requiring dusting. This is when she met Ralph Mirsky, a son or a nephew who played in the Juilliard String Quartet. They attended concerts and leftist meetings and fell for each other. He was my grandmother's first love. But the Mirskys wouldn't let them marry. Jean Addis might have been able to speak Russian, but she was, in the end, a Gentile.

So my grandmother took off to Russia and landed in the middle of history. Lenin had been murdered a decade earlier. Stalin sat as the head of the party and the USSR. He was the full promoter of his own cult, renaming the city of Tsaritsyn "Stalingrad." He had just launched his great purges, a killing spree of the very Communist Party members who had brought him to power. Aunt Cindy couldn't say what events her mother had witnessed. After three years, Russian authorities told my grandmother Jean that she had to either leave the country or become a Soviet citizen. She returned to California and married Milton Weiner, the New Yorker who drifted like a wayfarer from Harvard to Princeton to UC Berkeley.

"I was born and Milton was gone," Aunt Cindy said. "My mother was raising me by herself in a flat on Clay Street, right across from my grandfather's lab. She was working there as a nurse and trying to organize the theater group. This was the mid-1940s. I was five or six, and I remember seeing Arthur Menzies for the first time. He was in his army uniform standing in the kitchen kissing my mother. I thought to myself, *Oh, God, where did you come from?* He was damaged goods from the war. A brilliant horticulturalist but a disaster as a father and husband."

I kept hearing my grandmother's decree to her children—*Don't stand out. Be quiet. Nothing here shall be spoken on the outside.* These were the rules of the house on Stanyan Street. I wondered how much of my grandmother's paranoia—if that's what to call it—was a consequence of the Red Scare that had shadowed her parents, and then having to raise her own children during the fear that was McCarthyism. It wasn't as if she had let go of her strong political beliefs and activism. On more than one occasion, FBI agents (they always arrived in pairs before the dinner hour) visited their Stanyan Street house to chat with Grandma Jean. Grandpa Arthur would usually answer the door and send them on their way. Anne was oblivious to these visits, but not Cindy, who was a teenager by then. She suspected that their phone lines were being tapped, though it was hard to tell because the lines back then were shared and you could often hear the conversations of your neighbors. My mother and Anne were too young to understand how the trial and executions of Julius and Ethel Rosenberg, who were found guilty of passing atomic bomb secrets to the Soviets, roiled their house. Cindy saw my grandmother leaving in the dark of morning to mimeograph sheets of paper in support of the Rosenbergs. She tried to stop her as she headed out the door.

"You can't go," Cindy implored.

My grandmother would hear none of it. "I have to go," she

said. "The Rosenbergs are going to die in the electric chair if we don't stop this."

....

If Grandma Jean was complicated and crippling in her role as a mother, my grandfather Arthur Menzies was a far more troubled and destructive soul. I had no feel for him. He was dead by the time I was five. He hardly existed for me beyond the newspaper story in which he took a .38-caliber gun from beneath his pillow, put the muzzle to his head, and pulled the trigger. Before that, he'd been the assistant director of plants at the Strybing Arboretum in Golden Gate Park. Before that, he had left my grandmother and my mother and aunts and found a second family, in Stinson Beach, with a wife who had two teenage children of her own and was an expert in wild lilies and orchids. Before that, he was serving in the Philippines as a U.S. Army staff sergeant and was captured by the Japanese in the spring of 1942 and thrown into a prisoner of war camp.

Who was Arthur Liddel Menzies, standing six foot one and weighing 165 pounds, with black hair and brown eyes, narrow face and long nose? He was no stranger to my grandmother Jean Addis when they began their courtship in 1945. Indeed, their parents, my great-grandparents, had been friends for more than thirty years. Arthur's father and mother, Kenneth and Victoria Menzies, had lived in Marin and grown close to the Addis family over a shared past. Kenneth Menzies was a Scotsman from Edinburgh like Dr. Addis. Victoria Waithman Menzies came from a prominent family in England like Elesa Addis. The two families remained friends even after the Menzies clan moved to Southern

California in the 1910s. Hollywood is where Grandpa Arthur was born in 1916 and grew up.

By all accounts, his father was a wonderful man and his mother a beautiful woman who drank too much and was impatient with her son's botanical pursuits. Arthur's eye for rare native plants apparently dated back to a flower he grew in their garden when he was a child. It bloomed once every seven years, and he tended to it like a farm kid raising his pig. Before he could see it flower, though, his mother cut it down. By mistake or intentionally the story doesn't say.

At Hollywood High School, Grandpa Arthur wrote a ten-page paper on the wonders of the avocado, the single-seeded fruit that dated back five thousand years. My discovery of this morsel of family history brought a smile to my face because in my role as lieutenant governor, I once took advantage of Governor Jerry Brown's brief departure from the state to name the avocado California's official fruit. This was not a coronation without controversy, given that our state produced the finest table grapes, peaches, plums, nectarines, apricots, pomegranates, and mandarins in the world. Who knew that my grandfather and I shared such a passion for the *Persea americana*, a tropical evergreen native to Mexico and Central and South America?

My grandparents had struck up a friendship when they were teens. Grandma Jean had been sent by her parents to a private all-girls school in Pasadena called Westridge. The campus was close enough to Hollywood that she and Grandpa Arthur saw each other routinely. The esteemed school, which was committed to developing young women who were "intellectually adventurous thinkers," had done just that in the case of my grandmother. By the time Grandma Jean graduated and returned to San

Francisco, her heart was set on New York and Russia, acting and activism.

I am able to track Grandpa Arthur's movements for much of the 1940s by piecing together documents inside the three-ring black plastic binder I keep in my office—hundreds of pages of his official army records and letters home to "Dear Mother and Dad." He enlists in the U.S. Army on September 25, 1940, at Fort MacArthur in San Pedro. A month later, he is sailing to the Philippines to defend Manila Bay. "I feel rather funny today feeling I won't see California again for over two years," he writes. "Love to all. I will write my address when I know it. . . . P.S. #19048713. (This is my death tag#)."

A year and a half later, in a savage fight that will go down in history books as the Battle of Corregidor, Japanese troops numbering 75,000 attack U.S. and Filipino troops numbering 13,000. My grandfather Arthur Menzies is one of the boys. In the relentless Japanese bombardment and fierce resistance put up by Allied forces, nearly two thousand soldiers die on both sides. On May 6, 1942, American troops surrender, and my grandfather and other survivors are rounded up and led on a march. This is just a few weeks after the infamous Bataan Death March ended in the torture and murder of thousands of Filipino and American troops. As Arthur and his fellow captives endure their own horrors, the U.S. War Department informs his parents that he is "missing in action" and may be dead. A month later, to the family's great relief, he turns up as a POW on the Japanese island of Kyushu. His parents continue to write to him—about the family chickens laying well and his father picking a one-pound sapota off Arthur's budded fruit tree—but the letters are "returned to sender by censor." My grandfather will not be heard from again for another three years.

My record of him picks up on Sunday, November 16, 1947, when he writes to his parents from San Francisco on an afternoon of "the most beautiful warm rain, the clever San Francisco kind—one night and one day, and then today a magnificent clear Sunday, cold and crisp but not too cold." His father-in-law, Dr. Addis, has brought to the house fresh crabs that Arthur cooks, hating the cracking but loving the meat's sweet taste. The twin babies, Tessa and Anne, have cut their first teeth. "They chew up everything they can get their hands on. They are awful handfuls for Jean, of course, but one of these days they will be old enough so we can take them walking in the Sausalito hills."

He then sings the praises of Jean to his parents. "Jean is a wonderful person. I didn't know that people like her existed. After nearly two years our love is growing stronger. We understand each other's problems more and more and now we find ourselves really happy. Not the kind of false happiness that is ever present but the real honest-to-goodness thing that happens only once in a lifetime."

My grandfather closes the letter with an attempt to look deeper inside himself. "It only now just dawns on me how very juvenile I was before the war. It was a horrible experience—and not one to be forgotten—but now it pays its dividends. I have an understanding of life that few people have. I've seen it at its worst and I've seen some of its good side. But the important thing is the worst side. There, one sees life as it is."

The battle, the death march, nearly three years as a POW—it must have broken him. He tried to repair the damage by devoting his life to plants and flowers, but their beauty wasn't enough. He was so shy he could hardly speak, Aunt Cindy recalled. The only time he wasn't shy was when he was drinking, which was the reason he drank. "When Daddy was sober, he was very kind with a lot of sensitivity," she said. "Had he married a woman who truly gave to him, maybe things would have turned out differently. My mother was a lovely, elegant human being, but she was very self-ish in her pursuits. She would leave the house at the crack of dawn to work at the hospital, come home and take a nap, fix dinner, and then she'd go off to the theater to work with her troupe. She didn't drink but she was anorexic."

My aunts did see genuine affection between their parents. They never outwardly fought. She really did love him. At the same time, so much was repressed. There was the communist politics passed down from the Addis side and the alcoholism passed down from the Menzies side. Grandma Jean might have been a great thespian or at least continued her political activism, but she put those passions away and tried to give in to the conventions of family life. Then my mother and Anne were born and they didn't speak for years. They had a private language they invented, gibberish to everyone but them. They were basically mute their first six years. Even when they somewhat came out of their shells, they were very quiet.

"The private language your mother and I shared was our way to keep the rest of the world at bay," Aunt Anne told me. "I connected with the outside before Tessa did. I had much more of a voice, and she stayed mute for longer. You must understand our family. I wanted to protect Tessa from our mother and father because she was so fragile and always sick. 'It's your responsibility,' I was told by my mother. 'Tessa needs you.' My parents never tried to deal with Tessa's muteness. There were periods when she wouldn't even talk to me."

The house my grandparents built on Stanyan Street, for all its glass and redwood beauty, was a kind of repression itself. It was maybe six hundred square feet in all and so peculiarly designed that it made the newspapers when they built it in 1949. There were only two rooms: a living room and a bedroom. The three kids shared the bedroom and my grandparents Jean and Arthur slept in the living room. The tiny kitchen had a tiny stove, the only appliance my grandmother would allow in their house. She scrubbed the dirty clothes by hand and hung them outside on a line. Every offer by her parents to convenience their lives my grandmother rejected outright. Was it her pride? Bohemian asceticism? My mom and her sisters were left to guess.

The garden where my grandfather planted his rare seeds dwarfed everything. It was nearly a block long and was surrounded by a magnificent rock wall he built himself. That's where he stashed his bottles of liquor and would escape for hours at a time. Back inside, his mood more confrontational, he'd light a giant fire in a hearth that dominated the living room. The fires, my aunts recalled, roared, beastlike. The day after Christmas, he'd throw in the tree and watch it explode. "The fireplace was our source of heat," Aunt Anne said. "But it was also the thing we feared most. We were afraid he was going to burn down the house and we were going to burn with it and my mother would come home from the theater and find only ashes."

Grandpa Arthur was usually asleep by 6:00 p.m., my mother and her sisters sighing relief. But one evening, when Cindy was twelve or thirteen and Mom and Anne were six or seven, he couldn't calm his agitation and grabbed a gun from his hiding place. He told his daughters to line up in front of the hearth. Fire was bellowing. My mother, who suffered from horrible allergies and asthma, was out of breath and could not move.

"Tessa, get on the hearth!" Cindy screamed. "Now! He has a gun."

My mother lined up next to her sisters. Cindy was convinced he was going to shoot each one of them. The threat hadn't come out of nowhere. For the past year, Cindy had been putting herself to bed each night with the same prayer: "Oh, God, please don't make Daddy kill Mommy or me and the twins."

He waved the gun and then pointed it at them. "I'm going to shoot you," he said, his face aglow. "I'm going to shoot all of you right now."

Cindy could hear my grandmother coming through the door. "He has a gun, Mommy."

Grandma Jean walked in wearing her theater flats, calmly took the gun out of Grandpa Arthur's hand, motioned the girls to their bedroom, and persuaded him to put his head down on his pillow. Nothing more was ever said about it.

More and more, Cindy was called upon to play the role of caretaker because of the incapacitations and work schedules of my grandparents. She gave the twins baths in the morning, braided their hair, fixed them breakfast, and made sure they walked to school on time. If they didn't cooperate, she was forced into the role of disciplinarian, occasionally feeling the need to slap their faces. When my grandmother was at the theater, it was Cindy's job to keep my grandfather out of trouble. More than once she caught him visiting the house of a neighbor woman whose husband was away on business.

When she was seventeen, Cindy decided she'd had enough. She blew up at her mother and father, saying she could no longer handle the responsibilities of holding the family together. My grandmother couldn't believe her insolence. My grandfather threatened to leave the house if Cindy wasn't dealt with. "It's either me or Cindy," he said. Cindy left the house to cool off, meeting up with friends at the playground down the hill. When she returned home, my grandmother had made a decision. Cindy could no longer stay with the family. Cindy was being flown to New York City to live with my grandmother's sister, Elesa, who was married to Dr. David Karnofsky, a Stanford graduate doing pioneering work in oncology at Sloan Kettering.

Slowly, without Cindy, my mother and Aunt Anne sought their way into the world. The twins read every Nancy Drew mystery on the bookshelf. My grandmother would not allow them to watch any movies by Walt Disney, whom she detested for his right-wing politics. She took them to art-house theaters to watch movies with allegories, like *The Red Balloon*. My mom and Anne would find their refuge down the hill at Grattan Playground. Basketball courts, tennis courts, Ping-Pong tables, yo-yos, checkers—they played the way Hilary and I would a generation later at Funston Park. "Grattan Playground saved us," Anne said. In high school, the twins beat all challengers in tennis and found themselves facing each other in the finals of the city championship. My mother, who had been sick and frail only a few years earlier, was now lean and muscular. If need be, she could serve with either her right arm or her left. In a match that neither of their parents attended, my mother wore down Aunt Anne and was crowned champ. The photographer for the sports section said he couldn't tell them apart; they were both wearing the same white headband. He asked my mother to smile and Anne to frown, and that's how they made the newspaper for the first time.

"We had sort of parted ways by then," Aunt Anne said. "At Lowell High, the administrators thought it would further our development if we didn't attend the same classes or even share the same lunch period. Tessa started to blossom some, and I grew more isolated. I didn't have to be her voice anymore. Weirdly, she adopted a fake English accent after seeing *My Fair Lady*. 'Good,' I said. 'This is her way of differentiating herself from me.' She told me to stop being such a wallflower, which I was."

When it came time to pick a college, my mother chose Chico State in the far northern reaches of the Central Valley. The campus was plopped down in the middle of farm country with dairies and fruit and nut orchards watered by the lush snowmelt of the Sacramento River. She roomed with five other young women in a three-bedroom unit that abutted an orchard where the tracks of a supply train sliced across and horseflies as big as bees buzzed from spring to summer to early fall. I would locate years later one of her housemates, Shirley Tavernetti, and she would delicately tell me that Tessa Menzies was a bit of an odd duck, cultured and clueless at once. She was sophisticated in ways her housemates, several of whom grew up in rural towns, weren't. She dressed like a big-city girl, with clothes that had brand names that meant something. Her shoes weren't shoes but espadrilles. They'd make the loudest sound on the wood floor in the morning as she rushed out of bed and off to campus. Her roommate Barb, whose first class was a couple hours later, got so tired of being awakened by the clap of heels that she pushed Tessa right off the bed one morning. My mother had no idea what harm she had done. At dinnertime, each of them took turns cooking for the whole gang.

When it was Tessa's turn, she didn't know how to prepare a meal. Not even spaghetti with a jar of pasta sauce.

"She was a beautiful girl, tall and slender with light brown hair," Tavernetti said. "And she wasn't fragile, not in the least. But for all her big-city flair, she was clueless about so many things in life. She had no domestic skills whatsoever. But it was more than that. In so many ways, she didn't quite know how to function."

Early on, Tavernetti chalked it up to Tessa's living away from her twin sister for the first time. She talked about Anne a lot. The peculiarities, though, kept revealing themselves. Whenever horseflies entered the apartment, the girls took to killing them by flyswatter or hand. My mother would argue with a straight face that the flies deserved to live, too. I knew this story to be true, for it was a belief ingrained in her by her mother, my grandma Jean, who had tried to ingrain it in me. "Tessa literally would not kill a fly. She told us they would come back in a second incarnation and haunt her."

During a long weekend break, Tavernetti accompanied my mother on a trip back to San Francisco, catching a glimpse of her home life that would explain much. The redwood house on Stanyan was dark and tiny and beautiful in its own right. Perhaps, Tavernetti thought, it would lead to a sighting of famed poet, singer, and songwriter Rod McKuen, whose newest collection of verse in the mid-1960s was titled *Stanyan Street and Other Sorrows*. Instead, it offered a peek into the life of Jean Addis Menzies, Tessa's rail-thin mother, who was extremely quiet and bordered on the detached. My grandmother showed her guest around the spare little house, including the bedroom where she slept without a box spring or mattress. Her bed was made of wood planks, nothing else. The epic garden of the gifted botanist Arthur Menzies, who had left her for another woman, had been completely destroyed. Grandma Jean had removed by hand and shovel every plant and flower my grandfather Arthur had painstakingly and lovingly raised. Nothing was left back there but the upheaval of dirt. Dinnertime came and the little old woman, who had been such a prideful chef, disappeared. Twenty minutes later, she walked through the door with bags of hamburgers and french fries from a nearby fast-food joint. Around a small wooden table, the three of them ate with few words spoken. The next morning, Grandma Jean reached into her new refrigerator and grabbed the plate of leftover hamburgers and fries. This was a detail Tavernetti remembered distinctly, because she had never before eaten fast food cold and for breakfast.

It was a few months later that my mother dropped out of her second semester at Chico State to marry my father, who was thirteen years older. There was no wedding to speak of. She did not want a priest. A justice of the peace at San Francisco City Hall performed a civil ceremony. No one from her family was there. Only Ann and Gordon Getty, on behalf of my father, stood as witnesses. "Tessa's marriage to Bill made no sense to me," Aunt Anne said. "What was he thinking marrying a girl that young and then saddling her with two children in the span of thirteen months and then running for office not once but twice? I don't know what adult qualities he saw in Tessa, because she had none at that point. And then a few years later, he leaves her and the two children to pretty much fend for themselves. The whole thing was insane."

And that was the story of the Addis and Menzies side of my family, a puzzling out that allowed me to understand what my mother had to endure and overcome before she ever walked up the ladder of that lifeguard station at the old Squaw Valley Lodge and made the acquaintance of my father standing below her, lost in his own way. I could now see that her sad and stunted upbringing on Stanyan Street was all the preparation she had for her life ahead. She could not fill out what was missing in herself, much less what was missing in my father. They were woefully unprepared to share a life of marriage, children, and work. I am reminded of the oral history he left behind at the Bancroft Library, when he is given the opportunity to explain the sundering of their marriage and he heaps all the blame on his two failed runs for public office and the campaign debt he was saddled with. Out of shame or some psychological fracture, he takes off to Lake Tahoe and begins a life of bachelorhood. He briefly mentions my mother's callowness but only as a matter of her age. He was a fool to have married a girl of eighteen or nineteen, he says, and a fool to have introduced the volatility of politics into their lives. Where my father the storyteller never ventures is the terrain of that garden and wood house and roaring fireplace on Stanyan Street. He would not have wanted to paint for posterity such a portrait of Tessa and her parents. So the story he left to me and Hilary was not even half painted, a canvas almost entirely blank. I must say that there is something painful and cruel in the clear-sightedness I now own, the piece of canvas I have painted. Explaining the mystery of my mother all these years later allows me to understand and love her even more. And yet I am unable to act on that love in the time that it mattered. I am unable to reach back with what I know to be true and ease the pain of her living. Knowledge too late for anything but knowledge. This is the incapacity I am left with.

CHAPTER NINE

""

My blind date with Jennifer Siebel wasn't really blind. She'd been in TV shows and played small parts in movies like *Rent* and *Something's Gotta Give*. She was a Marin girl who'd been recruited to Stanford University to play soccer and graduated with honors in Latin American studies and a minor in human biology, before returning to get her MBA. Mutual friends in the Bay Area thought we might make a good match and set us up. We chose to meet on a weekend in the fall of 2006 when Jen would be flying up from West Hollywood to attend her college reunion. Our first outing (she arrived fashionably late) was very San Francisco, a fundraiser at the Yerba Buena Center for the Arts. *Yerba Buena*, meaning "good-smelling herb," was the name the Spanish missionaries had conferred on the mint-covered hillsides of the city-to-be, San Francisco. We started talking and discovered so many interests in common—nature and conservation, Montana and horseback riding, sports and travel—that the next thing I knew it was past midnight. The garage where she had parked her rental car was locked and the gates would not open again until morning. What to do now?

I drove her to my apartment and invited her to spend a platonic night with me. She didn't know what to make of the place. I had just moved in and wasn't planning to stay there long. The living room had no sofa and the windows had no blinds. To keep out the sun, I had taped rolls of black plastic over them. She later confessed that her first glimpse of my abode brought to mind a question: "Did this guy take his interior design inspirations from *American Psycho*?" We sat and talked for hours. She was the second oldest of five girls, smart and beautiful and warm and open and no-nonsense and civic-minded and gutsy and funny and fluent in Spanish. And a registered Republican. "This is a problem," I said, half joking. She explained that her party affiliation was a remnant of her upbringing and she was in the midst of a transition, from actor and producer to documentary filmmaker, that would challenge many of the conventions she'd grown up with.

Her father, Ken, was a transplant from Illinois who grew up poor in the river towns of Savanna and Rock Falls. Jen's paternal grandparents worked factory jobs, her grandma taking the morning shift and her grandpa taking the night shift. The Midwest might have kept Ken forever if it weren't for basketball. A high school phenom and valedictorian, he became a star at the University of Wisconsin and then a draft pick of the early National Basketball Association. His chances of breaking into the starting lineup, where the greatest players might earn twenty-five grand a year, seemed slim and he wound up taking a job with a financial services firm in New York and then in San Francisco. That's where he met Jen's mother, Judith Ann Fritzer, a flight attendant and daughter of an air force lieutenant colonel. Judy ran the home front and was every bit Ken's match. She became one of the founders of the Bay Area Discovery Museum at the foot of the Golden Gate Bridge. Ken poured his energy into his clients and coaching his girls in one sport after another. If he was a Reagan Republican who bristled at high taxes and government regulations, he was also a passionate outdoorsman, fisherman, and conservationist like my father.

Try as I might, there was no insulating Jen from the clamor of my world. Our dating life had no sooner started than my dalliance with Ruby Rippey-Tourk made headlines a year after the fact. Then we discovered that one of my stalkers, a forty-two-year-old man named Han Sup Shin, who dressed in purple ties and purple latex gloves, was trailing me with such diligence that he knew I now resided in a Russian Hill apartment building and that Jen was living with me. Late one night, Jen heard the doorbell ring and went to see who it was. It was the doorman, who had noticed Shin trying to enter our building with a roll of duct tape in his hand. The police arrived and tracked down Shin, who was in the throes of a psychotic episode. They found photos he had taken of me and a cassette he was recording titled "President Newsom."

This might have been a wake-up call, fair warning that being the wife of a lightning-rod politician wasn't the life for Jen. But she didn't seem fazed in the least. She had even accompanied me to some of those pummeling counseling sessions with Mimi Silbert. I couldn't imagine any of my previous girlfriends doing that. My commitment to Jen grew to a level I had never experienced with another woman. I could only describe it as soulful. This is not to say that Jen didn't have her very real questions about me. Gullibility and wide-eyedness were not among her traits. She would later tell me that my sessions with Silbert showed that I was willing to put in the work to become a partner in the fullest sense.

Our courtship lasted fifteen months. What sealed the deal for me was everything and one thing: whenever and wherever the music was playing, Jen got up to dance. I knew nothing about dancing but a few steps of Irish folk. I'd stand there and just watch her go. She would enter a zone, possessed, spiritual, a complete loss of self-consciousness, a flow that was mesmerizing to behold. I had never seen anything like it. She was completely in touch with her emotional side, an essence I found intoxicating because I had spent so many years trying to shield that side of me. I did not join her on the dance floor, but I let myself go. I fell in love with her deeply and could not help but wonder where her capacity for such joy came from. I would discover, as we made a life together, that it came from her own reservoir of pain.

Jen was not yet seven years old when she watched her eight-year-old sister, Stacia, die in an accident on a family vacation in Hawaii. She and Stacia and some friends were playing bumper cars with golf carts when Jen put her cart in reverse and hit the pedal. She did not see Stacia hiding on the cement right behind her. How Jen found a path through such an unforgiving tragedy, a decades-long process, is a story she has told me with many blank spots and blurs. I imagine its deepest reaches remain elusive to language. Both her parents came from strong Nordic stock. Their way of dealing with the sorrow and inevitable self-blame was to bear it privately. This was the early 1980s, before the proliferation of grief counselors and psychologists specializing in trauma and posttraumatic stress. Only once did her parents take Jen to see a therapist. She told me she spent the rest of her childhood trying to be two daughters, both of them perfect, for her parents. "I suffered in silence," she said. Because the family never talked about the accident, it meant that Stacia, the memory of her, couldn't be talked about either. And yet Ken and Judith Siebel intuitively reached for ways to heal themselves and Jen and her little sister, Brooke. Ken cut back his work hours and became a devoted coach for his girls and their teammates in soccer and basketball. A fourth daughter, Melissa, and a fifth daughter, Jessica, were greeted as blessings. The family began living months at a time at their ranch in Montana, where Jen rode horses and spent hours by herself exploring the nearby river and its wildlife. "Nature became my reprieve," she told me. Her parents bought her a little white Shetland pony named Sugar, dressed in red halter and western saddle and blanket. Jen and Sugar were inseparable. "Slowly, I learned to forgive myself," she said. "I learned that it wasn't my fault."

Anguish found her once more, this time as a young actress and producer in Hollywood who had her own terrible encounter with Harvey Weinstein in a Beverly Hills hotel. Instead of meeting in the lounge to discuss "future film projects" as they had planned, Weinstein changed his mind and told her to come up to his room. Jen did not tell me the details of what happened in that room for quite some time. We were attending a Hollywood function one evening when Weinstein intruded on our intimate space, lumbering within a few inches of Jen, ostensibly to say hello. He did not even pretend to notice my presence, but the way he looked at her I'll never forget. I watched the color drain from Jen's face and her body stiffen. When I later asked her to explain the awkwardness between her and Weinstein, she said she'd tell me about it when the time was right. It took years for her to reveal, little by little, what Weinstein had done to her.

Jen's wounds, I imagined, explained the way she danced when the music came on. They explained, as well, the subjects she would fearlessly tackle in her documentaries. Her way of dealing with pain, my way of dealing with pain, sometimes made us feel remote from each other, but more often it bound us together.

Jen and I had planned our wedding for July 26, 2008, at her family's ranch in Montana's Bitterroot Valley. The news didn't sit well with residents of the Big Sky State, who still blamed me for propagating the pox of gay marriages across America. Threats started to pour in. "Keep that faggot lover in his own state if he wants to get married," read more than one letter. Enough gun zealots were making a racket that our police chief, Heather Fong, thought it prudent that a security detail of San Francisco cops shadow me for the wedding. Some of my critics on the board of supervisors couldn't help but sense an opening. Why should taxpayers have to cover such an expense? Is the mayor attempting to turn the police department into his own private security force? On the eve of my wedding, a political dustup was the last thing I needed. I called Chief Fong and asked if a security detail was really necessary. "I'd be derelict in my duty if I sent you to Montana without one," she said.

With the ten-thousand-foot peak of the Bitterroot Mountains as backdrop and a pair of Canada geese flying overhead, Jen and I joined hands in a meadow beside a creek and exchanged vows in front of three hundred guests. Prominent Democrats sat on one side and stalwart Republicans sat on the other side. A smattering of tech titans—who knew if they were left or right?—were somewhere in the middle. Fourteen months later, on September 18, 2009, our first child, a girl, was born. Jen had prepared for a natural birth, but the baby was stuck under her rib cage, a complicated breach that required a Cesarean section. Montana Tessa Siebel Newsom weighed seven pounds, twelve ounces, and measured 20.5 inches long. Her name honored my mother and Jen's family, too, as well as the state whose wide-open country had been such a healing place. The breach had misaligned Montana's hips and slightly misshaped her head, and for her first few years she would have to wear a full-body brace and a tiny helmet to even things out.

How to quiet that crying voice—was it breast milk? was it diaper? was it upset at being uprooted from warm, floating confines to the cold cacophony of a crazy world?—was a question we asked ourselves many times a day on the worst days. We learned, as most parents eventually do, that there were some cries that could not be calmed, that the calming came from the crying itself, and it was best to let her be. For Jen, this lesson of parental detachment was the hardest lesson. I'm not sure she ever put it into full practice with Montana, though it became easier with Hunter and Brooklynn, and by the time Dutch came along, she was a seasoned pro.

Before Montana's birth, a year into my second term as mayor, I had felt an itch to turn the page. I had outgrown my persona as the brash young man-about-town; San Francisco, at least as a place to govern, began to feel too familiar, too small. My administration had done proud work on climate change, universal health care, and rebuilding the most neglected parts of the city. We had established a process to address the complexity of homelessness, even if we hadn't taken as many people off the streets as

I had hoped. Schwarzenegger would soon finish his second term in Sacramento, and this would clear the path for my run to be the next governor of California.

*****

In my final hurrah as mayor, a torch had to be carried. China was hosting the 2008 Summer Olympics, and the eternal flame of the games, lit in Greece, was traveling from Beijing along the Silk Road to the top of Mount Everest and across the world. The torch relay would log eighty-five thousand miles in 129 days through a score of countries. It would land in the U.S. only once, on April 9, and that was in my city, San Francisco. The "Journey of Harmony," the Chinese were billing it, though it had devolved along the way into a trek of protest and counterprotest that saw supporters of China facing off against supporters of Tibet. On the Paris leg, a disabled woman named Jin Jing was carrying the torch in a wheelchair when human rights advocates from the pro-Tibetan camp tugged and kicked at her to wrest the torch from her hand. The "angel in the wheelchair," as the Chinese dubbed her, fought them off. The next leg was ours.

No Chinatown in America is bigger or more filled with history than San Francisco's Chinatown. One third of our city is Asian. I became mayor on the strength of the Mandarin- and Cantonese-speaking vote. They liked that I was a businessman whose long hours had found success and a politician willing to take on the homeless issue. I had first passed through the Dragon Gate of Chinatown when I was a kid crossing between the two very different worlds of my father and mother. That demarcation would stir in me a deep appreciation of California history and a love and shame for my city. Back in the late 1870s, San Francisco had become a fulcrum of anti-Chinese animus, and the demagogue fomenting the hysteria was none other than Denis Kearney, an Irishman and leader of the Workingmen's Party. The *San Francisco Chronicle* served as his bullhorn, his fiery sandlot speeches always ending with the same four words: "The Chinese must go!" What started in San Francisco with Kearney blaming "coolie" labor for the low wages of white workingmen ended in Washington, D.C., with the passage of the Chinese Exclusion Act in 1882.

The Chinese community had endured in a city that had grown not only to accept them but to take much pride in their enterprise. As mayor of San Francisco and then as U.S. senator, Dianne Feinstein understood before any of us that California was part of the Pacific Rim. Though China's human rights abuses and occupation of Tibet presented real challenges, we would do well to build cultural and economic ties with the Chinese government and its people. In January 1980, one year after the U.S. and China established diplomatic relations, Feinstein led the way to creating a "sister city" bond between San Francisco and Shanghai. Over the next three decades, San Francisco celebrated "Shanghai Week" and Shanghai celebrated "San Francisco Week," and the exchanges of travel and culture, sports and commerce, grew into a shared language that transcended Cold War invective.

My first trip to Shanghai as mayor, on the occasion of the twenty-fifth anniversary of our sister-city tie, became one long, exquisite dinner with plate after plate of savory dishes and salutes of "Gan bei," "dry the cup," with each shot of alcohol. Libations notwithstanding, Senator Feinstein never changed her game face. What shines in my memory, however, was the small private lunch we shared with Jiang Zemin, the former mayor of Shanghai, who had just retired as president of China and general secretary of the Chinese Communist Party. Dianne sat on one side of him and I sat on the other, and each of us was assigned a translator. The dialogue from Chinese to English and English to Chinese hardly made for conversation. After the president's first dry cup, I ventured a rather personal question. "What's been the most difficult thing about stepping down from office?" His eyes grew large behind his big owl glasses, and he answered in English so flawless that it became clear that the two translators were something of a charade. "The fact that I cannot travel anymore to nations around the world," he replied. I then asked him what travel memory stuck with him most. "Easy," he said. "Bodysurfing in Hawaii. It's the one thing I regret I won't be able to do again in my life." Two dry cups later, I could see the conversation between the president and senator turn animated, maybe even flirty. They were reminiscing about the first time they had met, both of them younger and mayors of their respective cities who had come together for a first-of-a-kind partnership. Dianne was playful and Zemin was playful, and their playfulness took them right out of their chairs and onto the polished floor, where they began to dance, just the two of them.

None of this meant that San Francisco's leg of the torch relay was going to be trouble free. Senator Feinstein was talking in one of my ears and Speaker of the House Nancy Pelosi, not exactly a cheerleader for harmonious relations with China, was talking in my other ear. Dianne believed that smart planning and close coordination with a police department headed by Heather Fong would steer us clear of an international incident. Nancy, on the other hand, would have preferred I just cancel the whole thing.

For all our warm relations with China, none of us was naive about the need for "information security" during a high-stakes public event such as this. The head of my security detail, Jeff Lindberg, urged that we all switch from our cell phones to anonymous burner phones. Meanwhile, the Bush administration, never missing a chance to throw red meat to its base, was ratcheting up its attacks on China. I knew from talking to the mayors of London and Paris that pro-Tibetan and other human rights protesters were only half the powder keg. The other half were the Chinese special forces, clad in blue tracksuits, who surrounded the torch in a flying V formation and roughed up anyone they deemed a threat to the flame.

My former colleagues on the board of supervisors did all they could to heat up feelings. On the relay's eve, they approved a resolution that registered "alarm and protest at the failure of China to meet its past solemn promises to the international community, including the citizens of San Francisco, to cease egregious and ongoing human rights abuses in China and occupied Tibet." Word came that anti-Chinese protesters were planning to scale the suspension cables of the Golden Gate Bridge and unfurl a massive banner that shouted FREE TIBET. Thousands would be gathering at United Nations Plaza, gateway to city hall, in a protest led by Archbishop Desmond Tutu and actor Richard Gere, a practicing Buddhist of the Tibetan school. The Chinese government, for its part, was rallying Chinese college students from Nevada and Arizona and all across California. Organized battalion-style, they'd be riding in on chartered buses to join the throngs of locals who lived and worked in Chinatown. As the hours ticked down, the police command staff wanted to pull the plug on the relay, but Peter Ueberroth, head of the U.S. Olympic

Committee, cautioned that such a move would create its own international incident.

The morning of the relay, I was sitting in an unmarked car along the Embarcadero, the wind chopping at the bay. A mob of China bashers mistakenly believed a bus was carrying the actual torch and kept rocking its belly until they nearly turned it over on its side. Watching the flag-waving and chanting crowd surge to AT&T Park, where the torch would be lit and the first of seventy holders would jog along the Embarcadero, I grabbed my burner phone and pulled a fast one. I changed the route in wholesale fashion and mixed in enough subterfuge to ensure that the protesters wouldn't catch up. The first runner, just as advertised, emerged from AT&T Park with torch lit. But rather than running along the waterfront to hand it off to the next runner, he slipped into a cavernous warehouse at Pier 48 and disappeared. More than a mile away, the sixty-nine other torch runners were gathered at a hotel on O'Farrell Street waiting for the flame. A two-mile stretch of Van Ness Avenue to the Marina, half the length of the old route, became our new route.

It was some kind of magic trick, one that would have made the Great Gavini proud. Thousands of mystified protesters and counterprotesters were left stranded alongside the bay. On the other side of the city, hundreds of police officers riding motorcycles and bicycles flanked the torch runners down a peaceful path that took less than an hour to finish. Citizens astonished to see the flame pop up in their neighborhood were delighted. "This is a once-in-a-lifetime thing," Nancy Chan, accompanied by her four-year-old son, Christian, told the *Chronicle*.

One local politician was fuming. "Gavin Newsom runs San Francisco the way the premier of China runs his country," he said. "Secrecy, lies, misinformation, lack of transparency and manipulating the populace." The media, local and national, managed to get their shot of Willie Brown, clad in white athletic shorts and a white Olympics headband, jogging down Van Ness beside football great Herschel Walker, flame held aloft. We had not canceled the event. We had not denied the people the streets of our city. We had done better than Paris and London and dodged an ugly scene. We had just changed the route a little.

There would be no closing ceremony at Embarcadero Plaza. Instead, in a parking lot in the Marina, I piled into a black SUV with Chief Fong at the wheel. A smiling Peter Ueberroth and Nate Ballard, my aide and close friend, took seats next to me. The Olympic torch, still lit by a butane contraption, was safe and sound in a fireproof container packed in the rear. Chief Fong hit the pedal as if highway bandits were chasing us. She barreled down 280 and then 101 and pulled into San Francisco International Airport, where a short private closing ceremony was about to be held. Senator Feinstein was calling on one line, Speaker Pelosi on the other. Dianne could not have been more pleased. Nancy not so much. Onward to Buenos Aires the flame flew.

""""

That summer of 2008, confident the time was right, I announced my intention to run for governor of California. I set up headquarters at the Embarcadero Center in a space plenty big enough for the campaign. At the outset, my staff numbered a half dozen, if that. There was Nick Clemons, my campaign manager, and Paige Arata, my longtime trusted aide, and campaign consultants Eric Jaye and Garry South, and a kid out of Palo Alto with a history degree from Columbia University named Jason Elliott. We aimed to grow.

A campaign at its earliest stage is little more than a boiler room for fundraising, and ours was no different. We needed to raise tens of millions of dollars, and much of it had to be done in a vacuum, because we didn't know yet who our Democratic opponents would be, though I imagined Antonio Villaraigosa, mayor of Los Angeles, would be among them. I put aside my stack of white papers and tucked away my big ideas, and we did nothing but raise money. By the first reporting deadline, we had brought in our first $1 million, a decent enough start. The big donors, the unions, Hollywood, and the tech companies were waiting for other candidates to surface before making a commitment.

In March 2009, my candidacy caught the curiosity of *The Economist*, the London-based weekly that had been pushing its "radical centrism" since the 1840s. No expert on British mockery, I wasn't sure what to make of the headline: YOUNG MAN IN A HURRY: GAVIN NEWSOM WANTS TO RUN CALIFORNIA. SERIOUSLY. The piece pointed out the usual. As mayor of San Francisco, I was fodder for conservative media and had so entangled myself in the issue of gay marriage that I was probably radioactive, as well. But just when I thought the article was going for my jugular, it became a strangely backhanded endorsement of me: "Mr. Newsom is not the loony liberal of conservative tirades. By Bay Area standards he is a moderate Democrat; in San Francisco he is sometimes accused of conservatism."

I was determined to run for governor right up until the moment it became apparent that Jerry Brown was determined to run for governor, too. I didn't see how I could challenge the man.

Jerry had been a fixture in California politics since I was a kid, and my father had been close to him and I looked up to him. Once his second term as governor had ended in 1983, he had gone off to Japan to study Zen Buddhism, because "politics is based on illusions" and Far Eastern meditation would allow him to explore those illusions more deeply. With his move to Oakland in the 1990s he returned to political life, serving two terms as a mayor focused on downtown redevelopment. From there he served a term as California's attorney general. This later-in-life version of Jerry was more pragmatic than progressive, which meant there was no place for me to find a way around him unless I was willing to tack to the far left. Not only did the far left not fit me, but it was a position that wasn't electable in a California that had elected and reelected the Terminator. I was reminded that you didn't take on your elders, especially when you saw no way around defeat. This clear thinking made sense in my head, but what to tell my heart?

I considered taking a long sabbatical, as Jerry had done, or returning to our wine business. My team, however, made the case that I needed to throttle back and shift focus to the race for lieutenant governor. Officially, it was the second-most-powerful position in California. In actuality, it was a backwater where the only time you emerged from your burrow was when the governor flew off to another country. Lieutenant governor would keep me in the mix, they argued, and give me time to delve into the obscure policy issues that captivated my mind. I could learn more about California's water system, for one, and parts of the state I had only driven through on my way to Southern California. First, though, I had to unseat the incumbent, Republican Abel Maldonado, a former state senator who had been appointed lieutenant governor by Governor Schwarzenegger after the previous lieutenant governor, John Garamendi, was elected to Congress. Maldonado was the son of migrant Mexican farmworkers who toiled in the fields along the Central Coast and eventually saved enough money to buy their own small strawberry farm. He was not only a moderate but a decent person. He won inland California, and I won the more populous coast, which translated into my beating him by eleven percentage points. I had risen to state office in the same election that saw my longtime friend Kamala Harris win the job of California attorney general. It wasn't the first time our career paths had run parallel. Seven years earlier, we had come into local office together, me as mayor and she as district attorney.

I won't ever forget exiting the gilded, oak-paneled chambers of San Francisco City Hall for the last time, heading down the marble staircase a year shy of serving a full second term. No staffers trailed me, as they had every day for the last seven years. It was a walk I made alone. In that moment, it hit me that the young man in a hurry was now the young man made to slow down. I was no longer the leader of anything. As lieutenant governor, I sat on boards overseeing the university and college systems and chaired the commissions for economic development and state lands, which were not without consequence. But I had no power over legislation, no authority over the state's budget, no station to launch the next bold idea. I had gone from the guy who stood at the center of every decision impacting one of the most vibrant cities in America to a job so low profile that few people would have noticed if I'd gone AWOL for a month.

For the next eight years, I did my best to stay relevant. I turned the office of lieutenant governor into a hothouse to grow business, industry, and tech. I teamed up with the Brookings Institution and authored California's first economic development blueprint, "Regions Rise Together," which recognized the state's economy as an intersection of many different economies, each with its own strengths and weaknesses. As a businessman, this was familiar territory for me. With author Lisa Dickey, I wrote *Citizenville*, a book that became a rallying cry to revolutionize democracy in the digital age. Government was stuck in the last century, I argued, even as the private sector and the way we conducted our personal lives had leaped across the divide. How else to explain the California Department of Motor Vehicles, whose long lines and interminable delays caused more consumer heartburn than any other agency in the state? As high tech was giving rise to Facebook and Twitter, Uber and Airbnb, the DMV was still unable to process debit or credit card payments. Bill Clinton gave the book an enthusiastic thumbs-up. So did Michael Bloomberg and Newt Gingrich.

I was now a talking head with my own national cable show on Al Gore's Current TV, based in San Francisco. The audience for *The Gavin Newsom Show* was embarrassingly scant, but we were managing to break national news with the latest innovations from techies and revealing interviews with sporting legends. Sergey Brin and his wife, Anne Wojcicki, came on the show to tout the first Google glasses. With cameras rolling, Elon Musk drove me into our studio in one of the very first Tesla Model S's to come off his assembly line, an enterprise underwritten by hundreds of millions of dollars in California subsidies. Lance Armstrong sat across from me and insisted he had never taken a steroid on the road to winning seven Tour de France titles, a lie soon to be revealed. No guest mesmerized me more than Willie Mays, who sat for ninety minutes and patiently told his life story from the cotton fields of Alabama to baseball's Hall of Fame. When the interview ended, he smiled his beautiful smile and extended his giant hand and told me he had never spent that many minutes in one sitting recalling his history.

The Gavin Newsom Show lasted a whole year, at which time Current TV was acquired by the Al Jazeera Media Network and I moved on. I busied myself by making regular trips to the state capitol to meet with legislators and doing research at a tech incubator south of Market Street in San Francisco. I had a desk inside a space filled with kids in their twenties trying to pitch the next billion-dollar app. I was the old guy in shirtsleeves doing deep dives into employment insurance and offshore wind power and hosting academics, tech bigwigs, and labor leaders for long, drawn-out discussions.

****

The profile of lieutenant governor was low enough that I didn't have to move the family to Sacramento and we could continue to live in Marin. More important, it allowed me the chance to become a more present husband and father. I was home for dinner nearly every night and had time to bathe the children and put them to bed. As the son of Bill Newsom, my plunge into fatherhood came with its limits, of course. I could count on one hand the times I actually changed a diaper, and God knows that with three children under the age of three and a fourth one soon to arrive, there was no end to the diapers to change. Jen had devoted her documentary film career to interrogating the ways boys and girls were raised with different expectations—what society wished of them and what they then wished of themselves. It was odd to see these differences reflected in the very gifts and cards we received upon each of our children's births. Pink for the girls and blue for the boys, no surprise. Princess and fairy dreams for Montana and Brooklynn. Big jock and presidential dreams for Hunter and Dutch. As enlightened as people thought themselves, long-held conceptions of boys and girls, men and women, still ran in the bloodstream. If I found it curious, Jen found it infuriating. One of her first documentaries, *Miss Representation*, explored how conventional narratives in society and media were hamstringing women and girls, creating feedback loops that kept them from being all they could be. In a later documentary, *Fair Play*, Jen examined the uneven division of domestic labor between husbands and wives, which she assured me wasn't inspired by our home life, though I surely knew that it was.

I do recall a day before Montana's first birthday when Jen walked into my study and announced that she was taking a trip with her parents to the mountains of Rwanda to "hike with the gorillas." Would I like to come along—it was their fiftieth wedding anniversary—or stay at home with Montana and help out the nanny? That was the summer of 2010, election season, and Jen knew the answer. I would be staying in San Francisco and hitting the campaign trail for a shot at lieutenant governor. I would be taking over childcare duties when I could. In the ten days Jen was gone, I learned many things about babies. I learned that they are keenly aware that their mothers are missing. I learned that Montana had outgrown the soporific of swaddling, one of the few paternal skills I had mastered. I learned that all the frozen breast milk Jen had pumped out prior to leaving was the greatest gift I'd ever received. I learned that when all else failed across the long day, you strapped on the BabyBjörn and started walking with your daughter, so close you could smell the sweet of her beautiful head. I walked that way through the caverns of AT&T Park to see a Paul McCartney concert. During his sound check, the old Beatle caught a glimpse of Montana and hurried over to greet her. He kept cooing until the cooing turned into a song. He was making up the lyrics as he went. He sang to Montana for so long I had someone record it.

By the time Jen arrived home from Africa, I had come to realize I didn't have the time to be a full-time dad. I envied the fathers I knew who had that privilege, though when I looked around the office all I could see were fathers and mothers working insane hours on behalf of the public, just as I was. My hours were crazier only because I suffered from the compulsive notion that hard work led to a state of being ahead of all things I needed to govern. And to ascend to that state, I needed only to work harder. Then came Hunter. Then came Brooklynn. Then came, surprise, Dutch. Dutchie. Boy, was he different. Boy, did he pay no mind to the path his siblings had carved out before him.

As each child pushed into adolescence, we could see a combination of traits familiar and strange come into being. What was me? What was Jen? What was that thing we could not trace? Sometimes the questions were trivial. Whose eyes? Whose nose? Sometimes they were more far-reaching. Whose competitiveness? Whose anxiety? Whose attention deficit? Whose difficulty reading words on a page? The last one broke my heart when I saw it emerge in one of my children and then another. Dyslexia. There would be no dawdling, not for this generation of Newsoms. No sooner did the trait emerge than Jen had it diagnosed and a plan of remediation put in place.

How fun it was to see their skills emerge on the soccer field and basketball court and tennis court and ski slope. As a matter of nature, Jen and I could both take credit. As a matter of nurture, it was Jen who was with them for every practice and game, who showed them how to dribble a soccer ball and took them to the Sierra and taught them how to ski. On the way from my work office to my home office, I had maybe five minutes to shoot hoops with them in the driveway before my iPhone started buzzing with its one hundred calls a day, or two hundred calls a day, or five hundred calls and texts a day. Hunter and Dutch—no bragging—had the hand-eye coordination and explosiveness to be special baseball players, but baseball isn't a sport like soccer or basketball or football, where a kid's gravitation toward it is its own teacher. Most often, baseball requires a dad who played the game and is willing many times a week to pitch batting practice and hit grounders and fly balls and pass on the patience that teaches a kid that one hit in every three at bats, a dismal percentage in any other sport, is a ticket to the All Stars.

I wanted to believe I wasn't the distant presence in my children's lives that my father had been in mine. I wanted to believe that playing second fiddle to Jerry Brown or running for governor myself wasn't stealing unduly from my tending to the needs of family. But I did not have the time to pass on to Hunter and Dutch the game of baseball, a sport that had saved me when I was a kid. How to explain my hesitation to leap into the role of dad? Sure, the hours I worked were long and the pressures of the job never relented; I'd come home dog-tired and in need of an hour off the clock to escape my head and maybe watch the Giants game. And yet the roles Jen was juggling—mother, filmmaker, founder of a nonprofit advocating for gender equality—were long and intense, too. She had every reason to expect a full partner in me.

One of the slightly embarrassing stories Jen liked to tell people about our dating days was how her feelings for me grew fonder when she saw the way I interacted with children. I could home in on their wavelength without difficulty and linger there, in an animated space, for long periods of time. She knew my childhood had not been without challenges and that something of a latchkey child remained in me. As our kids grew, she could see that I was not completely at ease playing disciplinarian or deciding which one of them had a more provable case against the other. She could see that I was at my best during holiday seasons, when I went hog wild stuffing Christmas stockings with goodies I had wanted when I was a kid or putting little gems inside the plastic Easter eggs and hiding them in the most unlikely of places in our backyard. Complicating my parenting was the uncanny awareness of each child that their father possessed a weak spot. Guilt, they learned quite fast, was a sure path to clemency. And what dad in California lugged around more guilt than the one whose ambition was driving him to run for governor?

Had my parenting style been the subject of one of Jen's documentaries, here's what the camera would have recorded of one particular day.

I was folding clothes in the laundry room, one of the household chores that oddly brought a Zen to my being. Jen was in the kitchen, baking salmon and roasting a dish of potatoes and vegetables. Suddenly, the ruckus of one Newsom sibling upsetting another could be heard from some distant corner. There was no harm, I told myself, in letting the kids work it out on their own. But as their voices grew more indignant, I could hear Jen pleading.

"Gavin, the kids are fighting, and I keep hoping you might intervene without me asking. But I'm asking."

I waited another minute.

"Babe, they're at it again. I've had my fill of it all week. It's your turn."

I waited another thirty seconds.

"I told Hunter he needs to stop picking on Montana," she said. "He ought to be setting a better example for Dutchie."

I finally sprang into action, though I'm not sure it was the action Jen was looking for. I thought back to the relationship between me and my sister. Did I pick on Hilary growing up? Was she the recipient of anger I felt over my inability to decipher words? I grabbed the cell phone and dialed her number. She was a mother herself, one of the smartest and most emotionally attuned people I knew, who now oversaw all operations at PlumpJack. Jen and Hunter and Montana stood next to me. I put our voices on speaker.

"Hey, Hil, can you talk to the kids? Hunter is hassling Montana, and it's made me wonder how you and I got along growing up. I know we must have had our moments. But I want you to be brutally honest. Did I tease or bully you?"

"Really? You know I can ruin you," she said, laughing. "No, all in all, you were a pretty good brother. With all the crud of our childhood, you might have had a reason to be a bully. But you were the opposite."

To prove the point, Hilary recounted three small stories from our childhood. She told the kids that up until her thirteenth birthday she would wet her bed at night. "A friend of your dad's found out and threatened to spread the news," she said. "Your dad, who was fourteen at the time, told him, 'If you ever tell anybody, those will be fighting words.'"

Next she told them that among the houseguests and foster children who lived with us was one who possessed a slightly cruel streak. "He used to tease me because I was overweight," Hilary said. "He would call me 'Hil-a-fat,' and when your dad heard that, he put his foot down. Gavin was just a string bean, but he told him to knock it off. And that was the end of that."

Then she reached back further to recall Jim Meeker, who was so close to our father that we considered him an uncle. "When your dad was seven or eight, Uncle Jim gave him a hundred-dollar bill and told him to buy something for himself and something for me. Your dad came home with a sheepskin teddy bear for me. It cost something like eighty-five dollars. He bought a little plastic Snoopy sign for himself. It said, 'You're number one' on it."

The children were smiling. Jen and I thanked Hilary. I found myself deeply moved, in part because these were incidents I remembered only dimly, stories I could not tell.

""""

The groove of fatherhood came to me most easily not in California, where my obsessions kept me in work mode fourteen hours a day, but in Montana, where the Bitterroot River met Mitchell Slough and ran right through the acres that belonged to my in-laws. In his role as grandfather, Ken taught me how to be a more patient and engaged father. We shot hoops with the kids and rode horses from one end of the ranch to the other. We took them skeet shooting and showed Hunter how to hunt doves with a .22 and bag an elk with a bow and arrow. Despite my grandmother's admonitions about the sanctity of insect and animal life, I had come to hunting in my later years, though fishing remained my true passion. During those extended days at the ranch, whenever I needed time alone, I went looking in river's ripples for trout, rainbow and brown.

From the first rod and reel Boss Newsom had bought me, I'd come up through the ranks to join the sect that was fly-fishing. I'm here to affirm what Norman Maclean wrote about fly-fishing in western Montana in *A River Runs Through It*, the hypnosis of water and cast, sun and shade, quiet and buzz, solitary and in the company of multitudes native and farm hatched, hoping to catch the former but damn if I could tell the difference. This was my escape from reality, my catharsis, my meditation. Hours felt like minutes. "Where's Dad?" the kids would ask back at the cabin. I had no cell phone, no watch. How would I know that morning and noon had passed? I was thinking about my father and our first backpacking trip by mule and horse through Montana's Glacier National Park when I was eleven or twelve years old; a big brown grizzly bear arched its back on a distant hill and we made sure to stay downwind. The glacier was now gone. I was thinking about a summer day with Dad in Tahoe City, his law office next to the Truckee River, and how he worked all morning and afternoon and I went fishing with my rod and a bagful of tiny frogs I had hunted for bait. Though I had no state license permitting such activity, rainbow after rainbow came calling. I plucked so many of them out of the Truckee that I busted past the legal limit, making my crime a pair. Proudly, I hung the trout on a string and carried them back to Dad's office. Did I dazzle him?

Did he fry fish for dinner? Did he turn it into one of the stories about his son that he shared with his pals? I am left to wonder. This day, where the Bitterroot meets the slough, I let go the beautiful fat rainbows I catch—all but one. I try to remove the hook from his mouth but it's stuck. I hustle back to the cabin and retrieve sharp-nosed pliers. As I make my way again to the river, there's the rainbow I left safely on the line. And there's a great bald eagle that has swooped down in my absence and grabbed the fish. Both the eagle and I freeze in panic. As I move a step closer, she takes off with a great beat of wings. The rainbow, its eyes plucked out, its belly half eaten, stays alive long enough for me to remove the hook. I can hear Jen and the kids calling me in the distance. It is way past lunch. I put the rainbow still moving its gills back in the Bitterroot and walk home to join them.

CHAPTER TEN

·····

During my last term as lieutenant governor, it occurred to me that if I wanted to shape matters beyond the reach of my office, I needed only to grab the levers of California's initiative process. For more than a century, voters had held a power nearly equal to that of the state legislature to enact laws. All a citizen had to do was circulate the initiative, get it signed by 5 percent of the electorate, and watch it land on the ballot for a vote. Of course, there was the modern-day matter of having to raise millions of dollars to fund the signature gathering and campaign messaging.

I went straight to work on two measures for the 2016 general election: Proposition 63 to ban large-capacity magazine clips and require background checks to buy ammunition, and Proposition 64 to legalize cannabis for those twenty-one and older. Californians who had no idea what I did for a living were now referring to me as the "guns and weed dude." To steer the Prop 63 campaign, I hired a handful of staffers who raised millions of dollars to qualify and pass the measure. As part of our outreach, they collected hundreds of thousands of email addresses—access to voters that politicians would give their eyeteeth for. Over the years, that email list would grow to become one of the largest political databases in the country. I then assembled a separate team for Prop 64, led by Jason Kinney, a Princeton grad and gifted political strategist, and Sean Parker, the social justice warrior and first president of Facebook. We wrote a white paper making the case for legalizing cannabis and assembled a blue-ribbon committee to help raise funds and gather signatures.

Our messaging for both propositions appealed to common sense. The sickness of mass shootings demanded that Californians mobilize as a national force to push for new restrictions on weapons capable of killing so many with a finger's twitch. I was determined to use whatever bully pulpit I had to make the case, which included California's own failure to confiscate tens of thousands of firearms from those deemed too violent or mentally ill to possess them. State and local databases showed more than twenty thousand individuals in our state who fell into this category and yet were not required to surrender their arms. As for recreational marijuana use by adults, California already had been the first state to legalize the medicinal use of cannabis two decades earlier. Why not take it one step further? Tens of thousands of Californians, the great majority Black and brown, were arrested each year for nonviolent marijuana felonies. We were wasting the resources of cops and judges and taking up space in jails and prisons for cannabis, not to mention pulling families apart and worsening racial inequality.

On election night 2016, we gathered in the upstairs room of PlumpJack's Forgery Bar on Mission Street to celebrate what we thought was going to be a home run for Democrats. Jen and I embraced when both our propositions took sizable leads, and we did the same as the Electoral College map seemed to be tilting in Hillary Clinton's favor. As the night wore on, however, and Clinton lost the battleground states of Ohio, Pennsylvania, and Wisconsin, our worst fears materialized before our eyes. Donald Trump, fake business mogul and reality TV star, who just four weeks earlier could be heard bragging on tape about the lewd things he loved doing to unsuspecting women, was walking onstage with his family to declare victory. The look on his face, it seemed to me, was that of a man who could not believe the fraud he had perpetrated on the American people had actually come to fruition.

Driving across the Golden Gate Bridge late that night to our house in Marin, Jen and I remained in a state of disbelief. "Instead of one of the most accomplished women in the world, we've just elected a serial sexual assaulter," Jen said, tears in her eyes. What would we say to the kids, especially Montana and Hunter, who'd been so captivated by the race that they had watched the debates with us? Montana, who had met Hillary Clinton on the campaign trail, was crying on the phone. "I can't believe this," she said. "This can't be true." I told Jen that something fundamental had been revealed about our country, something I had missed in my now-and-then attempts to understand the red parts of California. I couldn't put my finger on it yet, but I was determined in my next race—the one for governor—to get a closer look. At the same time, I suspected that attacking Trump the personality, while it might do wonders for the gut, was a losing game. Dealing with a man of his makeup would require a subtler set of skills—and a determined focus on issues.

*****

With Jen's support and unsure how it was going to impact the lives of our children, I announced my candidacy for governor. My political team—Addisu Demissie, Ace Smith, Sean Clegg, and Dan Newman—had the map of California in their heads: its red-state interior, its blue-state coasts, its purple hues where farm met city. As the former mayor of San Francisco, I could count on my strong base in Northern California to free me up to campaign in other parts of the state. As lieutenant governor, I had spent enough time building relationships in Southern California that the turf there felt nearly like home.

In California primaries, Democrats and Republicans and independents run against each other, with the top two vote getters, no matter their party, moving on to the general election. In a state where Democrats outnumber Republicans two to one, conventional wisdom assumed that the challenger I needed to worry about most was fellow Democrat Antonio Villaraigosa, the former mayor of Los Angeles. We expected Villaraigosa to employ the same geographic strategy as us, only in reverse. Because Southern Californians knew him well, his big push needed to occur in Northern California, persuading voters in the Bay Area, Silicon Valley, and Sacramento that he was a credible candidate for the entire state.

Instead, curiously, Antonio spent an inordinate amount of time trying to find a foothold in the San Joaquin Valley, where the lower number of voters and their overall conservative bent argued against such an effort. Good for Antonio for talking early to the farming community, but there was no metric that justified the amount of time he was spending there. We, on the other hand, knew that Northern California was ours to lose, so we stayed focused on making further inroads in Southern California while not ignoring the Central Valley either.

This was a campaign where everything went right from day one: the internal cohesion, the execution, the ideas, the strategy. Then, about midway through, my political team executed a cunning move that seemed counterintuitive but proved quite effective. It was a trick that the frustrated magician in me couldn't help but love. We began to focus the lion's share of our advertising on attacking not Villaraigosa but the strongest Republican candidate in the race, John Cox. Our calculation was simple: Cox had little chance to win California. An attorney and housing developer, Cox was a Chicagoan who had lost every race he ever ran in, including those for Cook County recorder, U.S. senator, and U.S. president. His chances in this race weren't boosted by the fact that he was an enthusiastic supporter of President Trump.

What happened next was fascinating to watch. The more our ads attacked Cox, the bigger his name recognition became and the more support he garnered from the Far Right. In essence, we were helping Cox build his MAGA base and gain enough votes to place in second. We were boosting Cox as our opponent for the general election, not Antonio. I don't think Antonio, a skilled and charismatic politician, knew what hit him at first. Here he was spending all his resources attacking me in his ads, and here we were going after Cox. The thinking was, we didn't want to run against Antonio, so we didn't focus on Antonio.

The minute I won the primary and Cox came in second, we had the general election matchup we wanted: a MAGA Republican and a Democrat running for governor in a state dramatically at odds with Trump. The president, in essence, was on the ballot, a millstone Cox had to bear. We did not let up on the gas; we never left a thing to chance. I ran as I always did: presuming I was twenty points behind. Heading into election night, however, we knew the outcome. The only drama was how big our margin of victory would be.

My memory of that evening, November 6, 2018, begins and ends with my father. The two of us were awaiting the results with Jen and the children and a dozen other family members and longtime friends in a room on the second floor of the old Los Angeles Stock Exchange. It was an opulent Art Deco building that fronted Spring Street and functioned as a four-level nightclub on most nights. Its renewal was part of a remarkable transformation of Downtown LA that had begun three decades earlier. On the ground level, where the bar and dance floor met, campaign workers and supporters were well into their inebriated celebration, though the polls had barely closed. On the second level, in our war room, the Irish contingent took care not to jinx anything. This meant sitting on the edge of our seats and watching the big-screen TV until the race was officially called.

Superstition aside, I had been in close races before, and this did not feel that way. Sealed off from the hoopla, moving between TV and computer, I kept checking on the numbers and then checking on my father. He was sitting in his wheelchair, a woolly scarf around his thin neck and a caretaker at his side. He was not well. In fact, he was dying from the complications of esophageal cancer. My sister and I couldn't believe he was hanging on. He had lost all five of his siblings, each to a different version of cancer. His youngest sister had died in her midforties; his youngest brother had died in his early fifties. At eighty-four years old, Dad counted himself the lucky one. He had wanted to stay at his beloved Dutch Flat, but his body had grown too weak from the treatments to live alone. Gordon and Ann offered that he stay at their house until he got stronger. She gutted a space on their top floor and put in a special bathtub and sitting area. From the window, he could see the Golden Gate Bridge.

Dad lived there for six months, riding the elevator between floors, and then decided he did not want to impose on the Gettys any further. By that time, Hilary and my brother-in-law Geoff had bought a house in Marin, and they moved Dad into their converted pool house. We lived only a few minutes away and visited often. Though the pain had stolen much of his verve, he worked to make a connection with his six grandkids: Hilary and Geoff's two daughters, Siena and Talitha, and our four younger ones. They called him Popa-pop, and he just lit up in their presence. He wasn't there to tell a story. He wasn't there to flash any wit and erudition. No lines from Yeats did he pass on to his grandchildren. He felt their love and gave it back. It was something pure. Watching the beauty of three generations mingling in the air of Marin, I could see my father's spirit whole. As the strength of his body slipped away, he worried more and more about the burden he was placing on Hilary and Geoff. He told us he missed San Francisco and his old pals, and that's when he made his final move to an apartment in Pacific Heights with its own view of the Golden Gate. As a tribute to my father's lifelong friendship with the Gettys, Gordon and Ann insisted on an arrangement where they would cover the costs of his rent and medical caretaker.

Dad's heart had grown so weak that his body filled up with fluid. There was no medical explanation for why he was still with us. The reason, we were all convinced, was this moment. He had summoned the last bit of life force to see his only son become the fortieth governor of the state he loved so much. As his body shut down, his mind found its sharpness again. He had taken himself off the pile of medications that had sustained him over the years—the SSRIs that helped him endure long stretches of depression, the heart medications that steadied his erratic beat. The fog in his brain cleared. The physical decline was stark, he couldn't really move, but his mind . . . It was as if he had come back to us.

Those who approached him in his wheelchair that election night did so gingerly. In their tender reaching out, you could sense their awareness that this would be their last encounter with him. "Uncle Bill," they called him. No reason to fret tonight, they assured him. Gavin's race is in the bag and so is the fight to take back the House. They knew he was a Dem's Dem. They knew how proud he was of me and my political career, because he had told them so time and again. It was a good thing he did, because he wasn't one to express such sentiments to me. "You need to get on more national news shows," he'd say. "I like this Chris Matthews. Why not his show?" "Dad," I'd reply, "I'm running for local office." "Local office?" he'd shoot back. "You're running for governor of the biggest state in the union."

His caretaker, Lisa, had grown close enough to him to notice that in my presence he always held something back. It wasn't that he was flinty or stinting, but when it came to his son there seemed an absolute commitment on his part to never cross the line into sentimentality, which seemed a curious trait for an Irish lover of verse. As I sat next to him in the war room, his caretaker began to goad him. "Come on, Mr. Newsom, say you love your son." As much as Lisa coaxed him, he would not utter those words. And yet I had not one ounce of doubt that he loved me dearly.

My father's oldest childhood buddy, John Francis Mallen, had a theory to explain Dad's reserve. He believed it was an instrument of his personality long before he became a judge. "He's a tough guy," Mallen had told me, and then he related a story. "We grew up a block apart. I met him when I was eight years old. I was sitting in an empty lot in our neighborhood, minding my own business, when he showed up with two older guys. They were sort of parading him around, showboating him. A scruffy kid who wasn't afraid to fight. The next thing I know we were in a fight, and he beat me up. A strange way to begin one of the strongest friendships two people could have for the rest of their lives."

*

The TV declared a NEWSOM VICTORY around nine o'clock that night. I hugged and kissed Jen and bent down and embraced my father, who had a twinkle in his eye and a Jackie Gleason smirk on his face. As they wheeled him to the right of the stage for my victory speech, Jen and I stood behind the lectern and waited for the children to join us. Montana and Hunter were smiling and Dutchie had a pacifier in his mouth. Brooklynn was stricken with stage fright and stayed backstage with our beloved nanny, Abby, who had assisted us since Montana was a baby and had three grown children of her own. I met eyes with my father as I launched into my speech, echoing themes that were as resonant with him as they were with me: In a nation gripped by rancor, lies, and hysteria, now is the time for facts and truth. Now is the time for decency. To those who question whether a melting pot of forty million people—different colors, different faiths, different narratives—can live and prosper together, California is your answer. We don't criminalize diversity, we celebrate diversity. We don't reject the most vulnerable, we protect them. We don't put profits ahead of clean air, clean water, or clean coastlines. We don't regulate a woman's body more than we regulate an assault rifle. We don't separate families, and we don't lock children in cages. And yet the California Dream is still too distant for too many Californians. Too many families priced out of housing, health care, and higher education. Too many workers feeling the ever-tightening squeeze of automation and wage stagnation. Too many children growing up poor and starting school from behind. Too many people living without a roof over their heads.

By the time I recited the last line and looked to the side of the stage to find my father, he was gone. Maybe his caretaker had wheeled him off to meet the boys, I thought, which wasn't really possible because we were in Los Angeles, not San Francisco, and those who hadn't yet died were broken down like Dad. The Lonely Hearts Club. My father, John Mallen, Jim Halligan, Lou Felder, Chris Malarkey, Lloyd Fabbri, and Art Groza, most of them forever pals from St. Ignatius High and the University of San Francisco. They knew every restaurant and bartender on the North Beach circuit, the old Italian quarter. A meal and a couple of bottles of wine at one place and a "final-final," a whiskey or scotch, at another place. They hung out with George Moscone, the thirty-seventh mayor of San Francisco, who was shot dead at city hall, and John Burton, the congressman and chair of the California Democratic Party, and Quentin Kopp, the state senator and judge. The restaurant owners were their best buddies, none more entertaining than Lorenzo Petroni, founder of North

Beach Restaurant, who'd stand on the corner of Columbus and Stockton during every Columbus Day celebration, dressed as Bacchus and pouring free cups of wine to passersby.

This was the world my father began to reveal to me when I was eight or nine, in part because he had such difficulty spending time with me alone. Rather than letting his silence prevail, he'd take me out with his friends to places where he was the life of the party, the one with the best stories. I celebrated my twenty-first birthday with the Lonely Hearts Club, a black-tie affair at Stars, the landmark California cuisine restaurant on Redwood Alley, opened by Jeremiah Tower, the former chef at the Balboa Cafe. When the conversation turned to Hilaire Belloc, one of the Big Four of Edwardian letters, my father rose to recite Belloc's poem about Lord Lundy, the lad so freely moved to tears that he could not sustain a political career.

> It happened to Lord Lundy then,
> As happens to so many men:
> Towards the age of twenty-six,
> They shoved him into politics.

Dad in his element connected me to things that my mother could not. Rivers and mountains. Fishing and backyard tents at Dutch Flat. Mountain lions and hawks. San Francisco and dinners out. I remembered one evening in the grand penthouse of the Fairmont Hotel when an audience gathered around my father and his brother, Patrick, and Daniel Patrick Moynihan, the senator visiting from New York, who believed that "to be Irish is to know that in the end, the world will break your heart." Beneath a domed ceiling painted in gold leaf, the three of them were holding court, seeing who could captivate the crowd most with his wit, blarney, and lore. It was like a death match, each one taking his turn, and then around it went again. The final showdown was a performance of the limerick, which was a specialty of Uncle Patrick, who had memorized pretty much every limerick known to man. Moynihan spoke with a slight stutter and drew out his vowels, making his speech sound even more patrician. And yet his limericks were perfect Irish. I wish I could remember the verses that rolled off each of their tongues, five lines, a single stanza of rhyme. In the end, neither Moynihan nor my father could compete with Uncle Patrick, whose ribaldry radiated pure joy.

When Dad received his diagnosis that the disease was terminal, I told myself not to shut off emotionally and enter the hole I had hidden in when Mom was dying. I began asking him questions I had never asked him before, and though he opened up some about one period of his life or another, my curiosity did not make him comfortable. He repeated his old stories, their beginnings, middles, and ends the same as they always were. I was not surprised that there would be no dying revelations, much less confessions, for Judge William Newsom. Over the years, I sought out his pals, longtime friends such as Joe Cotchett and John Burton and Bill Prezant. I only wish I could have had a chat with Art Groza, the incomparable ladies' man who had taught me how to hit a curveball at Redwood High. But Art had died a decade earlier just the way everyone imagined he would. After a day of sailing, he tied up his boat, *Connemara*, "Hound of the Sea," at the dock in Tiburon and headed to Sam's Anchor Cafe for a drink and a big fat steak. He was going to meet up with his newest lady but complained of indigestion on the way out. He died of a heart attack at the fire station in Tiburon, a block and a half from the restaurant.

Several of my dad's pals were more than pleased to chat with me, but they weren't quite sure what I was up to and out of their deep respect for him larded me with stories of the brilliant man of letters and linguistic genius who could bend the English language to his will. No one could outdo Bill as raconteur and bard, they said. Fluent in French and Italian, he was a master of allusion and superb with accents and impressions. It wasn't until I reached Bill Prezant, the lawyer who took over some of the duties of the Getty trust, that something less than hagiography was presented to me.

He told the story of a night in Mexico, where he and my father and Gordon had gone for a Getty trust meeting. They had dinner and wine, and then the others went to bed and it was just Prezant, Gordon, and Dad. "Gordon and Bill started this contest to see who could better recite lines of poetry from Shakespeare and Yeats. They were going back and forth, on and on, one perfect line after the other, and it was near midnight and we had polished off nine bottles of wine. The two of them kept going. I was in my early fifties then, and I thought to myself, *These guys are indefatigable.* Bill had his 'brown' drinks and his 'white' drinks. The brown drink might be a Manhattan or a Rob Roy or in later years tequila. The white drink would be vodka."

It was a drinking story that then turned into a larger story. "It was magical the way your father was able to bring out Gordon, who was deeply inside his head composing his music," Prezant recalled. "Bill was the medium who made for the conditions that allowed Gordon to engage with the real world. What a gift he gave him. But Bill had his own discomforts. He was in need of his own medium."

He went on to describe the "couples' trips" that he and my father and some of their pals took from time to time, each of them bringing along a partner or a date. "Bill had these women in his life who were just terrific. Smart and accomplished and pretty. As we'd check into the hotel, each of us would pay for our rooms. Bill paid for two rooms, one for himself and one for his lady friend. Jim Halligan, who was boisterous and fun, finally asked Bill, 'What's wrong with you? These are good-looking women you're with. And you're getting two bedrooms?' Bill would get sort of shy and try to brush it off. He later told me that he had a problem with intimacy that dated back to his honeymoon with Tessa. It was so much Catholic repression. Some of the guys who had known him since St. Ignatius said something had happened to him in childhood. There was a theory about a priest molesting him when he was young, but I rather doubted it, because Bill had been a feisty kid."

Had I been compelled to push back, I might have offered up the notion that my father operated with a different standard in mind. His upbringing and years on the bench acted as their own restraints. Call it an old-fashioned respect for women, but the values he carried might not have allowed him to display a girlfriend in such a manner. Was he more reserved than he was repressed? Prezant undoubtedly had more such stories and speculations to share, but I sensed that he, too, wasn't exactly comfortable delving deeper into my father's psyche, at least not as an exercise with his son. I wasn't sure where to go next, certainly not back to my father. And so I let it rest there.

*

The morning after election night, thinking I might take a walk, I opened the door of my hotel room and found the hulking presence of two California Highway Patrolmen, who were now part of my security detail. I did not fully grasp it at the time, but I had crossed a divide. As far as the outside world went, I would almost never find myself alone again. The chamber would become my world. This was partly a function of the job. Jerry Brown had his own chamber and so did Arnold Schwarzenegger. But my chamber would also become defined by a particular visceral reaction I triggered in a subset of Californians. It wasn't simply my politics that rubbed them the wrong way. It was my personage—my perceived privilege and how I spoke and walked through the world and even wore my hair—that would turn me into a different sort of lightning rod. I would not come to regard myself as a victim. I was a fifty-one-year-old man and this was part of the job. Buck up. But it was a complication I would need to grow accustomed to, even as I bridled against the chamber's confines and even as my security detail, reacting to the record number of death threats, sealed me off from the world. From home, I'd crawl into the black SUV and be transported to the governor's office for work. The same morning meeting with the inner circle, same faces, same blocks of time, never enough, to tackle a complex issue, and then I'd crawl into the SUV for the drive home. Only the angle of the sun would change. Monotony would replace serendipity. Choreography would replace freestyle. Freedom—it would be the greatest price I'd pay for the privilege of the job.

Late that post-election morning, we headed to the Redbird restaurant in Downtown LA for a brunch with staff that lasted five hours. It was like we were living in Europe, I told Jen. Fortunately, we had no official duties that day. My closest aides were wiped out; they'd barely slept the night before. Everyone was drained of adrenaline, relaxed. The sun felt like a tonic, and there was lots of easy talk across the table. We were having fun, and maybe it was the last carefree time we would have, because whether we understood it or not that first morning, and I don't think we did, the task in front of us would be all-consuming, a realm of such endless demands, complications, surprises, tragedies—man-made, nature-made—that you simply could not prepare for it. You had to wait until you were immersed in it to come up with a way to respond. The challenge was embedded in the geography of California itself, in the overreach of our settlers, who had taken a sprawling landmass—Death Valley near the bottom, redwood forest at the top, many different states of nature in between—and administered it as one state. When it came to governance, California was of a magnitude beyond that of New York, Florida, or Texas. No model we played with could capture the reality of what we were about to face. The perpetual state of challenge and uncertainty would become its own sameness.

That afternoon, we made our way back to the Bay Area with the kids and my father. The grind began bright and early the following morning. A mass shooting had taken place twelve hours earlier in Ventura County at a bar and grill called the Borderline. Thirteen people had been killed, including a sheriff's sergeant who was the first officer on the scene and the gunman, who, after carrying out the carnage, had killed himself. He was one of those mass shooters who left me questioning who we were and what manner of aberrant society we had constructed.

He was a twenty-eight-year-old Marine Corps gunner who had done a tour of duty in Afghanistan and returned home with a case of PTSD so debilitating that he could no longer eat spaghetti because of the flashbacks of eviscerated bodies it triggered. He had attended Cal State Northridge but lacked the development of a language—a healthy notion of self and community—to deal with the young students he encountered who did not regard his service as heroic. The grudge he nursed was fed by websites preaching hate and glorifying guns, mass killings, and suicide. And so when it came time to pick his target, he chose a bar in Thousand Oaks crowded with young people on a night promoted as "College Country Night." Beneath the Borderline's trademark giant cowboy, he opened fire with a .45-caliber Glock designed to feed endless bullets into its chamber through one of the seven large illegal magazines he carried. By the time the carnage was over, he had fired sixty-one rounds and dropped a smoke bomb to elude capture.

The details of the shooting were still emerging as Jen and I traveled to San Francisco's Tenderloin that morning to join volunteers helping feed the homeless at St. Anthony's Dining Room. I had chosen St. Anthony's for my first event as governor-elect because it was a place that connected me to my past, how the junction of mental illness, drug addiction, and homelessness was why I had even pursued a life in politics in the first place. To work the line at St. Anthony's was to understand profoundly that no matter what government had done to ease the hunger and suffering, it wasn't enough. Eight years after I left the mayor's office, San Francisco was now home to 7,500 homeless. Nearly 150,000 souls were left out in the cold of California—a quarter of our nation's homeless.

The tragedy in Thousand Oaks had forced me to pivot from the Franciscans feeding and clothing the homeless to another mass murder in America. I told the assembled reporters that in an era when heroism is sometimes exaggerated, the sheriff's sergeant, Ron Helus, had displayed true bravery by walking into a situation he could not control and diverting the attention of the gunman long enough that some families would be able to hold their loved ones tonight. If only politicians in the clutches of the gun lobby could show such guts. Instead, their response to each mass shooting was a tired variation on the old saw that guns didn't pull their own triggers, that mental illness was the true cause—this coming from politicians who gutted mental health budgets and laughed at madness as a legal defense for murder.

As the press conference wound down, a reporter asked a question about two wildfires that had broken out at opposite ends of the state. It was November, a month that once fell comfortably outside wildfire season but no longer. Hearing the word *Paradise* that first day, it didn't register in my head as a real town that had risen between two river canyons in the northern Sierra, an accidental suburb where forty thousand people, looking for a cheaper version of the California Dream, were living in the direct path of wildfire. Disaster was about to make its first grim showing on my watch, and I wasn't even the governor yet.

CHAPTER ELEVEN

''''

I was sitting in an SUV at Beale Air Force Base, outside Sacramento, on a Saturday in mid-November 2018, when Air Force One landed under a grim sky. Paradise had burned nine days earlier and had taken eighty-five lives, and President Trump was making one of his rare appearances out west. It wasn't enough that Governor Brown would be here to greet him. He wanted me, the governor-elect, to show up, too. I had never seen or spoken to Trump. His act on TV and Twitter was all I knew. The invitation from the White House had caught me and my staff by surprise. Surely he knew how we felt about him. He had made it abundantly clear how he felt about us.

I had called him a "small, scared bully" whose plan to shore up our borders included the absurd idea of getting rid of federal judges in immigration courts. At a rally in Nevada, he fired back. "How about this clown in California who's running for governor? He wants to open borders and then wants to give them health care, education, everything." I replied that *clown* was an interesting word choice for a president who locks up kids in cages like Pennywise, the demonic clown in Stephen King's *It*. He used the tragedy of our wildfires to lob more insults. In the aftermath of Paradise, he had tweeted, "There is no reason for these massive, deadly and costly forest fires in California except that forest management is so poor. Billions of dollars are given each year, with so many lives lost, all because of gross mismanagement of the forest. Remedy now or no more federal payments." His assessment was wrong, of course, right down to whose forestland was burning. Most of the acres of forests in California belonged to the federal government. The state owned scarcely 3 percent. Private parties owned the rest. I tweeted right back at him: "Lives have been lost. Entire towns have been burned to the ground. This is not a time of partisanship. This is a time for coordinating relief and response and lifting those in need."

There was no use pretending. California was at war with the Trump administration. No other state in the union had a more antagonistic relationship with the White House occupant. Our state attorney general, Xavier Becerra, would file an astonishing 122 lawsuits against the Trump administration to stop one assault or another on values California held dear. The president and his people were viscerally opposed to our commitment to protecting immigrants and our global leadership in the fight against climate change. The yo-yos he had chosen to "drain the swamp" at the Environmental Protection Agency and the Interior Department were gutting the very safeguards that kept the nation's water and air from ruin and our wildlands from being mined. The White House was doing the bidding of the oil, gas, and coal lobby with a level of shamelessness that not even the Bush administration had approached.

Trump was hell-bent on revoking California's unique author-ity, granted under the Clean Air Act, to regulate tailpipe emis-sions. This special power, first championed by Governor Ronald Reagan in 1967 and then codified into law under President Rich-ard Nixon, had been extended to California to fight the nation's worst smog. Fast-forward a half century later, and we were poised to use this authority to compel the big automakers to phase out the gasoline-powered engine by the year 2035. But our leverage resided in more than the act alone. Because one out of every four cars and trucks sold in the U.S. was purchased in California, General Motors, Ford, and Chrysler had little choice but to go along with our decision. This sway over the country's enormous vehicle market perturbed Trump and his oil company backers to no end. He was going to employ every strong-arm tactic in the book, including stuffing the Supreme Court with justices who cared little about climate change, to wrest away California's long-held authority and make sure that carbon emissions kept spewing into our skies.

Right up to the moment I left for Beale that morning, my transition team was arguing over whether I should even be seen with Trump. We had set up shop at an old office building in downtown Sacramento to translate my campaign promises—all two hundred of them—into a working agenda. I had selected as my chief of staff Ann O'Leary, a lawyer who had held top legis-lative and policy jobs for Hillary Clinton. Ann was whip-smart and had grown up in a small town in Maine with a mother who was a social worker and a father who was a tough Irish union boss. It was Jen who had introduced Ann to me; they had served together as board members for the main NPR radio station in the Bay Area. Our first conversation lasted three hours, and Ann never sighed once as I recited obscure policy papers and numbers from budgets past. She struck me as someone who would not allow the wonk in me to get lost in the weeds.

In the first days of transition, Ann had made a forceful case for why I needed to accompany Governor Brown and President Trump on their tour of Paradise. Her position had put her at odds with one of my most trusted political strategists, Ace Smith, who dismissed the visit as a MAGA production that would only serve Trump's warped agenda. Ace stuck to the view that California was on war footing with the Trump administration—and needed to maintain that posture. "The governor-elect doesn't need to be a prop for Trump," he said. Ann was more concerned about what lay ahead. "This won't be the last wildfire that's going to hit California," she said. "And this won't be the last disaster declaration we're going to need from the Trump administration."

Before I decided, I wanted to hear what Dan Newman and Jason Kinney had to say. Dan was a communications guru who had shaped messaging not only for me but also for Jerry Brown and Kamala Harris. Jason was the political strategist who had helped me conceive Prop 64 and written some of my speeches. Both of them saw Trump's visit as a chance for me to measure the president up close and maybe even make a personal connection, an opportunity I could not pass up. This is what my gut had been telling me to do, and I was glad to hear the majority of my team concur. At the same time, I wasn't about to pretend that Trump was coming to California to learn about the complexities of western wildfires. His mind could not be bothered by the fact that six of the ten largest wildfires in state history had occurred within the past decade, a distinct indication of climate change.

A few years earlier, visiting California as a candidate, Trump had unleashed his thunder on an adoring crowd of drought-mad farmers who believed that their lack of water wasn't the work of nature but the trick of socialists. There was no drought, he roared. The drought was a fake. The Dems were refusing to build more dams. The Dems were refusing to turn on the massive pumps that moved water from the Delta in the North to the vast orchards, vineyards, and fields in the state's middle. It did not matter to the candidate or his crowd that California rivers were rivers of snowmelt, and there had been no snow to speak of the previous two winters. By dam and canal, 80 percent of the river flow already had been appropriated by agriculture. The endangered run of Chinook salmon received little more than a trickle. But facts did not resound in reality TV land. What Trump could see was that he was standing on the fertile soil of California's heartland, and the rural crowd in MAGA hats believed that only he could bring them rain.

""

As I exited the SUV and walked in the direction of the president and his aides, I found myself wondering about the ways he might try to involve Governor Brown and me in whatever charade he was cooking up. The governor was dressed in loose-fitting black, appearing almost monklike. He seemed to be feeling his own ambivalence. He was clutching a book as if it might help him fend off whatever pummeling was about to come our way during a six-hour day with Donald Trump. We would be riding together in the Marine One helicopter to survey the ruins of Paradise and then hopping aboard a flight on Air Force One to

Southern California to see the Woolsey fire, which had erupted in Malibu.

"So how many times you been on Air Force One?" I asked Jerry.

"Never."

That was certainly true for me. But he'd been the thirty-fourth and thirty-ninth governor of California and at least three times a candidate for president. "Give me a break," I said.

"First time."

Years ago, Jerry did fly on Trump's private plane. Trump's vainglory back then extended to works of art he displayed in the aircraft's cabin, including a painting of two young sisters wearing colorful hats on a terrace in France. This was a Renoir masterpiece worth $10 million, Trump told his guests. That it ended up being a master fake might have been one of our early clues.

Chief of staff General John Kelly greeted us warmly, and then we got a nod from Trump's son-in-law, Jared Kushner, and finally handshakes with Trump himself. He was wearing khaki pants, a white button-down shirt, and a slick black windbreaker zipped two thirds of the way up. He had on his USA ball cap, broad crowned so it wasn't possible to see the swirl of contrivance that was his hair. I knew a thing or two about creative hairdos and was disappointed not to have the chance to study his. Maybe it was the windbreaker, but Trump looked more fit, less ponderous, in person.

He did not waste a moment trying to capture me and Jerry in his orbit. It was first names only, an air of casualness, as we hopped aboard Marine One. He wanted us to know that there were different versions of the helicopter, and this wasn't the fanciest one. This was the traveling version, slightly more cumbersome than the newer model. Trump and Jerry took the first two seats. I sat parallel to them with Kushner to my left. Kelly was seated to my right, just behind Trump. It was a tight fit, but thankfully the ride to the Chico Municipal Airport wouldn't be a long one.

"Hey, Gavin," Trump said, motioning out the window to the Osprey helicopters that would be flying around us as security. "We could have taken the Osprey. The Osprey is a lot faster, but it's got too many moving parts. Right, General Kelly? Too many moving parts."

"That's right, sir."

Trump sort of slapped my knee with his hand, one of the chummy gestures he would use throughout the day to establish an intimacy, a confidentiality among men. This was his shtick: smiling, engaged, generous, as if to say that we, too, could be part of his club if we played along. It was an initiation I found fascinating, and not a little bit intoxicating, and it paid no mind to the Twitter tantrum he had thrown just days before. This was a different Trump, a thoroughly accommodating Trump. He had come ready to engage. Jerry, on the other hand, with book in lap, was pecking at his cell phone. *Who's he calling?* I thought. *Man, he's sure intent on being standoffish.*

"Hey, Anne, can you hear me?" Jerry asked. The number he had dialed was home. Anne was Anne Gust, his wife.

"Yeah, I hear you, Jerry."

"Mr. President, can you talk to my wife, Anne?" Jerry handed the phone to Trump, who began talking to Anne as if he'd known her for years.

"Hey, Anne, I'm here with your husband. Hey, we're all friends. He was on my plane back in the day. Right, Jerry? I'm here to deal with some tough stuff. Tough stuff. These fires. Big fires. We're going to work through this. Jerry is doing great. How are you doing? That's great. We're going to work this stuff out."

He said goodbye to California's First Lady and handed the phone back to the governor. I considered myself a student of the gruff Jerry Brown, the iconoclastic Jerry Brown, the detached Jerry Brown. But this Jerry Brown seemed thoroughly taken by the moment. In some second-class model of Marine One, above the wide-open dirt of the Central Valley, a lesson in the seduction of ultimate power was being conducted.

Trump then turned to me with a sly grin. "Kimberly," he murmured. "Kimberly." That would be my ex-wife, who was now ensconced in the world of Trump as the girlfriend of Donald Trump Jr.

"Okay," I said, smiling. "I was wondering if that would come up in the first few minutes or in the first few hours."

He laughed and I laughed, and nothing more about Kimberly had to be said. "I knew you and I would be good," he said. "You and I, we're going to be okay. This is going to be good."

To juice him up, I began praising his building, 555 California Street, in downtown San Francisco, the city's fourth-tallest skyscraper, which was once the headquarters of Bank of America. It was now owned by Steven Roth and his Vornado Realty Trust, with a minority interest held by the Trump Organization. Roth was one of Trump's top economic advisers.

"Mr. President, your building in San Francisco must be doing really well," I said.

"One of the best buildings in the city, right?" he gushed.

"No doubt," I said.

Kushner, who'd been nearly silent, began listing its attributes.

"Probably the best building in the city," Trump said.

"It's a fine building," I nodded.

"Magnificent," he said. "What a spectacular place."

I mentioned being in the wine and hotel business myself, and that's when Trump shifted to autopilot, talking about his properties across the country and around the globe. As the president recounted the details of one project, Kushner suddenly became animated. And then—I don't recall if there was even a transition—a glowing Trump began to talk in almost reverential tones about NFL quarterback Tom Brady.

"Gavin, you know Tom Brady?"

"Of course, Mr. President."

"Tom Brady is a friend of mine. He's one of the fastest guys on the football field. You wouldn't think that, right?"

Tom Brady was a lot of wonderful things on the gridiron, but fast he was not. In fact, his forty-yard dash time was one of the slowest for a quarterback in the NFL, and that was when he was fresh out of college. But before I could reply, the president cut me off.

"He just dances." Trump began to move his feet in frenetic fashion, trying to mimic Brady's movements to elude a pass rush. "He dances, dances. Nothing like him. He'd be a scratch golfer, too, if he played a little more."

And then his riff took a strange turn. He recounted that when Brady was single, the two of them were at a function and Brady expressed an interest in dating his daughter Ivanka. The quarterback asked for her number, and Trump gave it to him. Brady called Ivanka and left a message, but she never called him back. Soon after, Brady related the snub to Trump, who then called his daughter, wondering what was up.

"I said, 'Jesus, you know, Tom Brady. What the hell is going on? Why aren't you calling this guy back?' And she tells me, 'Oh, I'm in love.' 'What do you mean you're in love?' And that's when she mentions this guy," Trump said, pointing to his son-in-law. "This guy right here. This Kushner guy. I said to Ivanka, 'Not the guy whose father just got out of prison?'"

It was dead air for a moment. Kushner wore a face that somehow retained its impassivity. He finally muttered, with the slyest grin, "Yes, sir. I know I wasn't your first choice."

And then Trump turned to me and said, "Not even close, right, Gavin? Tom Brady. Tom Brady."

I think I might have winced or stifled a laugh. In front of the governor and future governor of California, Trump was making his son-in-law feel two feet tall. And Kushner just let him do it. General Kelly, who after sixteen months as chief of staff must have been accustomed to his boss's cruelty, averted his gaze. I could only imagine that he was feeling embarrassed that Trump didn't feel embarrassed by his pure joy in humiliating another person. Here we were fifteen minutes into our first meeting, and he did not bat an eye, showing me how callous he could be, and at the expense of a family member. I asked myself days later: What kind of ego could do that? And what kind of ego could be on the receiving end of such treatment and respond with little more than silence? Any awareness of what he had just done completely passed over Trump; he was already dazzling us with another unbelievable tale, this one about a government plane, the F-something, that was invisible. You could be flying next to it and not see it. "The greatest plane you've ever seen," he said.

We landed at the Chico Municipal Airport and up marched a crisp team of white-gloved marines to open the door of the helicopter and let out the president of the United States. "See that? See that?" Trump said, soaking in the spectacle. "Can you believe it? Stephen Schwarzman doesn't get this treatment." Stephen A. Schwarzman, of Yale and Harvard, member of Skull and Bones, founder of the Davenport Ballet Society, CEO of the Blackstone Group, could only dream of such service.

I was about to exit the helicopter when General Kelly, the last to leave, leaned over in my direction.

"Just so you know, none of that was true," he said.

He might have been referring to any numbers of things, but it was Trump's mischaracterization of the F-something that had perturbed the general. The commander in chief had inflated a unique feature of the plane, its 360-degree cockpit, and turned it into a flying phantom. "Those planes aren't invisible," Kelly said.

I chuckled. "No worries. It's all good."

The general meant no disloyalty, it seemed to me. He was simply trying to clean up one more adulteration of the truth his boss had left behind. If such cleanups were a full-time job, they wouldn't be for very long. General Kelly would leave the White House the very next month.

""""

After a meet and greet with Butte County officials, Governor Brown and I followed the president into the cramped back of his SUV, and off we went past a line of citizens holding up protest signs. IT'S CLIMATE CHANGE! MORON, one read. Butte County was Trump country, that was certain, but the city of Chico was a college town sporting a subversive bent. "These are amazing people, beautiful people," the president said. "Look at that. They love me. They love me here." He was looking right at the people, right at their GO TO HELL signs, but the shtick wouldn't die. The motorcade drove from the valley floor to the ridgetop, where the devastation of Paradise, the loss of nineteen thousand structures and eighty-five lives, the deadliest fire in California history, now came into unremitting view. Here was a place that dated back 160 years, if you passed over indigenous times, a place wiped off the map by one of the manifestations of climate change, a reality that the Trump administration was doing all it could to deny.

Now, amid the smoke and ash, the significance of what had been erased appeared to impact even Trump. He kept telling Paradise mayor Jody Jones how unbelievable the scene appeared to him. It was as if a bomb had blown up the place, he said. He called her constituents "my people," even as he couldn't get the name of Paradise straight. Throughout the day, he called it Pleasure, putting a pained look on the face of Governor Brown. I had to avert my eyes. "We have to do management and maintenance," the president told the huddle of press. "I think everybody's seen the light. I don't think we'll have this again to this extent. Hopefully, this is going to be the last of these because this was a really, really, bad one."

Then, as was his wont, he careened to a place that few of us expected: Finland. It was a "forest nation" that knew how to keep wildfires from igniting, he said. "They spend a lot of time raking and cleaning and doing things, and they don't have any problem. I know everybody's looking at that." In the wake of his visit, as comic relief, MAKE AMERICA RAKE AGAIN would become a banner for the beleaguered progressives in the state's far northern rural counties. Here in the moment, the chief of CAL FIRE, like the rest of us, could only grin and bear it. Trump thanked the firefighters for "fighting like hell." He thanked the law enforcement officers and elected officials in attendance, among them House Minority Leader Kevin McCarthy ("my Kevin") and Representative Doug LaMalfa, a Republican who represented this part of Northern California. LaMalfa didn't believe in climate change and McCarthy wasn't far behind.

Marine One ferried us back to Beale Air Force Base, where Air Force One was waiting to fly us to Southern California and the Woolsey fire. As governor-elect, I made sure to follow protocol and trail behind the president and governor. I was no different from anyone else in Trump's presence, which is to say I wasn't immune to the power of his office or his eloquence for bullshit and flattery. For him, it was all about physicality, the connection, how things look and feel, the stage, the set. He was sizing me up. The aesthetic was what mattered most. He climbed up the steps of the Boeing 747 with a display of vigor. My climb was more drawn out. I read the words I could almost touch, *United States of America*, emblazoned on the side, along with the seal of the president and the U.S. flag at the tail.

Inside the main cabin, I was greeted a bit too warmly by Kevin McCarthy, who represented the MAGA stronghold of Kern County, at the southern end of the San Joaquin Valley. McCarthy was so comfortable inside Air Force One that he assumed the role of second host. He knew exactly how to play Trump. Accentuate the ass-kissing. And Trump knew exactly how to play McCarthy. Return the ass-kissing. As we prepared for takeoff, Trump pointed to a flat-screen TV. It was time to turn on Fox News to see how our visit to Paradise was playing. Trump knew the timing, the cadence of Murdoch's cable news, better than anyone. He was riveted. "Turn it up," he said. "Hey, Gavin, look, look. We're looking good there." He critiqued the angle and the choreographed shot, the images still fresh in my head: the carcasses of trees, the air hung with smoke, the twisted, melted metal of what was once a mobile home park. He soaked in the coverage and couldn't have been more pleased by it.

When the plane reached its altitude, we posed for group photos. Jerry then wanted one of himself, sitting in the conference room at the head of the table, in the president's chair. It was funny seeing the governor let go and embrace the incongruity of it all. Trump whipped out his black Sharpie, designed by the company to his specifications, including a sharper tip. As a keepsake, he signed his name on a piece of paper and handed it to me, along with the Sharpie. "This is for your kids," he said.

He introduced me to his press secretary and a nice gentleman who typed out his tweets. Presumably, it was Trump who whispered all those CAPITAL!!! words into his ear. The president's graciousness extended to his staff and Secret Service agents. He seemed to genuinely interact with each of them. And then, pleasantries dispensed with, he grabbed me by the shoulder and whisked me off. "I want to show you something," he said. The royal tour of Air Force One, just the two of us, had commenced.

He became a giddy child. As we moved from one section of the cabin to another, he was literally petting the plane. "Gavin, take a look. A hundred and seventy-one million dollars. That's how much it costs to remodel this every two years." Every bell and whistle seemed to give him great personal satisfaction: the aircraft's ability to refuel in midair and travel unlimited miles; its onboard electronics hardened to protect against electromagnetic pulses; its communication system with the highest grade of security that could function as a mobile command center in event of an attack on the U.S. He guided me into the cockpit. "These are the greatest, the finest, pilots," he said. "Thank you, sir," they replied in unison.

He ushered me into his office and showed me his perfectly polished desk. "Last week there was a nick on it," he said. "This week, the nick is gone." I naturally assumed, as the former manager of nicks for Walter Shorenstein, that a crew member had buffed it out or perhaps replaced the desk with a new one. But no, the president explained, it was a magic trick. There were actually two identical Air Force Ones. In the first months of his presidency, this luxury had caught him by surprise. Two of the world's most spectacular jetliners for one man? Can you believe it?

I was about to turn left and head back into the main cabin, but he had one more room to show me. "Come into my bedroom," he said. A White House photographer or some staffer was trailing us. The press had dubbed these quarters the "Imperial Bubble." One account told of Trump's inability to fall asleep on overseas trips and how he would spend all night consuming cable news, arguing with the tube, awakening his staff to praise or complain about how certain channels were covering him.

"You need to go to the restroom?" he asked me. The presidential lavatory was just off to the side.

"No, I'm good."

"You sure you don't need to go to the restroom?" It was a toilet with plumbing unlike any other.

"Thanks, I'm all good."

This was the chamber where he and Melania, on trips to distant places, retired. A room with two beds, I could see, separated by more than a few feet. He did not wait for me to mentally fill in the blank.

"Melania wanted one bed," he said. "But two beds, you know, two beds next to each other." He seemed to be winking.

We posed for a last photo, but if the tour was done, that didn't mean the fun had to end. "Let's call somebody," he said. "Who do you want to call?" This was the second time he had asked me that question. Before the tour, he suggested we call President Xi of China and have a friendly chat. Even though China was fifteen hours ahead, he asked his operator to put through the call. I knew it was a gag, but I played along. This time, though, he wasn't gagging. "Go ahead, Gavin, make a call." I paused for a second, pondering who in my world would want to hear from Donald Trump. Surely not Jen, who was directing a new documentary called *The Great American Lie* that examined how "extreme masculine ideals of money, power, and control had glorified individualism, institutionalized inequality, and undermined the ability of most Americans to realize the American Dream."

"How about your wife?" he said. "Let's call your wife. Just lift that up and ask them to make a call for you."

"Okay," I said, but I was praying Jen wouldn't answer because there was no telling what she would have told him.

"Sir, we're so sorry, the person on the other end didn't pick up," the staffer informed me. Thank goodness, I thought.

It was time for sandwiches and salad in the main room with Jerry and Kushner and Kevin McCarthy. Straining to show his progressive side, Kushner wanted us to know that he favored changing the law so that low-level drug offenses no longer landed people (i.e., Black and brown people) behind bars. McCarthy, for his part, wanted to make sure I grabbed all the packets of M&M's I desired.

We landed at Point Mugu, the naval air station along the Pacific Coast near Oxnard. On the tarmac, I must have been lagging too far behind the lead group, because Trump was asking, "Where's Gavin? Get him back up here." Once I caught up, he insisted that Jerry and I ride with him. We piled into a limo even more locked down than the first one. The driver and a fancy guy carrying a long gun sat up front; the president and Jerry took the middle seats, and McCarthy and I sat in back.

The whole way to Malibu, Trump didn't stop talking. The ease with which he spilled details extended to any number of topics, including our enemies and allies. I lost count of how many state secrets, or what should have been state secrets, he divulged. He was tossing them off almost as goodies to impress his guests. His unwillingness to practice the discretion expected of a president must have presented our nation's security agencies with quite a challenge, not to mention the gold mine it provided for countries spying on us.

"Jerry, you and Gavin, you're politicians. You can't say the stuff I can say. My base, my base, they love me. I can say whatever I want. I'm giving them what they love."

He told us that California was "so lucky" to have him as president, that he was taking care of our multitude of problems. "You guys need me," he said. To his credit, Jerry kept trying to engage Trump on the complexities of wildfire and the realities of climate change, but he was hopelessly incurious.

"Hey, Jerry, who was it that you were dating back in the day?" the president asked.

Jerry knew that he was referring to Linda Ronstadt even before Trump added, "You know, the one who hasn't aged so well." But Jerry wasn't going to dignify any of Trump's denigrations concerning women, especially about a singer whose talents were legendary and whose agile mind had captivated his own mind and who remained bright and beautiful even as she struggled with Parkinson's disease. In fact, Jerry was now going to mess with Trump.

"You mean Natalie Wood," Jerry said.

"Natalie Wood?" McCarthy and I both repeated. "You dated Natalie Wood?"

Trump chewed on this tidbit—Governor Moonbeam gallivanting with the beautiful star of *West Side Story*—for a second. "So, who killed her?" Trump asked Jerry, referring to Wood's mysterious 1981 drowning while yachting off Catalina Island with her husband, actor Robert Wagner, and actor Christopher Walken.

Jerry fed Trump an answer, but the answer wasn't important. What stuck was the realization that this was the sort of drivel that engaged the curiosity of the president as we drove to a blaze that would burn nearly 100,000 acres, destroy 1,643 structures, force the evacuation of 300,000 residents, and kill 3 people. The future was burning, and this was the type of thing he idled himself with.

In my later attempts to decipher Trump, so that I could be the best advocate for California I could possibly be, I would return again and again to this first peek. His act on TV was easy to dismiss as pure carnival. But this flick-you-on-the-knee Trump was not so simple to pin down. It seemed to me that he wanted to connect and be loved, but it was illusory. He couldn't connect in a genuine way. I felt sympathy for him because, despite his attachment to cruelty, there was a surface kindness he tried to express and maybe even a longing for something more. And yet he had a deep, almost congenital capacity for feeling aggrieved.

When a line from my inaugural speech later landed on national cable news—"We will offer an alternative to the corruption and incompetence in the White House"—a wounded Trump called me on the phone.

"Gavin, hey, you know, I had to explain to Melania because she asked me, 'Did you hear this?' I thought that was a little tough. I thought you and I had something."

He sounded truly hurt. "I know," I said. "It was a tough line."

"I get it," he said. "It's politics."

I was about to explain myself more, and perhaps soften the blow, but he interrupted me.

"Politics. That's what I told Melania," he said. His tone then switched as he talked about the visuals of my inaugural speech: Jen and the children joining me onstage; Brooklynn overcoming her fright of the crowd, Dutchie climbing into my arms with his pacifier and blanket and falling asleep as I delivered my lines. "Hey, Gavin, hope I don't get in trouble for saying this, but that wife of yours is pretty hot. And the kids. Beautiful family."

This was, from his vantage, the essence of my inaugural. The telegenic, the aesthetic, the image. How was I to reply? "I appreciate it, Mr. President," I said.

"Gavin, I think we're good."

"We're good, Mr. President."

"We're good," he said, hanging up the phone.

It had not been my intention, upon accepting the invitation to share a day with the president, to explore the mind of Donald Trump. That said, our first curious encounter became a prelude to a rather extraordinary relationship between the leader of red-state America and the leader of the biggest and bluest state in the union. What we had in common wasn't much. He was East

Coast; I was West Coast. He grew up with wealth. I grew up around wealth, though it was a different sort from Trump's grift. What we did share—my past, his present—was a link to Kimberly. I did not realize it back then, but my fate as governor, and the well-being of our state, would rest on my ability to make Trump, ever more mercurial, care about me and California, even as he was sowing the seeds that would threaten to upend my governorship in a way I would not see coming.

////

My father, bedridden, was directing Hilary on which Christmas gifts he wanted to buy his six grandkids from the World Wildlife Fund. He'd been an ardent supporter of the fund for years, in part because of its efforts to save the grizzly bear, which was still fighting for survival across the West even though the last known California grizzly, *Ursus arctos californicus*, had been shot to death in Fresno County in 1922. He chose a different stuffed bear, T-shirt, or canteen for each child and then fell back asleep.

He was bleeding internally now, and Hilary and I understood, after his sixth or seventh trip to the emergency room, that there was nothing more the doctors could do. Hilary turned the living room into a bedroom so he could see the Pacific in the distance. For five days he went in and out of consciousness. Gone was his fluency in French and Italian. Gone were his wit and mastery of verse and allusion. Gone were his uncanny impersonations, though we could hear him muttering something to "Tessa, Tessa." Had we thought of it, we would have filled the room with Chesterton and Belloc, Yeats and Heaney, Shakespeare and Verdi, Twain and

Stegner. But we let his silence be the last word. We were all there beside him, family, friends, Gordon and Ann. He was looking out to the Golden Gate Bridge when he closed his eyes. There was now in the window a hawk perched on the cornice.

It was strange in that moment of abandonment what came back to me: an afternoon when I was nine or ten and he introduced me to the world of Chinatown. I had conned my way out of Madame Bergez's reading class and into the nurse's office by faking a headache. I bit down on the thermometer to make it register higher because that's what I had done countless times before. The thermometer never broke ninety-nine degrees, but it didn't seem to matter. Without fail, sick or not, the nurse set me free. Mom was fed up with my malingering—I had more absences than any other kid at school—and she refused to pick me up. My father, about to be appointed to the state court of appeals in downtown San Francisco, did not make me present a case. He pulled up to the school sidewalk in his car with two of his friends, and off we went.

He was incapable of saying no to me, though his *yes*es were sometimes less than reliable. He once said if I never took up the habit of smoking, he would buy me a new car when I turned sixteen. He even wrote down the promise on a business card I kept. I never smoked, but he never came through with the new car, though he did make good on a lease for a used one that I drove to college. My mother thought his lack of execution was a lack of money, but how could that be? He was a working judge who always made good on his gifts to others, handing out first editions of *Huckleberry Finn* to my cousins and the Getty boys and girls on their birthdays, attaching lovely notes that they cherished for life. "Uncle Bill" was a role that came naturally to him. Dad?

Not so easy. Not unless he was gifting me some exotic piece of the world, which Chinatown at the lunch hour certainly qualified as being. All the better if his friends came along.

Before I knew it, the colors, sounds, and smells of San Francisco had changed again. We were in the heart of Chinatown. Festooned above, from one side of the street to the other, were thousands of red and gold banners and red lanterns hanging on strings. They were there to commemorate the dead, he explained. The alleys were narrow and the buildings pagodalike. The general idea was to follow your nose. There was a hole-in-the-wall where duck after duck, plucked and seasoned, sizzled in roasters, and the little bakery where the sugary scent of fresh cookies drifted out the door, and the bustling market on Stockton Street that knocked you over with the odor of things still clucking and croaking.

On its face, this was a mission for food. But what I didn't grasp back then was that it was also his mission to give me a slice of San Francisco, our city, and the story of California. There at the intersection of Bush and Grant, we had crossed the great divide between what I knew and what I was about to discover. He wanted me to see past the pagoda facades to the people themselves, to the humble entrepreneurs and immigrant parents building better lives for their kids—to the journey that had brought them from East to West to enrich our city and state. After our two-hour lunch we might have called it a day, but this was Friday with the boys. I was given a tour of the Chinese Culture Center and learned that after the 1906 earthquake, some of the city fathers regarded the widespread destruction as a perfect excuse to clean up Chinatown and remove "the Celestials" to a ghetto on the outskirts of town. Other city fathers, not exactly civic-minded but inspired by the potential for tourism, brought in white architects to redesign Chinatown into a kind of movie set "Chinatown." This explained all the pagodas.

Near evening, we piled back in Dad's car and headed in the direction of North Beach for drinks and dinner at the Washington Square Bar and Grill—"Washbag," he and his buddies called it. Or maybe we ended up, for my sake, at the heartier confines of Romano's on Lombard Street in the Marina District. Romano's was perfect. It served pasta and all the bread you could eat, and the Golden Gate Transit line was just a half block away. Dad deposited me, belly stuffed, on the 8:00 p.m. bus back to Marin, back to my life with Hilary and Mom and what would become of our California Dream. Dad was headed to La Rocca's for a final-final with his friends.

Epilogue

####

In the fall of 2020, not long after Jen turned forty-six, she approached me one evening with some stunning news. "I'm pregnant again, Gavin." I stopped in my tracks. I didn't know what to say. The times before, four times before, those words had brought a jolt of joy. This time, my mind started to race. The complications of carrying a baby to full term posed a significant risk to Jen and the child. "Okay, so where does that leave us?" I asked. She didn't have an answer. Our lives, she knew, were already overwhelmed with the demands of four children, to say nothing of the demands of forty million citizens, hundreds of whom were filled with such venom that they camped outside our house in daily protests and shouted insults at our kids. At night, in bed, confused and scared, she awakened me. "Gavin, as much as I believe in choice, I just don't think I can terminate this pregnancy. Abortion isn't an option for me." I told her that I was confused and scared, too, and wanted her to consider our lives as they were, the noise inside, the noise outside, the already impossible juggle of state and family, and the strains that were pulling at our marriage. Into this tumult could we bring a fifth child?

The doctor told her it was likely the fetus would not be viable, but Jen had been a supreme athlete and believed in the resiliency of her body. She waited for a heartbeat to appear. She heard it during the first ultrasound and again during the second ultrasound; she told herself that if a fifth child was to be, she would consider it a blessing. Then, at nine weeks, the heartbeat was gone. The machine could not detect it. Had the fetus died? Had the fetus never really been alive? All those abstractions over the question "When does life begin?" were beside the point. To remove it from her body, she would need the intervention of medicine. The doctor prescribed pills to empty her uterus, and she took a single dose. She began cramping and convulsing and burning with fever, symptoms that pointed to a rare side effect. The pain was so severe she was writhing in bed. It was New Year's Eve, dark of night, when our security detail rushed us to UC Davis Medical Center. Would I lose my wife? Would my children lose their mother? These are the questions you ask yourself at such an hour.

The surgery that Jen never wanted in her life became a matter of medical necessity. Thank goodness this was California, that there was a doctor, a female, who was an expert in such a procedure and had at her disposal the most modern of tools. Jen received the health care that would very soon be denied to countless women in red-state America because of the decision of Supreme Court Justices Thomas, Alito, Kavanaugh, Gorsuch, and Barrett. In one of the most medically advanced countries in the world, we had gone backward a half century in time. The next day, I brought Jen home to Fair Oaks, to the cacophony of Trump's little haters.

""

The winter of 2023 has come, reminding me of an old California admonition: When drought times end, they are never broken by mere rain. They're busted open by flood. Watch out for the boulder on the mountain and the mud sliding down the hill. Watch out for the sinkhole beneath the asphalt road and the gully you may have forgotten was a creek. When drought turns to deluge, it can make for an unkind death. Nine "atmospheric rivers" have rolled off the Pacific in the past four weeks. Twenty-five trillion gallons of rain make for the first billion-dollar disaster of the new year. Twenty-two Californians died in the waters, including five-year-old Kyle Doan, on his way to kindergarten with his mom, swept away by the surge of a creek that feeds the Salinas River. Month after month, they have yet to find the boy's body. This was no aberration. This was California returning to form.

I pull a book off the shelf and read about the great flood of 1862, a biblical deluge that inundated much of California, swallowing cities and farms, drowning people and pets and cattle whose bloated forms bobbed over the vast landscape upside down, four legs pointing straight into the sky. A supplication for those gold-crazed fools who dared to tame such a place, perhaps. Leland Stanford, the railroad magnate turned governor, had to row his boat from the second story of his flooded mansion in downtown Sacramento to the state capitol for his swearing-in. The speech he delivered spoke not a word of the people and their epic fight to hold back the waters. Rather, he warned those assembled that their future generations must never carry the smirch of Asian immigrants. He did not mention that these were the very people who were about to build his railroad. "There can be no doubt but that the presence among us of a degraded and distinct people must exercise a deleterious influence upon the superior race," he said. "It will afford me great pleasure to concur with the legislature in any constitutional action having for its object the repression of the immigration of the Asiatic races."

Reading history helps me make sense of Trump, if nothing else. As extraordinary as pundits on both sides of cable news try to present him, he's cut out of an old archetype. His compendium of lies emanates from a deeply American place, belonging to the tradition of folklore as much as it belongs to the manual of psychological disorders. The syntax he attaches to them is often quite funny. More times than not he lies to convey optimism. This gives his lies the appearance of braggadocio, a minor sin. He lies so much that the lies seem like no big deal after a while. He lies so much that his lies erase his lies. His base of people, sensing some kind of genius in the habit, attaches a higher purpose to his lies. He is lying to challenge authority. He is lying to get around the bureaucracy. He is lying to speak truth to the liars in the swamp. He is lying to get reelected and stay out of jail and not pay the injustice of settlements and fines. Those who love him and those who despise him struggle to find the words to capture him, and this is when they reach for legend and turn him into a homespun euphemism. He is an American manifestation, the peddler at our door. The more he stretches the truth in the name of the sale, the more desperate he becomes. Once inside our living room, however, he is far more malignant than any of that.

There would be no Trump if there were no Murdoch. Consider me an expert on the matter, having endured decades of Fox News portraying San Francisco and Los Angeles as totems of civilization's decline, modern-day Sodom and Gomorrah. California's moral decay has become practically a fetish of Murdoch, a myth as zealously pursued as the recurring fantasy of Christmas under mass assault. If a media empire can have an operating principle other than making billions, the creed at Fox is morally destitute: sell fear and panic when the subjects are big-city crime and poor minorities infesting the suburbs and Mexicans invading the country, but sell utter calm and indifference when the threat is greenhouse gases destroying our planet.

If I find myself in the mood for California bashing, I much prefer the words of Bernard DeVoto, one of the West's most eminent historians, who wrote that "California was almost entirely a dream, a dream vague but deep in the minds of a westering people." They came with grit and ingenuity, a spirit to invent and reinvent. As to the question that has long confounded Americans residing east of the Rockies, there is no characteristic Californian. There is no one type truer than the other type. DeVoto, a child of the Utah frontier who died a long way from home, in New York City, spent much of his writing life trying to explain the paradox of Californians to East Coast readers of *Harper's Magazine*. In a 1946 essay titled "The Anxious West," he wrote: "They [Californians] are the only Americans today who look forward toward the future with hope and confidence, and they ignore the elements in themselves which brings both into question. They are children of paradox and begetters of paradox."

The Newsoms, hailing from the ridges and hills and rough pastures of County Cork, threw their own paradoxes—we were bards and priests, drunks and nobles—into the mix. There, in the mud of Yerba Buena, the land of the good herb, the Newsoms and Brennans joined hands with the Addises and Menzies. My father, for one, wasn't sure what to make of this legacy. At some point after leaving us, he headed to the hills like the 49ers themselves. He came upon a town called Dutch Flat, dotted with Victorian homes and surrounded by pine mountains, that had been founded in 1851 by two brothers from Germany, Joseph and Charles Dornbach. *Dutch* was shorthand for *Deutschland.* Here had arisen one of the great chapters in hydraulic mining, where high-pressure hoses blasted away mountainsides to unearth the gold that lay beneath. In its heyday, Dutch Flat boasted a population of six thousand, half of them immigrants from China, nearly as many Chinese as in San Francisco itself. They did the work of the mines and the work of the railroad, and when the gold was all grabbed and timber became the new extraction, Old Chinatown burned down like so many other Chinatowns in California. The Chinese were sent to the open dirt beside the railroad tracks. The Dutch Flat Hotel, the stone jail, the Odd Fellows Hall, and the Masons building were still standing when my father arrived. The old opera house that featured evenings with Mark Twain, had, sadly, burned down as well. Being a man with a regard for history, my father bought the original house of the Dornbach brothers and moved in with his thousands of books. This is where he found his peace, cherished his solace, recalled the best times, grieved the losses, read Yeats and Belloc, and brought my mother's body to bury in the old cemetery. This is where we buried him, too.

Two summers after his death, we drove up to Dutch Flat to celebrate Hunter's ninth birthday. Everyone was outside and I decided to get a closer look at things inside. I hadn't stepped foot into my father's bedroom since the funeral. When I opened the door, I could see that everything was in its place as he had left it. I could hear through the window the kids playing outside and knew I had only a few minutes before they'd start to wonder where I had gone off to. I walked over to the bookshelf and started rummaging through his collection. These weren't the first editions, the classics bound in leather, that filled the living room, but they were good paperbacks and hardcovers written by writers he cared to read. There was one book, however, that didn't belong with the rest. It was sitting there crooked, bound in beautiful red leather, and it had no title, no author's name. There were three words of Latin embossed on the cloth: I Comici Oci. What did they mean?

I opened the book and there was my father's handwriting, page after page. Each section was dated, and the dates went back to the 1970s and connected to people and places all over the map. Rivers and mountains in California, ruins in Rome, town squares in England. I had my father's diary in my hands—the book I had always suspected he had written—filled with thoughts and feelings he had never shared with us. The handwriting itself, wouldn't you know it, was nearly indecipherable. I had to work to even read a few lines. July 15, 1987: "Down the middle fork of the American River. Great River." August 6, 1998: "Debra has left me for a new beau. Much as I love her, I am powerless to retrieve her. I feel a surge of jealousy and impotent rage. And I'm too old (64) for the experience." May 26, 2002: "Tessa died in San Francisco last week and we buried her at Dutch Flat." Strangely, I did not want to read more. Because of the trespass, I reasoned. Because of Hunter's birthday. I closed the cover, carried it outside, and hid it in the car. I would get to it later, spend the time needed to decipher his scribbles, for I was making my own scribbles, writing a memoir I thought I might title *Young Man in a Hurry*.

It's now late fall, 2024, and I've yet to return to Dad's diary. The young man in a hurry is now an older man slowed in his ambitions by a succession of events beyond his reach. The diary rests in the bookcase behind my desk in the study. I feel its presence, the red cover practically shouts, but I'm not sure I have the desire to read what's inside. I've gone where I've gone. I know what I know. Every once in a while, Brooklynn will walk in, remove it from the shelf, and try to read a line.

"Popa-pop had bad handwriting, Dad."

"Yes," I say, smiling.

But he had a wonderful grasp of comedy.

ACKNOWLEDGMENTS

This is the page where writers are expected to pay their debt of gratitude for the completion of a book. It is where they confess that no book, however solitary the endeavor, is written alone. For the author who happens to be dyslexic, the tally of dues is hardly obligatory. *Young Man in a Hurry*, for all the reasons you might guess, called upon the efforts of many.

It began with a great borrowing, the muddle of family history five generations back. How to make sense of it? How to do it justice? To serve the purpose of a readable story, the past had to be distilled. Along the way, regrettably, much was lost. I imagine a furrowing on the brows of my forebears, my parents and grandparents and great-grandparents, had they been alive to read what I took of their lives. I can only hope that the love and admiration I have for them, and their wonderful complexities, comes through.

Where documents were nonexistent or vague, where time erased a trail, where myth obscured truth, I had the good fortune of being able to rely on the vivid recollections of my mother's two sisters, my aunt Cindy and my aunt Anne. Returning to their own harrowing childhoods was not easy for them—indeed it was quite painful—and I cannot thank them enough for the stories they generously shared.

More than once, my own childhood memories eluded me because language back then had eluded me, too. When in doubt about the events of my early years, I consulted often with my younger sister, Hilary, and she almost always was able to fill in the gaps or at least confirm what was hazy in my head. When it came to my role as husband and father, my wife, Jen, never failed to round out my often shortcut versions of our family life. For an overbooked politician, it only helps to have a documentary filmmaker as a patient and loving partner.

Even the stories of past and present firmly planted in my head required a process of extraction and rendering into structure and language so that the finished product might read differently than the books of other politicians. I enjoyed the privilege of having Mark Arax, one of the great chroniclers and storytellers of California, in my corner. His role went beyond mere ghostwriter. He asked for one thing: that the memoir would go where it needed to go, no matter how personal and wrenching, and I agreed.

Before the book reached New York and Ann Godoff, one of the legends in publishing, I burdened my own staff and consultants, both current and former, with many readings, edits, fact-checks, and research. This they did on their own time. I want to thank Jason Elliott, Lindsey Cobia, Bob Salladay, Dana Williamson, Nate Ballard, Ann Patterson, Jim DeBoo, Ana Matosantos, Sean Clegg, Anthony York, Una Corbett, and Trevor Rodgers for enduring what turned out to be a four-year book journey with me. I want to thank my literary agent, Elyse Cheney, for never losing faith in the project.

A memoir that pokes into private places can try the patience of loved ones. And yet I can honestly say that never once did my words on the page tear at the fabric of the bond I keep with my sister and her husband, Geoff Callan. This is a testament to the love my parents, William and Tessa Newsom, had for their children and the love we have for our children: Montana, Hunter, Brooklynn, and Dutch Newsom, and Talitha and Siena Callan. This book, after all, is for them.

INDEX

INDEX

Marichal, Juan, 60
Marine One, 247, 248, 255
Marin Independent Journal, 58, 77
Marks, Milton, 18
Marshall, James, 2
Martin, Dorothy "Del," 155, 157
mass shootings, 226, 240, 242
Matier, Phil, 136, 161
Matthews, Chris, 232
Maxwell, Gavin, 17
mayors
    Brown, Jerry (Oakland), 213
    Jones, Jody (Paradise), 254
    Nickels, Greg (Seattle), 171
    Villaraigosa, Antonio (Los
        Angeles), 208, 212, 228
    Zemin, Jiang (Shanghai), 208
mayors (San Francisco)
    Agnos, Art, 164
    Alioto, Joseph, 145
    Brown, Willie
        Burton as confidant to, 125
        ending of term of, 145
        Fagan as new chief of police
            installed by, 147
        homeless crisis and, 165, 169
        offer to Newsom by, 123
        overhaul of taxicab system
            pledged by, 128
        request by, 121
    Feinstein, Dianne, 164, 207
    Jordan, Frank, 164
    Moscone, George, 234
    Newsom, Gavin, 16
        act of contrition by, 174
        Bayview–Hunters Point project
            of, 149
        climate change (administration's
            work on), 205
        dredging of pond while mayor, 48
        election of, 145–47
        first trip to Shanghai as
            mayor, 207

as fodder for conservative
    media, 212
importance of police reform to,
    146–47
"Journey of Harmony" as final
    hurrah of, 206, 208
new public housing built by
    administration of, 150
Newsweek headline on, 158
new torch relay route engineered
    by, 210
police reform under, 147, 151
same-sex unions (admonition
    regarding), 153
    Rolph, James, 12
Mays, Willie, 215–16
McCarthy, Joseph, 43
McCarthy, Kevin, 255, 258
McCarthyism, 185
McCartney, Paul, 218
McGowan, Ross, 124–25
McKuen, Rod, 195
Meeker, Jim, 222
Meeker, Martin, 16–17
Mental Health Systems Act, 163–64
Menzies, Arthur (father of Tessa),
    191, 196
    background of, 187–88
    courtship of Jean and, 186
    epic garden of, 191, 196
    first look at, 185
    friendship struck up between Jean
        and, 187
    letters from, 188–89
    military service of, 188
    as one of the boys, 188
    parents of, 186
    shooting threatened by, 192
    suicide of, 14, 186
    wife of, 54–55
Menzies, Jean Addis (mother of
    Tessa), 15, 57, 186, 190,
    192, 195

284

INDEX